DARKNESS SUNLIGHT

DARKNESS
TO
SUNLIGHT

THE LIFE-CHANGING JOURNEY
OF ZAID ABDUL-AZIZ
("DON SMITH")

ZAID ABDUL-AZIZ

FOREWORD BY OSCAR ROBERTSON

Published by Sunlight Publishing, Inc.
PO Box 75184
Seattle, Washington 98175-0184
1-877-244-4009

Visit our website at
www.darknesstosunlight.com

Cover design and text design by Mi Ae Lipe
Printed and bound in Canada by Hignell Book Printing

First Edition

ISBN: 0-9778861-0-7

Library of Congress: 2006902347

In the name of God the Merciful and Compassionate.
Peace be upon all the Prophets and their families.

I offer this book, in gratitude, to my wonderful family.

To my wife, Mina, and to my deceased parents,
Juanita L. Smith and Bert Smith.

To my children—
Atiya, Mariam, Adam, Yusef, Saara, and Nurah.

To my courageous sister, Beverley, and brother Rasheed (Duane).

To M'barak, Fatima, and all of the Baracht family.

CONTENTS

IOWA STATE UNIVERSITY

GOING PROFESSIONAL

A GREATER PURPOSE

FOREWORD

I first heard about Zaid (then named Don Smith) when he was playing for Iowa State and I was playing for the Cincinnati Royals. He was an outstanding player and he had the vertical jump and rebounding skills that the Royals really needed. At that time, professional basketball was integrated but racism still permeated the business. There was an unwritten rule that only so many slots in the league were available to African-American players. As a result, an African-American had to be a phenomenon in college to be noticed by scouts, let alone be identified as an early draft pick. Zaid's outstanding performance at Iowa State made everyone sit up and take note. Those of us who were watching this upright, gifted young player were moved to compare him with veterans like Elgin Baylor and Bob Pettit.

When Zaid was drafted by the Royals, he had more natural talent than any of our other young players, but he was on the team just a year before he was traded. He simply wasn't given enough time to prove what he could do. He landed with the Milwaukee Bucks where Kareem was playing, and later that year, I also joined the Bucks. Soon, Zaid was traded again. To this day, Zaid, with his big, easy smile, gives me a hard time every time I see him. Instead of "Hello" he says, "Oscar, did you get me traded?" To which I always respond, "No way, Zaid! It wasn't me!"

African-American athletes too often write books aimed at an African-American audience. White athletes are more likely to write a book assuming that any sports fan is part of their potential audience. Frankly, I feel that Americans of every race and creed should be interested in the stories of African-American athletes whose careers were affected by racism. Zaid's career spanned a time of radical change, and this book provides a very personal perspective of the challenges African-American athletes faced in the 1960s and 1970s. The tales of his tenure as an elite basketball player are surrounded by other reflections on his life before and after college and pro ball. All of these stories are told by a man who views his life with gratitude and a refreshing sense of awe. As a result, he has written a memoir that is bound to touch hearts and open minds.

Welcome to Zaid's journey.

Oscar Robertson
Fairfield, Ohio

PREFACE

If you think that the mind of a champion athlete is focused and sure, I wish you could have seen inside my mind when I first considered writing this book. There was a mighty struggle between the part of me that knew I could write it and the part of me that doubted my motives and skills.

For years, caution prevailed. I was afraid to reveal aspects of my past to many of my friends and family. I feared that I might hurt the feelings of people whose stories intersected with mine. I was also concerned that the whole project might simply be an egotistical exercise.

Besides all that, I wondered if I had lived long enough to write an autobiography. Maybe I hadn't when the idea first came to me. I wrote down some of my memories about twenty years ago, but I literally threw my hands up at the immensity of the project. It was like putting my arms around an ocean and trying to control each wave.

Two years ago I started again and the timing just seemed to be right. This time stories unfolded before me, so many that I had trouble choosing what to include and what to leave out. At first they were just separate little memories. Other than the fact that they were my memories, they seemed unrelated. But as the book took form, three things happened.

First, all those seemingly unrelated memories started to weave together into a reasonable outline of my time on earth so far. This allowed me to reflect upon my past as I had never done.

Second, it became clear that if I wrote down as honest a picture of my life as I could—including moments of clarity and confusion, humor and sorrow, highs and lows—my story might help others.

Third, writing this book has forced me to step beyond my tendency toward shyness. As I complete this labor of disclosure and happily contemplate sharing it with others, I realize that this is not the attitude of a shy person! I have learned to reveal more of myself without concern about approval from others, and I hope that is a lasting effect.

I want to make a short note about offensive language that comes up in some of the stories I tell here. When I was growing up, my friends and I used profanity casually and frequently. I consciously omit these words from my life now, so I was torn about how to simultaneously maintain the authentic voice of those times and avoid excessive profanity in the book. I struggled with this for a while, and I've decided to reduce the worst of the profanity to the first letter of the offensive word.

Some names have been changed to protect individual privacy.

Finally, no book is complete without readers. I am grateful to all of you who take time to read my story. Maybe it will inspire you to take a closer look at your own story—starting with just a few memories.

I hope I hear from many of you in the future.

Zaid Abdul-Aziz
Seattle, June 2006

ACKNOWLEDGEMENTS

I have met so many wonderful people in my life that I could never give them proper acknowledgment, because I know that I cannot possibly remember them all. But let me try...

To Jean Smith and Donna. To Karen, James, Kevin, Binky, and Sheryl (who always says "I love you Uncle Zaid!" when she sees me). To Rodney Johnson and his family, and to my late cousin Tia and to Barbara, Inez, and Uncle Al, who have passed on. To my two grandchildren Jalen and Anissa Iman. To my Uncle Don. For Chahrazad, who has a wonderful spirit.

To Roy and Ray Killens and Duane Jones. To Khalid, Jami, Lukman, Amin, Khidr, and their families. To Abdul-Haleem Muhammad and his family. To the legendary Ahmad Jamal, Yusef Lateef, and the late Rahsan Roland Kirk. To Russell, Natalie, Josephine, and Lucy.

To Nelda Danz, who trusted me and helped me in the grueling editing process, and to Sarah Sweeney, who helped edit an early version. Michael Campbell for his help and Irene for her kindness. For Frank, in loving memory of Joanie. For Patty Manley, who helped obtain permissions but passed away before the completion of the work. Mi Ae Lipe for her help with book design, editing, and permissions. To her father, Dewey. Loxie, Karen, Jamila, and Ayana. To Mohammed Nor Awang and his loved ones, and Kareem Abdul-Lateef and his family. To Chris Anderson, Fatiha, and Haitem.

For my late coach, Gene Smith, who taught me all I know about the game of basketball. To Howard, Stanley, and Butch. To Deanna, who helped me immensely. To Lola, Corrie, and Kobbie. Awad and Bilal. To Beth Fleming and her family. Gary Erskine and his mother, Dorothy.

To Oscar Robertson, to whom both active and retired players owe an enormous debt. To Kareem Abdul-Jabbar and Bob Dandridge. To Mahdi Abdur-Rahman (Walt Hazzard) and his wife Jalessa for their support. Abdul-Hakim Olajuwon and family. To my attorney, Robert C. Mussehl, who believed in me when many people didn't. Senator Bill Bradley and Coach Phil Jackson. To Spencer Haywood, my personal "Hall of Fame" candidate. Fred and Linda Brown. Garfield Heard and Emmette Bryant.

To Mike Newlin, and all my Houston Rocket teammates. To Coach Lenny Wilkens and all my Seattle SuperSonics teammates. To my late trainer Dick Vandervoort. For Ray Patterson, Jim Foley, and Eddie Doucette. To Fred Crawford and his loved ones. To Sam Lacey, who paid me a compliment I surely needed. In memory of John Brisker and the late Ed "The Czar" Simmons. Mel Davis and Cal Ramsey.

To my childhood teammate Mike Davis and to John Hunt. To the late Howard Cosell, who would say "Don Smith of Iowa State" in his unmistakable voice when we would meet at airports. To UCLA Coach John Wooden, whose compliments are still major highlights of my career. For all NBA players, no matter how long or short their careers.

Hank Whitney and Coach Wayne Morgan. The Iowa State University Athletic Department. Gary Thompson and Kay Lande. To the late Eppie Barney. Coach Glen Anderson, Lyle Frohm, and Arnie Gaarde. Bill Cain, John McGonigle, Tom Goodman, Dave Collins, and all my ISU teammates, friends, and associates.

To George Hamilton IV, Charles Steadham, and staff at Blade Agency. To all the staff at the Shoreline Library. To Leo ("The Lion"). Ron, Chris, Cameron, Baby Girl, and Tiny. To Ed and Barbie Benshoof. To Dan Neal, whom I am proud of. To Sary, Yusef, Nasir, Tohir, and all at the Olympic Express Restaurant. To Shelly and James at Starbucks. The "Rock" in Atlanta and wife, Paula. Chris Dendrinos, who gave positive feedback. Catie and her daughter Sadie. Jack and Michael in the park and parents. Jim, Takae, Paul, and all in our Tai Chi class. To Rudy Walker and his wife Jill. To

Brian, Kelly, Aaron, and Leah. To Hajj Abdul-Malik. To Matt McCullough. To Imogene and Marda and all the Schroeders. To Shoeb Ishmael, his wife Rosa Linda, and Leila. To Mitch and the staff at Grinders Hot Sands. To Dan Raley and Dan DeLong of the *Seattle Post-Intelligencer*. To all the Seattle Metro bus drivers for their kindness over the last two-and-a-half years.

To Dr. Wardak, Joanne, and staff. Dr. Bilal, Dr. Kazi, and Dr. Vern Cherewatenko. Sonny Chu, Sensei Bomini, and John Shibuya. Brother Renae and his family. To Hassan Ali and Abdullah Penick and their families. To the late Yah Yah Abdullah and family. Ibrahim Faraj and family. To Hajji. To the late Dr. El-Muslimani and the late Mustaq Junejo and their families. Akel Kahera and family. Willie and Kathy Robinson. The Taylor family in memory of Rupert and Edna, and all the Whites. The O'Keefe family in St. Louis.

To all the souls who died in the World Trade Center and all their families. To all the chemical dependency professionals who have waged wars against alcohol and drugs. To all the people who are dying in Iraq and their families. To the dead and afflicted in Louisiana, Mississippi, Pakistan, and Thailand. For all creatures on earth and beyond.

CHILDHOOD

BEING A BISHOP—SUMMER OF 1959

My friends and I never planned to be in a gang. It just happened.

We were a bunch of kids with a wide range of temperaments, ages, physical capabilities, and attitudes. We came together because we all lived in the same neighborhood on the edge of the Bedford-Stuyvesant section of Brooklyn. We fought, drank, and smoked with one another and the gang just evolved.

Lots of the things we did were considered unacceptable, negative behavior by our parents, but it was *our* unacceptable, negative behavior. It felt natural to us, and it made our life feel exciting. We were just kids. We saw life as permanent, ourselves as indestructible, and loyalty to one another as sacred. We didn't realize that our existence was ephemeral and that all bonds would break with the passage of time. One summer day seems particularly vivid.

The cheap Thunderbird wine burned as it went down my young throat. At thirteen, I was the youngest member of my gang, but on this night I had the most important assignment—making Molotov cocktails.

They were easy to make. I learned what to do from the older guys in the gang. First, I would just go to a gasoline station and collect drops from the gas nozzle. It took about two hundred drops to fill a glass Coke bottle half way. Then I would wet the end of a cloth with a little gasoline and stick the other end of the cloth in the bottle. When the time was right, I'd touch a match to the cloth and quickly throw it at a target. Upon impact, fire would break out all over.

That night we were fighting the Hill Toppers. Why we were fighting this gang with Mafia connections is beyond me. They had real weapons. Our crude zip guns were no match for their arsenal, and sometimes our weapons even blew up right in our hands.

On this particular night, we were fighting simply because we were black and they were white. My ego argued that we must not allow the Hill Toppers to take over our turf, but my conscience told me that this is God's land, and we must all learn to live together. I could not express my deeper thoughts to my gang because I was afraid of ridicule. I was full of conflict, because I wanted to appear brave and unyielding, but inside I felt loving and concerned—even toward our sworn enemies.

Lefty shouted at me, "Hey Poochie, you got the bombs ready yet?"

"Yeah!" I hollered. I nervously stacked the Coke bottles in a straight line.

Lefty was older, about twenty or twenty-one. He took a few swigs of the Thunderbird, then yelled,

"These white boys can kiss my a__!"

"Mines too!" I replied.

From the peak of the hill, we saw a bicycle heading our way. As the rider approached our gang of fifteen, we recognized Bruno, the War Counselor of the Hill Toppers. Hanging from his right side was a sword. The bike stopped right in the middle of my gang. Bruno dismounted and headed over to Lefty, drawing the sword from the sheath.

"If there are any of you niggers who want to do something, do it now!" shouted Bruno. My gang was suddenly at a loss for words. Bruno remounted his bike and pointed his finger at each one of us.

"You know where any of you can find me," he said, as he turned his bike and headed back up the hill.

My gang began to talk about how we didn't want to hurt him. I was stunned.

"What's this?" I wondered. "These guys are supposed to be so bad, but they can't live up to their own hype."

I walked away, grief-stricken, as I realized that the gang that I relied on for support and strength was weak and afraid. After that night, I gave more weight to my gut feeling that there was a better way to spend my life. I learned I would have to be strong for myself.

Shaken, I made my way back home, with the refrain of Billie Holiday's beautiful song in my head.

♪

Mama may have,
Papa may have,
But God bless the child that's got his own,
That's got his own.

The Bar

"Where you been to, boy?" asked my grandmother as I opened the door to our two-bedroom apartment.

"I was just out with the guys," I replied. I walked around, trying to figure out who else was in the house.

"Where's ma?" I asked. I always asked, although I knew where she was.

"Across the street," was my grandmother's automatic reply.

There wasn't a day when my mother wasn't at the bar. Time after time, I crossed the street and opened that heavy door. My senses would be hit with the smell of pigs' feet and alcohol. The jukebox was always playing. When I was much younger, the men and women there would pick me up and say how cute I was. I was chubby as a little kid and they nicknamed me "Poochie," which stuck with me throughout my teens.

The regulars gave me lots of attention, but I really wanted to see my mother. She would look at me and mumble something, then continue drinking. After a while, I would slowly walk to the door and exit with a forced smile on my face.

"Where you been to, boy?" my grandmother would ask as I re-entered our apartment.

"Across the street," I would reply.

That night after the failed fight with the Hill Toppers, my older sister Beverley was in the house. She is four years older than I am, and at times we would discuss the important things of life—our dreams and aspirations. My sister wanted to be a secretary for her career. Bert, our father, never paid too much attention to Beverley or her aspirations. I didn't see much of him either, but by comparison he showered me with attention and affection. If she ever felt that my gain was her loss, she never let on that it bothered her. But it bothered me. I felt sad for her.

I wanted to talk to Beverley that night, but I didn't know how to start. I walked through the apartment to a small room in the back, opened the window, and took out a rolled reefer. (I didn't smoke marijuana habitually, but by the time I was a youth, I used both pot and alcohol occasionally to overcome my shyness.) I lit the joint, took a few drags, put it out, and finally decided that I had the confidence to tell my sister what was on my mind. I walked into the living room where she was sitting.

"You know, Bevy, I will be somebody one day and rescue you from this madness. Grandma is always telling me that God has a mission for me to follow. I feel that's true!"

≫≪

The Black Athlete: A Shameful Story
By Jack Olsen, *Sports Illustrated*, July 1, 1968

… Don Smith fidgeted nervously on the bench one night late last winter. Iowa State had just lost to Kansas State in the crucial game of the season, and ever since the final horn had blown in the big armory in Ames, Iowa, the students and fans had been sitting patiently in their seats. This had been the last home game for Smith, a 21-year-old light-skinned Negro from the slums of Brooklyn, and statisticians were busy working out the final summation of his brilliant college athletic career. It developed that he was the second best Big Eight rebounder of all time, behind Bill Bridges, and the third best Big Eight scorer behind Clyde Lovellette and Bob Boozer. He had been All-Conference each year, Sophomore of the Year in 1966 and Big Eight Player of the Year in 1968. He had made the Helms Foundation first-string All-American and half a dozen

other All-Americas as well. Earlier in the season he had matched up against Lew Alcindor of UCLA, scoring 33 points and picking up 12 rebounds. Somebody asked Alcindor what he thought of Elvin Hayes of Houston. "He's one of the best," said the taciturn Lew, "along with Don Smith of Iowa State."

Now Smith waited shyly in the armory while his jersey was officially retired, the student body presented him with a plaque, the mayor of Ames presented him with a handsome piece of luggage and Dr. W. Robert Parks, the university president, presented him with a color photograph of himself in action. Smith said only a few words in response. He said he was grateful for the gifts and for his years at Iowa State. Mostly, he said, he was sorry he had missed three free throws in the last six minutes.

"Just like him," said an instructor in the audience. "Everybody's telling him how great he is and he's apologizing for missing free throws."

"Yeah," said a man sitting alongside. "For a shine, that is one good boy."

Yeah, one good boy. …

454 VANDERBILT AVENUE

My house was on the corner of Vanderbilt and Fulton, 454 Vanderbilt Avenue. Vanderbilt and the four blocks east of it were an ethnic and economic buffer zone that separated downtown Brooklyn from the Bedford-Stuyvesant area. Most of the businesses in that four-block area were white-owned retail businesses and offices. Diagonally across the street from our apartment, there was a liquor store with a huge pulsating neon sign in front that spelled out "LIQUOR," each letter a different color.

A block east of our apartment, on Clinton Avenue, was Ratner's Candy Store. My grandmother cashed all her welfare checks there. The Ratners were a Jewish family who ran a fantastic business where everyone was welcome. Their store was the heart of our neighborhood. It was conveniently located at the A-train subway station entrance at Clinton and Washington.

In those days, race within our neighborhood was not an issue. We accepted one another because we knew and appreciated everyone's contribution to the neighborhood. There was some racial conflict between the youth of different neighborhoods, but I think that was as much about "protecting turf" as race. A color distinction became more visible as you headed three blocks east of my neighborhood on Fulton Street to Washington Avenue. After this boundary point you could say that you were in Bedford-Stuyvesant proper. It was like gradually going from day into night, or white into black. That section of Brooklyn was almost exclusively black compared to the integration of my neighborhood.

Outside of our unusually integrated area, racism was definitely present. Even within the black community, the shade of one's skin aroused racist attitudes. My family was considered "high yellow" because our skin color was light—a holdover from the racist categorization of skin colors by the slave industry. (Historically, "high yellow" slaves were considered more desirable for certain domestic jobs, which created resentment between darker- and lighter-skinned African slaves.)

Some folks in our neighborhood assumed that, because our skin was light, we must be "uppity." This resulted in very different behavior by individual family members. Bert, my father, whose family was from Barbados, did have that "uppity" attitude. He acted like "blacks" were less competent. My grandmother, on the other hand, who was lighter-skinned than many Caucasians, culturally identified completely with the black community, and she showed it in her style of speech—which was more "black" than many darker-skinned African-Americans. As a really young kid, this speech confused me. I wondered why my grandmother, who looked like she was white, "talked black."

My mother's boyfriend, Jess, was Italian. He was a small man with strong Italian features and mannerisms. Because he lived in the neighborhood, he was just "Jess" to us—different from the way we viewed Italians who lived in a predominantly Italian neighborhood. It was rumored that Jess was the father of my half-brother Duane, but none of the kids knew for sure or even dared to ask. Jess would come over to our apartment, where he and my mother would play pinochle until very early in the morning. When I awakened, he was gone as if he had disappeared. Kazzam! The next weekend, he would reappear, and the whole process would begin again.

Occasionally, while my mother was preparing chitlins, potato salad, and greens for some special occasion, Jess would tell us Mafia stories like they were the truth and like he possessed some secret, firsthand knowledge. Even then, I doubted he had Mafia connections, but he sure seemed to want us to believe that he did. For a long time I didn't know where Jess worked, but eventually I found out that he worked for a cigar maker.

To the right of 454 Vanderbilt was a parking lot, and just beyond that was a large factory called Schreder's. They built rubber tires, and you could smell the rubber for blocks. Sometimes, on the way to school, I would peek through the metal mesh window and watch the workers roll huge slabs of rubber through a press. The extruded product was carted off and mysteriously formed into tires in another section of the factory that I couldn't see.

Many Schreder's employees frequented the soul food restaurant that was located right below our apartment. I never knew the real name of that place as there was no sign outside, but my family called it "Downstairs." My favorite Downstairs foods were macaroni and cheese and sweet potato pie. Downstairs was always jumpin', especially on weekends, and it provided my music education. I heard "God Bless the Child" by Billie Holiday, the Platters's hit "Only You," "Blueberry Hill" by Fats Domino, and hundreds of others. That jukebox sang me lullabies, taught me lyrics, and started my lifelong love of music.

Across the street was that bar where my mother spent most of her free time. She would come home from work around six in the evening and drink beer until the bar closed at one in the morning. The next day she would awaken at seven, eat a light breakfast, and take the bus downtown where she worked as a telephone operator. She never missed a day's work, nor was she ever late. Even with all those hours in the bar, I never saw her drunk or out of control. However, that bar stole countless hours from her family.

I remember crossing the street one day. I must have been five or six years old. I just wanted to hear my mother say, "I love you!" or show me some affection. I spotted my mother sitting at her usual place, sipping her drink.

I asked, "How ya doin' mom?"

She replied, "What are you doing here?"

The tone of her voice was not angry, but concerned—filled with that "you-crossed-the-street-and-could-have-been-hit-by-a-car" tone. She scooped me up, threw a few dollars on the counter, and told the bartender, "I'll be right back!"

She took me across the street to our apartment and told me, "Get upstairs!" I scurried to the top of the stairs and she headed back across the street. I ducked into the bathroom. Struggling with tears, I peed in the toilet, flushed, and went into our apartment to wash my hands and cry!

It was a Saturday and the music downstairs was blasting. I could hear the conversations of the patrons and smell the luscious aroma of collard greens and ribs. The merriment of black folks dancing and socializing drifted up through the floor, and it eased my sadness. I heard coins clicking into the jukebox as folks played the same songs over and over again.

Over the months and years, I memorized many song lyrics and phrasings that drifted through those floorboards. Sometimes I would climb out of bed to press my ear to the floor. I cried when I first heard Billie Holiday sing. It seemed that she was singing to me. This paradox was amazing. My flesh-and-bones mother, whom I loved dearly, was just across the street, but she could not give the affection I wanted so desperately. My soulful, spiritual mother was below, singing to me, telling me her story, and my own.

My childhood inspiration, Billie Holiday.

Years later I learned that Billie Holiday and I share birthdays, another special connection with the woman who sent me much-needed maternal love through her exquisite songs.

My mother carried a deep sorrow that may have been a reason for her emotional distance, but she never acknowledged it to her children. She didn't divulge much personal information to anyone. She was a proud woman who worked long hours to provide for my sister, half-brother, and me, and when she had free time, she drank to drown her memories. I learned about my mother's sorrow through the neighborhood grapevine.

A Strange Family

Inez, Mother, and Loretta

Just after World War II ended and when Joe Louis was the Heavyweight Champion of the World, my grandmother Hattie Coombs moved from Norfolk, Virginia to Orange, New Jersey with my mother, Juanita Louise, and two of her sisters, Inez and Loretta. There were two other sisters who stayed in Virginia. I never met them, nor did I hear much about them.

I don't know exactly why my grandmother moved, but in those days it was common for African-Americans to move north in search of work. Looking back, maybe my grandmother was just tired of the South's segregated water fountains and "colored" and "white only" bathrooms. During the 1940s, the Ku Klux Klan was very active in the South, fomenting abuse and intimidation fueled by racism. My grandmother was raising these girls on her own, and maybe Brooklyn seemed like a safer place for her family. As a kid, it seemed that nothing scared my grandmother. Maybe by the time I showed up she had been through so much that she was just too tired to be scared.

Aunt Inez was the oldest sister. She lived with us for a while when I was young. She had short, matted hair and a gloomy, pallid complexion by the time I knew her. What I remember most about Aunt Inez was that she hummed while she picked her ear with a needle. At times I could not tell whether her humming was a cry for help or an expression of satisfaction as the needle scraped her eardrum. Like a rooster's familiar crowing, we were always aware of her proximity throughout our apartment.

Inez had a daughter named Barbara. Cousin Barbara was very slow cognitively and suffered from diabetes. One time she fell asleep while smoking a cigarette, and we all awoke to toxic fumes and a small fire burning the mattress. My grandmother called the fire department and they put out the flames. A fireman asked Barbara about the incident. She said, "I fell asleep and when I awoke, I realized the problem, but I didn't want to disturb anyone, so I just lay there in my bed as the smoke and fire got worse. I'm sorry!"

When they were young, Juanita and Loretta were extremely beautiful girls with long black hair and fine features. They were close, like two peas in a pod. I have heard that my Aunt Loretta was vivacious, and folks thought she looked like the entertainer Lena Horne. Lo-

My mother, Juanita Louise Smith.

retta began dating a Pakistani by the name of Ali. For Loretta, the relationship was totally platonic. He took her to dinner and bought gifts for her. She would kiss him on the cheek and he would blush with delight. He had no idea that my Aunt Loretta had not one iota of genuine affection for him. Ali thought it was a love affair.

One Sunday afternoon he came to see my aunt unannounced while she was talking with her girlfriends. His unexpected arrival embarrassed my aunt, who got a ribbing from the crowd. To save face, my aunt casually and condescendingly asked, "What do you want?"

Ali tried to answer with confidence, but felt awkward and ashamed. Eventually, he managed to say, in his thick Urdu accent, "I want to take you out."

My aunt angrily snapped back, "This has got to stop! Please stay away from me!"

The naïve Ali was shocked.

"But I love you!" He was at a loss for any other words for the woman who was breaking his heart.

My aunt sneered at Ali's lovesick proclamation and finally came forth with the truth, loud enough so all who were present could hear,

"I don't love you and never did. I just wanted the gifts!"

My aunt's girlfriends doubled over in hysterical laughter at the misfortune of this young man. A dejected Ali turned and left without saying a word.

The next day, Loretta walked the one block to Ratner's and bought a newspaper to read on the way to work. As she exited the store and headed down to board the A-train, she heard someone yell her name from the top of the steps. She turned, looked up, and recognized that the voice was Ali's. That moment ended as he pulled out a .38 special and shot my aunt six times in the chest. She collapsed and died on the cold concrete steps to the A-train.

In the turmoil, Ali fled the scene. He worked as a longshoreman and probably boarded a ship. Wherever he went, he was never caught. My mother lost her sister and was devastated. She began drinking from this juncture, and kept it up every day of her life.

Grandma Coombs

One of the things that confused me most while I was growing up was that my grandmother, Hattie Coombs, looked white, but her style of speech was completely black. It seemed like she was two people in one body.

"Boy," she would yell in a crisp mix of Virginia and New York accents, "I told you to get your butt in the bed!"

Upon that command, I would drop everything, run to my mattress on the floor, pull the covers over my head, and try with all my might to go to sleep. Some nights I dozed off instantly. But on others, like in the summer when it felt like it was 110 degrees, I'd lie there swatting at the mosquitoes. On the nights I couldn't fall asleep, I listened to the sirens of ambulances and police cars. If I wasn't being serenaded by the lullaby of the sirens, I was engrossed in the conversations of prostitutes and their pimps, or the transactions of a junkie trying to acquire a fix.

At times, addicts would shoot up right in my hallway (which prompted my grandmother to frequently holler at us to close the door when we came home). Some mornings I awoke to find liquor bottles in our hallway. I would pick up the fifths and pints and heroically drop them in the trash bin. I felt proud to able to help out.

My grandmother was born just before the turn of the twentieth cen-

My beloved grandmother, Mrs. Hattie Coombs, with my cousin Kim.

tury, so by the time I knew her she had lived through a lot of variations on racism. Despite her fair skin, she was extremely black in her outlook and convictions. She was dignified without a trace of arrogance, and she had true patience.

My grandmother was also a very practical thinker. She always made us aware of how fortunate we were. She would remind us by saying things like, "The poorest man in America would be the richest in some other countries!"

Nothing much scared Gran, but I was fearful of two things that we dealt with daily—roaches and rats. Thousands of roaches lived in the walls of our building. They came out when our apartment was dark. I dreaded turning on the lights because for a few seconds I could see them everywhere—on the table, the floor, the refrigerator—and then they would scurry into the walls the moment the light hit them. Gran fought those roaches for a long time. We called the exterminator and tried all kinds of insecticides, but what finally worked was simple baking soda.

One time, Gran cooked kidneys, rice, and beans and I was alarmed to find a large roach in the rice as I dished up my plate. Before I could even start complaining, my grandmother interrupted and said,

"Praise the Lord, more meat on the table!"

Spiders never frightened me, but rats were a different story. The way they moved and squirmed was scarier to me than their actual potential to do harm. One afternoon when I was really young, I was with my grandmother while she was cleaning the outside hall bathroom. Suddenly she came face to face with a huge rat. My heart almost stopped upon seeing it! It had extremely red eyes. When the rat spotted my grandmother he arched his back, bared his teeth, and hissed.

My grandmother grabbed her broom and limped down the steps after him. I held onto her apron for dear life, in total fear. As she cornered the rat, he hunched his back and hissed again. She quickly smacked him on the head with the broom and he let out an awful screech. Grandmother had no mercy on him, and she smacked him again and again until his gray body went limp. She picked him up by his tail, opened the door to the outside, and calmly threw him onto Vanderbilt Avenue. My poor little heart was about to beat out of my chest.

My grandmother was good-natured, but she was also the disciplinarian in the house. Everyone in the family knew better than to get on her wrong side. When we called her "*Grand*mother," we meant it. She was our general and we all took orders.

I learned how strict she was the hard way. I recall one lesson I learned from her when I was about eight or nine years old. Like just about everybody in our neighborhood, Grandma played the numbers. One summer day she had hit for five hundred dollars. I was home that afternoon when I noticed Sammy, the numbers man, in the kitchen. He was paying off my grandmother in crisp twenty-dollar bills, which she happily placed in her purse.

"There is no way she is going to miss one of those twenties!" I thought.

That night I went to her purse, took out one of those bills, and put it under my pillow. I went to sleep dreaming of how I'd spend my money.

The next morning, I got dressed, retrieved the twenty, and caught the train to the amusement park at Coney Island. I had a ball. I rode the petrifying Cyclone Ride, played game after game, and ate hot dogs and knishes. The hours flew by, and the fact that I would have to go home and explain where I had been never entered my mind.

Near the end of the day, I decided that I'd better quit while I still had enough money for the ride back. The subway ride home was great, too, as I relived the day in my mind. However, when I emerged from the subway and saw the big Williamsburgh Clock, I panicked. I had been gone since nine that morning and now it was nearly eight in the evening! I raced through the neighborhood, up the steps of our building, and down the hall to our apartment.

My grandmother was sitting in her chair with a Viceroy cigarette hanging down from her clamped lips and smoke circling above her head. She looked like a tough Bette Davis character, and I knew I was in trouble. I had rationalized that I had a right to the twenty. I had also convinced myself

The famous Cyclone rollercoaster at Coney Island.

that my grandmother, at nearly sixty-five years old, could not possibly know that a bill was missing from twenty-five twenties! My hole-card excuse was that I could blame Sammy, and say that perhaps he had mistakenly given her twenty-four twenties and not twenty-five.

"Where ya been, boy?" My grandmother asked. She took a long drag on that Viceroy.

"I went to Coney Island," I responded, hoping that my honest answer would be enough.

"How'd you get there?" The smoke escaped her lips as she spoke, and she locked her gaze on my eyes.

"Subway," I said simply. The less information I could give her, the better.

"What's that on your sweater?" she asked.

I pulled my sweater away from my chest and tucked my chin down to see what she was talking about. Right there in plain sight was a big mustard stain from the hot dog I had eaten. My cool began to melt.

My grandmother limped over, plucked something off my cheek, and asked, "What's this?"

It was a piece of cotton candy. My cool was history. I began to panic.

"Boy, did you take anything out of my purse last night?" she asked point-blank.

"I don't know what you're talking about Grandma!" I lied.

"Where in the world did you get the money for hot dogs, cotton candy, and the train ride to Coney Island. You workin'?"

I was stumped. I had no answer, and I had forgotten my lame, planned excuse. I decided to continue my lie.

"I didn't take no money from your purse Grandma."

"Take your clothes off boy!" she snapped.

"What you gonna do Grandma?" I asked in a trembling voice.

"Just take your clothes off!" she demanded.

I unbuckled my belt and slipped out of my trousers (also stained with tell-tale mustard). I pulled the sweater over my head and in frustration and anger, threw it impudently on top of the kitchen table. I was left with only my underwear, T-shirt, and socks.

"Take off the rest too, boy!" said my grandma. I complied, feeling very embarrassed as I stood in front of her, stark-naked.

"This is going to hurt me more than it hurts you!" she said. I looked at her right hand, which was gripping the cord to our iron. The first blow stung like nothing I had ever felt before. The next blow was about the same in intensity.

"I won't do it any more!" I wailed.

"You're d_ _ _ right you won't!" she said, as she struck me again.

I ran into the bedroom for safety, with Grandma right on my tail, iron cord flying relentlessly. I scrambled under a bed but she grabbed my left ankle and continued to strike me.

"I'm sorry, Grandma!" I whined, but to no avail.

Then I got this bright idea to play dead. If I could make Grandma feel guilty, she might use more restraint or give me some sympathy. I went limp.

"Oh, you're dead, eh? I'll show you what dead is!" Grandma shouted, even more determined. Finally, Grandma got tired of hitting and the whole thing suddenly ended. My crying turned to sobs and then sleep.

That was the only time my grandmother ever spanked me. In hindsight, perhaps that spanking could be viewed as child abuse, but I also see it as a desperate measure to stop me in my tracks when I abused her trust. My grandmother's strict disciplinary action made me realize that I hadn't fooled anyone but myself. Not only did I need to respect my grandmother, but I also wanted her to respect me. I appreciate that she took her job as my guardian so seriously.

I love her very much, and although she has been gone for decades, I still miss her.

⤜⤛

I'll be the first to admit it; my family was a strange one. Even though my grandmother, mother, sister, half-brother, and I were technically a family, most of the time there was a distance between us. We didn't express that we loved one another. Although we shared a small space, it seemed that everyone was just doing their own thing. My sister had her own lifestyle, my half-brother, Duane, had his, and I had mine. We rarely shared stories or worked together for the collective good of the family.

My grandmother did almost all the cooking. When the food was ready, she would place a big metal pot on the table, and one by one we would fill our plates and return to wherever we were sitting before the meal was served. When we got our weekly welfare hog headcheese loaf, it was the same. Family members would emerge from wherever they were in the house, cut the headcheese into slices, get out the loaf of Wonder Bread and the bottle of Hellmann's Mayonnaise, and prepare their sandwiches. Everything was done individually.

The only time we ate together as a family was on holidays like Christmas and (my favorite eating day) Thanksgiving. But even after receiving our Christmas gifts and chomping down Grandma's turkey and stuffing, our interactions felt superficial and awkward. When I went to other homes to show off my presents, I could see and feel more warmth and togetherness.

What made holidays feel even worse was the fact that I knew Bert, my father, was celebrating the same holiday festivities just a couple blocks away.

Bert Smith, my father.

It felt like "forbidden" secrets would

be revealed if we got too close together. Somebody might ask, "Is Jess Duane's father?" or "Why was Loretta murdered?" Maybe someone would ask my mother why she drank so much. Our family life seemed like one big cover-up, since every topic of importance was off-limits. At Christmas, I played with my few toys, but I even viewed the toys as just another way to mask the deeper issues in my family. As a child I just wanted to yell at the top of my lungs at my family, "OK, what the heck's going on around here?"

But I didn't. Instead, I adopted the family habit of keeping the secrets that I did know about under wraps. I think only my grandmother knew everything about the family. I'm sure she kept those secrets inside, thinking it was for the good of the family, as if by ignoring them she could will them away. But I also think it is possible that the stroke she suffered was a result of the things she knew and blocked from her mind so she wouldn't be in a state of constant worry and heartache. Denial can be a powerful shield. Why would she want to ponder whether her daughter was an alcoholic? Or acknowledge how much she missed her beautiful young daughter who had been savagely murdered?

As I got older, I am sure she worried about me hanging out with the wrong crowd, too. She never mentioned it, maybe because she felt she couldn't control it. I was one more tragedy just waiting to happen. This was what my grandmother worried about and why she perpetuated the secrets. It seemed safer than facing the truth.

BERT

I really don't know the details that led to my parents' divorce. They never talked to each other during my entire life. Not one word!

I suppose it was partly due to pressure from the child support agency, but Bert Smith, my father, would call and sometimes take me out. When he did call, he never spoke to my mother. He always got a third party on the line. My sister Beverley would relay the message to me. She never referred to him as "Father" or "Dad." That was too personal. Instead, she used his first name, Bert.

She would yell from the living room, "Poochie! Bert wants to take you to Ebbets Field to see the Dodgers play. Do you want to go?"

Of course I wanted to go! I rarely ever saw Bert and I liked the Dodgers! Even though Bert lived about two blocks from our apartment, I knew very little about him. He was pretty much the "mystery man." One thing I knew for sure was that he had a sharp mind. He could do the *New York Times* crossword puzzle in about an hour, and he could tell the quality of a three-piece suit just by looking at it.

He would say, "Wool, tightly knitted, one hundred stitches per square inch," with great authority.

He was keenly aware of details, and when he spoke, he would usually act as if the topic were top-secret information. He was highly suspicious, bordering on paranoia. He could also be very critical without justification.

When I was eight, I spent a week at his house. I was sent there because my mother didn't know what to do with me. At that time about nine people were living in our apartment. With so many people coming and going, I found I could easily disappear and no one would notice. I was always looking for ways to make money, and some of my early, unsupervised efforts included breaking into parking meters and selling newspapers on the subway.

Usually I stole the papers off the back of the *New York News* delivery truck and sold them for five or six cents each. Sometimes the buyer would give me a quarter, or even a buck. Maybe they felt sorry for that little kid! I had also taken to sleeping on the subway.

My mother had my sister call Bert to make the arrangements for the week. At first, I was happy. I thought that if I stayed with Bert, maybe I could solve some of the mysteries that surrounded him. Maybe this would be the beginning of a closer relationship with Bert. But despite my expectations, our week together pushed us farther apart.

At that time, Bert lived with his mother and stepfather, Sully. (His birth father, my grandfather and namesake, Donald, had committed suicide when Bert was a kid.) Sully had recently retired from forty-five years as a caterer and was given an expensive Bulova watch as a going-away present. The second night I stayed at their house, at about three in the morning, Sully woke me up. He pleaded with me to put the watch back. I didn't know what in the world he was talking about.

He said, "Son, I know you took it. Please put it back sometime this morning!"

At about eight that morning, Sully again woke me and said, "Thank you, son, for putting it back."

I hadn't touched the watch, so I figured that Sully must have just forgotten where he put it the night before. But I had a history of theft, so I was the prime suspect and was blamed for the deed.

Bert and his mother were one hundred percent sure I was guilty, which was obvious as we ate breakfast. I stayed there the whole week, but afterwards I only came back on Christmas to get my gifts. They never trusted me again, and there was nothing I could (or wanted to) do to change their attitude toward me.

Bert was of Barbadian heritage, but I never knew if he was born in Brooklyn or in Barbados. He used to lecture me about the distinction between the blacks in Bedford-Stuyvesant and the West Indian culture, as if the West Indians were superior.

He once told me that he could sell snow to an Eskimo. I didn't understand that he was bragging about his powers of persuasion. He seemed so proud that I thought it must be an honorable thing to do. I tried to make sense of his statement by thinking, "Maybe the Eskimo needed the snow."

As I grew older and continued to observe Bert, I saw that his intelligence was wasted. He felt that he could convince people to believe anything. During the 1950s he was a New York City police officer. He was promoted and became an inspector in the Division of Weights and Measures, probably one of the first blacks to ever achieve that honor. Unfortunately, he abused his power and it cost him dearly.

One day, during one of his rare visits, he decided to take me to down-town Brooklyn to buy some clothes. An inebriated man came up to our car and began speaking to Bert. The man reeked of alcohol and his clothes were filthy. I was frightened, and after the conversation ended and he left, I asked Bert, "Why do you speak to bums like that?"

"That was Detective Fisher," he told me. "He's an undercover detective. I used to work with him, years ago."

Another Saturday, he picked me up and introduced me to his partner, Detective Ryan. We drove over to Delancey Street in Lower Manhattan. Detective Ryan then got in and out of the car at meat markets, haberdasher-ies, and clothing stores. I was all eyes and ears. Bert would print out health violations to storeowners. At one meat market, Bert pointed to a roast in the freezer and told me,

"That hind roast is about three days old. The owner has also put red dye in it to cover its age."

I didn't get it. "So what?" I thought.

We did this investigative thing for about two hours. Finally, at the last stop before heading back to Brooklyn, my "So what?" young mind got an answer. I saw a butcher place an envelope in Detective Ryan's right hand. The butcher seemed to let out a sigh of relief. Detective Ryan left the store and climbed back into the gray Pontiac Bert drove for work. He gave the envelope to Bert, who opened it and took out five crisp one-hundred-dollar bills. He handed Detective Ryan two, and soon we were on our way back to Brooklyn via the Manhattan Bridge. I knew something was wrong, but it would be a long time before I really understood what Bert and his partner were doing.

A couple years later, my grandmother, sister, and I were watching the evening news on television. We were shocked to see Bert in handcuffs. My grandmother, who never showed much surprise or sorrow in her face, let out a shriek of horror I will never forget. As we watched police officers lead him away, we were mortified, because we knew where he was headed—to the Tombs to await trial.

THE BUST AND THE TOMBS

The Raymond Street Jail, an old medieval-style building known as "The Tombs" was Brooklyn's notoriously atrocious prison. It was finally abandoned in 1963, but when Bert was arrested, it was still in use. Everyone in the neighborhood had horror stories about The Tombs. This was the confinement Bert now found himself in.

It was the winter of 1959, right before Christmas, and I was just entering my teenage years. Even though I didn't know Bert that well, I had enormous sympathy and concern for him. The bust made local headlines, and when I read that he needed fifty-thousand dollars for bail, I worried.

The newspapers reported that Bert, a former inspector in the Bureau of Weights and Measures, was indicted for extortion involving butchers, along with the head of the citywide Salesmen and Poultry Workers Union. The cheating methods including substitution of inferior or lighter-weight meat for the piece the customer saw weighed correctly on the scale.

I felt bad for Bert. But I also felt bad that the real victims in this scandal were poor housewives who were cheated as they shopped, finding their five-pound chickens weighed only three when they got home.

❧❦

Bert pleaded guilty and made a deal. He lost his badge and almost lost his mind. In about a month, he was paroled. It was like a Shakespearean tragedy in which great potential was thwarted by poor judgment and greed.

After Bert's release from prison, he never worked for anybody but himself. He became a successful photographer and promoter, but he never really gave up the attitude that fast-talking was the way to make it big. I really didn't look to him for guidance, although he provided it in a sort of backwards way. When I had tough decisions to make, I often found myself consciously choosing the opposite of whatever I figured Bert would have done in the same situation.

Brooklyn Then

The first time I heard *"Watermel…watermel…watermelons!"* ring out through the neighborhood, I was about four or five. I looked up and saw a charcoal-colored man wearing a huge straw hat. In his left hand, he was holding the reins of a massive horse who was eager to prance. Sometimes the rider had to pull the reins in a bit to restrain him.

Behind this beautiful animal was a wagon filled with fruits and vegetables. Apples, oranges, and grapes were neatly boxed. There were many similar wagons in Brooklyn in those days. Some vendors carried chestnuts, peanuts, and different types of spices, too. These wagons were scarce on the weekdays, but on Saturdays and Sundays they could be found everywhere.

I wanted to be a helper on a wagon. It paid a whopping twelve dollars per day. Unfortunately, when I was old enough to do it, I couldn't get myself going early enough to be at the stable by 5 A.M. sharp. I blamed myself as I saw five fruit wagons heading down Washington Avenue, each with a driver and helper. I don't know if the drivers owned the horse and wagon or just leased them by the day, but I remember that they were very businesslike and they seemed to be really happy in their work.

Brooklyn was a great city to grow up in during the late 1950s and early 1960s. On summer mornings the kids in my neighborhood would chip in to buy a broom and pink rubber balls. We pulled the straw off the broom and had a stick for a bat. Everybody met at Claremont Avenue to choose sides and play stickball. The pitcher threw the ball "on one bounce" and the batter got only one swing. The best pitchers used a little spin on the ball (or "English") to fool the batters. One strike and you were out. Balls were hit to the heavens and caught with the grace of a major-league outfielder. Each player emulated his or her favorite player—Jackie Robinson, Whitey Ford, or Roy Campenella.

The neighborhood kids who played were from lots of ethnic backgrounds and included ages eleven to nineteen. We were just there to play. Afterwards, we usually had lemonade and occasionally a six-pack of beer was shared. We played only on the weekends, so we looked forward to these games with much anticipation.

There were so many things to do and see in Brooklyn back then. I enjoyed going to the library on Flatbush Avenue, which was about a mile away. There was also Ebbets Field, where the Dodgers played, and Prospect Park, with the Brooklyn Zoo and famous Botanical Gardens. For three dollars and fifty cents you could rent a horse and ride around the park. If you fell off, there were no lawsuits like today, because you rode at your own risk.

This was also the area where Barbra Streisand, Jackie Gleason, Woody Allen, Michael Jordan, and Tupac Shakur grew up. I attended summer school at Erasmus Hall High School, located in the predominantly Jewish Flatbush neighborhood. I liked it a lot more than my regular school because the classes were more challenging and I learned more.

My childhood Brooklyn neighborhood, with the Williamsburgh Bank Building in the background.

Just a few blocks from my house, at the base of the Williamsburgh Bank building, was the Long Island Railroad Station, a major conduit for getting to and from the other boroughs. If people needed assistance all they had to do was ask the train conductor. To check the time, you could look up at the four-sided Williamsburgh Clock, which still towers above the neighborhood. People also gathered here and fed the hundreds of

The Williamsburgh Bank Building. We kept time from its clock, which was visible from all directions.

pigeons that came out en masse.

On November 22, 1963, about six blocks away from this station was where I learned that President John F. Kennedy had been shot. I was taking the bus home from John Jay High School when we made a left turn on 7th Avenue at Flatbush. The bus halted, and I saw people in the street crying. The driver had stopped the bus in total shock. Then, on a transistor radio, I heard the news that shook the whole world: "John F. Kennedy, the 35th president of the United States, died today at 1:38 CST."

I cried and cried and cried. To this day I cannot remember how I got home or how I even got off that bus.

➤⟆

Brooklyn was an interesting place to live, but it also had its rough side. There were lots of neighborhood gangs. I aligned with the Bishops, who were uptown, even though the Chaplains were closer to downtown and my apartment. Right where I lived was pretty neutral turf, so I joined the gang that some of my friends were in. A Bishop knew never to get caught in the Chaplain area or vice versa. If you did, you could very likely lose your life. Each gang could tell where a person was from by looking at the way he dressed, walked, and spoke. Another gang active during that time was the SBB, or South Brooklyn Boys, an Italian gang who had courage, or "heart," as we would say. My brother-in-law Sonny belonged to the El Covons, who were in the Red Hook area. The Hell Burners prowled Manhattan, and Chinese gangs roamed Chinatown.

I remember an incident that happened between the uptown Chaplains and another gang called the Corsairs. A member of the Corsairs was caught and stomped to death by the Chaplains. At the funeral, as the teen lay in the casket with his family weeping and dressed in black, the same group who took his life entered the funeral parlor. They took the body out of the casket and slammed it onto the floor and began stomping him again! You can imagine the grief-stricken family's reaction.

During those days, a major deterrent to gang violence was the Payne brothers. They were detectives, but they operated according to their own rules. I don't think they were twins, but they sure looked like it. At six foot six and about two-hundred-seventy pounds, they were feared all over Brooklyn. Their name explained it all—these brothers could inflict serious pain. When a gang fight broke out, or if some illegal transaction was taking place, all anyone had to do was call for the Payne brothers. They would arrive and begin cracking heads with their steel billy clubs. The crowd would disperse almost immediately. This wasn't a perfect solution, but these guys were allowed to continue what was basically police brutality because almost everyone in the neighborhood—black, white, and Puerto Rican, despite social and cultural differences—supported their tough tactics.

The first line of discipline was family and friends. If a youth did something wrong or was shameful to someone, he knew that he would have to face uncles, cousins, and friends for an accounting. The folks would say, "I brought you into this world and I'll take you out!" The phrase was an exaggeration, of course. None of my friends were ever actually beaten to death by their parents, but they knew they had to "toe the line" or face the consequences. The police very seldom got involved in domestic disputes, since it was up to the neighborhood to intervene. We applied the philosophy "it takes a village to raise a child" long before the phrase was fashionable.

On the other hand, when a gang youth was involved in a violent act, he knew that a likely result would be an encounter with the Payne brothers, and his relatives and friends would consider the punishment logical. One characteristic of that time was that everyone had a sense of his or her place in the fabric of the community, no matter how tough or eccentric he or she might be.

It all boiled down to minding your own business, and that was Brooklyn during those times.

Unforgettable Characters

Judson

Outside of Atlantic Avenue, Fulton Street was probably the second-most-traveled road in Brooklyn. Kitty-corner from my house was a triangular block with a florist shop at its eastern point. On the same street going northwest and at the end of the block was a pest extermination company. Right across the street was a candy store near the beginning of Gates Avenue.

One of the more eccentric characters in our neighborhood was Judson. Above the candy store was the apartment where Judson and his mother, Lottie, lived. Lottie was a very small lady, about three-and-a-half feet tall, with a huge hump on her right shoulder. Judson had a job as a messenger, but he was an entertainer at heart. He both looked and sounded like the late singer Tiny Tim, minus the ukulele.

The youngest neighborhood children loved to go to Judson's house to play and be entertained. Judson was in his twenties then, and he swore that he would never grow old. We believed that and everything else he said, because he certainly was not like other adults.

Most parents knew Judson and no one worried about kids spending time with him. He was unusual, but he was a good person who enjoyed sharing his fairy-tale mentality with kids.

He played nursery rhymes for us on his phonograph player. When the "Three Little Pigs" played, Judson would sing and prompt us to do the same. Out of the blue he would just yell out, "Fee Fie Fo Fum, I smell the blood of an Englishman!" and start cackling, and we would shriek and laugh at the top of our lungs. From Snow White to Humpty Dumpty to Rapunzel, he would entertain us and we loved every minute of it!

Judson even made up a song about me, which he titled "Poochie," after my childhood nickname:

♪

Dirty hands,
Dirty face,
Leads the neighbors on a chase,
Making noise,
Breaking toys,
Always fights with the boys,
But to me
He's an angel of joy.

He was also a master craftsman who showed us how to make papier-mâché puppet heads, starting with a light bulb. We patiently helped him apply layer upon layer of paste and paper and let it dry. About an hour later, he added the puppet's facial features. On another day he would paint it. It was amazing how lifelike these puppets looked.

One day he showed us what he could do with what he called clippings or "shivers." He collected them from 78-rpm records by pressing on the needle to cut into the plastic. He had us follow him into the kitchen, announcing, "I want to show you something!"

He then applied about a handful of plastic shivers to the top of a broom. He lit a match, blew it out, and quickly applied the hot match head to the broom. Suddenly a huge puff of smoke hid him from our view. Judson had disappeared! Then we heard a laugh and saw that he had reappeared in the living room. Every kid who was there was impressed and we talked about this for weeks.

Halloween was Judson's mission in life. One Halloween Judson and about six of us kids went out trick-or-treating. My costume was Davy Crockett, with a holster, two guns, and a coonskin cap. Judson's was the Wicked Witch of the West, complete with wart on his nose, black dress, black shoes, and a black hat. We were little kids, so we didn't see anything strange about his choice of costume, and it didn't seem to bother our parents. We knocked on doors and received Hershey's bars, candy kisses, and my favorite, candy corn. We went from home to home and through alley after alley. Judson knew the way, so we just followed his lead.

At Waverly Place and Gates Avenue, we were heading back to Judson's house when we passed a street gang. One of the members did a double take at Judson and yelled,

"What the f_ _ _ is that?"

We were too little to get beat up, but our leader wasn't. They began chasing Judson and he ran as fast as he could, his witch's dress flying behind him. The rest of us followed for blocks, and to this day I don't know how we all kept up. Then Judson, who knew all the pathways in the neighborhood, made a mistake—he turned down an alley that was blocked by a brick wall.

The wall was too high to scale, so we were trapped when the gang showed up. Judson reached into his pocket with his right hand and put a handful of shivers onto the broom that he was holding in his left hand. Then, just as he had done in his kitchen, he lit a match, blew it out, and touched it to the plastic. Smoke rose again, but this time Judson didn't disappear. The gang moved in and began to beat him up.

There was nothing we kids could do but run away to tell our families. I can't remember if the police were summoned or not. Days later, a friend and I went to Judson's house. From what we could tell, he had received only a huge black eye and a busted lip. We were relieved that he had not been killed.

As I grew older, my interests shifted to stickball and basketball, and I quit going to Judson's house. Judson has continued to celebrate Halloween even to this day, keeping his word that he would never grow up.

SAMMY

Cross the street from my apartment, and walk one block north. Cross Gates Avenue, walk twenty feet, look up to your right, and you'll see Sammy the Bookie's tenement building. He lived there with his wife, who was rarely seen. She never seemed to leave the apartment, but she used to wave to passersby. Rumor had it that this wasn't really his wife, but a male companion.

Sammy was very private because of his line of work, and we never were sure of Sammy's last name. Everyone just knew him as Sammy the Bookie.

He was also the man to call when our television was on the "blink," as we called it. Gran never agreed to a price for his services before he did the work. He just arrived and worked on the TV for about an hour until it was fixed. Delighted, my grandmother would place a bill in his hand.

Their conversation always went from TV repair to gambling. It seemed like everyone in Bedford-Stuyvesant played the numbers. A little extra cash could go a long way in relieving financial stress, so everybody played, hoping for a hit.

A bookie was the term used for a person who could place bets for you. The numbers racket was illegal, run by organized crime. However, the punishment for a small-time bookie (the person who could place bets for you) wasn't too serious if he got caught. A couple of days in jail and a fine were the occasional inconveniences of the job, and hardly anybody got busted for playing.

Playing worked like this: You picked three numbers—like 1, 2, 3. If that number came out straight—that is, in the same sequence you chose—you won five hundred dollars on a one-dollar bet. Just think, five hundred-to-one odds!

You could bet as much as you wanted. Once, my mother hit for three dollars and received fifteen hundred dollars in cash. If the number was not played straight, then you could combine it. For instance, 3, 2, 1 or 2, 1, 3 would be a combined sequence of 1, 2, and 3. If you hit on a combination, the payout was eighty-to-one.

The three numbers picked were the last three digits of the number of people in attendance at the track on that day. For instance, if 12,345 people paid to see the race that day, the number would be 3, 4, and 5—the last three numbers of the total attendance. Today, the Daily Game, part of the legal state lottery, replaces the old numbers game that was played in Brooklyn, and three numbered balls are picked instead.

Some bookies wrote the number and the name of the person who placed the bet on a small piece of paper to keep track of the bets. Sammy figured if he were caught, these pieces of paper could be used as evidence against him in a court of law. So he kept all the numbers that he gathered throughout Bedford-Stuyvesant in his head, memorizing all the combinations of his clients. When you gave him your number, Sammy would point to his head with both index fingers, proudly saying, "I got it, hope you hit!" while laughing in his strange "Hee-he-ha-ha" manner.

As the years passed and Sammy got older, his memory began to fail him. People would hit on winning combinations, but Sammy told them that they had not played that number.

One night out on Fulton Street, an old lady approached Sammy. She claimed that she had played 3, 2, 9 for five dollars, and wanted her twenty-five hundred bucks.

Sammy denied that her bet was ever placed.

The old lady raised an umbrella over her head and screamed at the top of her lungs, "Weasel! You're gonna give me my money!" She proceeded to whack Sammy all over his body with the umbrella.

Sammy had no choice but to run away in fear.

Over time his dementia increased. I was saddened when we got the news that Sammy had died. In those days, no one knew about Alzheimer's, but that was probably what killed the man who had run his entire business by memory. When I think of Sammy now, he seems both a comic and tragic figure.

Doo Wop and George IV

Living over the soul food restaurant at 454 Vanderbilt Avenue opened up my musical talents. By the time I was ten I found myself instinctively singing lyrics when going to school or stuffing a stolen salami up my sleeve at the local A&P grocery store. I had never taken a course in music, but I had a natural gift for pitch and phrasing and a high, clear voice, like the lead singers in popular groups of the time.

In the bathtub I would pretend to be Frankie Lymon (of The Teenagers) and sing,

"Why do fools fall in love?
Why do birds sing so gay?
And lovers await the break of day?
Why do they fall in love?"

My grandmother would yell out from the kitchen, "Boy, you better clean behind your ears and forget all that lovebird nonsense!"

Or I would be Jackie Wilson, and sing,

"Lonely teardrops
My pillows never dry off
Lonely teardrops…"

Then I'd throw my head back and imagine that my wavy process went back too.

A couple of years later, I had been to a few shows at the Apollo Theater and others around town. Some members of my gang liked to sing too, and four of us formed a singing group. We named ourselves the "G Clefs" and met three evenings a week for rehearsal.

The heart of the Bishop turf was at Bergen Street and Classon Avenue. The most direct route from my house was to turn right on Vanderbilt and when I reached Bergen, take a left and walk about five blocks to Classon. In the winter when it was cold, the distance seemed longer, so I used the neon lights of Tony's Pizzeria as a beacon. Our group would sing in the evenings across from Tony's, or on the west side of the street.

My group knew that I had a problem with shyness. They told me I was a good singer, but I didn't believe them. We had talent, and the word got around. Every now and then a group of about fifteen people would gather around our practice gig area to listen.

The first time this happened, my heart raced, and I thought, "I hope they don't want me to sing tonight!"

Then a member of my group said, "OK, guys. Let's sing."

I crawled deeper into my shell.

"I really don't want to!"

"Hey, come on, man," they encouraged me, "What's wrong with you? The people want us to sing!"

"I just can't!" I then tried to sing, but the shyness just choked off my voice.

Then the group huddled, reached into their pockets, and started to collect change. When enough coins were collected, one member left and returned with a bottle of Hombre red wine. We passed the bottle around, taking measured sips. I started to have more confidence as we drank the sweet synthetic wine, and, like magic, my shyness disappeared.

With no downbeat, our group went into Louie Lyman and the Teenchords's "I'm So Happy."

Then, pretending to hold a microphone in my hand, I said to the crowd, "Now we will slow it down for the women in the audience." We began singing "I Only Have Eyes for You" just like The Flamingos. We finished with the Cleftones's great hit "Little Girl Of Mine." The crowd wanted more, and it was just like a real rock-and-roll show right there in the street. We kept singing, and folks said it was hard to tell the difference between our group and the ones we were emulating. But once that wine wore off, my shyness returned and I took the long quiet walk back to 454 Vanderbilt Avenue.

That's pretty much how it went whenever an audience gathered around our practice spot. Eventually, my shyness isolated me from both my singing group and my gang. To make matters worse, my voice began to change, and those high notes were no longer effortless, which concerned me. The solution was to sing an octave lower most of the time and get a handle on my falsetto, but for the extra work it took, I had no patience.

≫≪

Around that time, I began to follow the rock-and-roll shows in New York City. If a show was on, I was there. I remember standing in line at the Apollo Theater in Harlem to see James Brown with his band, The Famous Flames, featuring Maceo Parker. What a show they would put on! The people went crazy, and there was so much hype that it was like a world-wrestling event. I was also fortunate to see Little Stevie Wonder, who also put on a spectacular show.

Since I didn't have much money, getting into these shows was difficult. I would meet kids my age and devise creative ways to slip inside. At times we would pay for a ticket and have the person go in and then open the back fire escape door. The problem was when that door opened, it created light that emanated throughout the darkened theater. Ushers would spot us, and, we'd run and blend into the large crowd.

Another thing we did was to find two used ticket halves and glue them together. This only worked sometimes. When desperate, we used to wait for the show to end; then we would walk backwards into the theater as the rest of the crowd exited. Then we watched the next show. There were at least three or four shows a day.

No one could emcee a show like Alan Freed! Even though he had no musical talent, he was blessed with a gift for communication. His curly hair and raspy voice only added to his mystique.

"We have a whale of a show for you tonight! So kick back and relax as we start off the show with Screamin' Jay Hawkins!"

That night Freed pointed over to the wing of the stage, where a black man dressed in a dashiki made his appearance. In his left hand he held a human skull, and in his right hand he held some kind of a stick. He began singing, "I Put a Spell On You" and hitting the skull with the stick. The first time I saw him, he scared the living daylights out of me, but I reassured myself by thinking, "If Alan Freed feels Screamin' Jay is okay, then Screamin' Jay is okay with me."

Jo Ann Campbell, nicknamed "The Blonde Bombshell" by Freed, was next, followed by George Hamilton IV. He came out wearing cowboy boots. Up until that time, the only people I could remember wearing that type of attire were my TV idols Gabby Hayes and Gene Autry. I looked at him and thought, "What you wearin' those pointy shoes for?"

His southern drawl sparked a memory that completely turned me against him. My singing group and I had heard the rumor that Elvis, early in his career, while he still lived in Tupelo, Mississippi, had said,

"The only thing a nigger can do for me is buy my records or shine my shoes!"

So when George IV began singing his hit "A Rose and a Baby Ruth," my mind was closed. He began to sing a second tune and I thought, "Get the hell off the stage, redneck!"

He finally finished and I said, "Thank God."

After the show ended I went outside to get autographs and a closer look at the stars I idolized. It was an extremely cold day. I had no gloves and wore a long

George Hamilton IV.

leather coat that was two sizes too big for me (convenient for shoplifting). My nose began to run, so I wiped it with my left sleeve.

I was gazing at the ground when I saw the same cowboy boots that I had seen inside the show. I slowly looked up and found myself looking into the eyes of the country singer George Hamilton IV.

I thought, "Not another song!"

He spoke to me in that southern twang.

"Boy, you must be cold," he said.

I didn't like the emphasis on the word "boy," but then I thought, "That's what I am—a boy."

Then Mr. Hamilton pointed to a diner about half a block away.

"What about something to eat?" he asked.

"Sure," I said, puzzled. I wondered what interest he had in me, and I definitely had my guard up.

We went to the diner and sat down at a table. A waitress came over with a menu and two glasses of ice water. Mr. Hamilton then asked me, "What do you want?"

My daughter Nurah and I, reunited wtih George IV, whom I had met 45 years earlier, and his wife Tinky in 2004. Without knowing it, George was a mentor throughout my entire life.

"Would a bagel and cream cheese be okay?" I asked cautiously.

He responded, "If you're gonna eat with me, you're gonna eat more than that!"

He took the menu and asked, "What about sausage, hash browns, and eggs?"

I was astonished, and I started to drop my attitude. "Okay," I said.

Mr. Hamilton placed the order with the waitress. Then he asked me what I wanted to be when I grew up.

I put my hands on the table, stuck out my chest, and proudly said, "I wanna be a bus driver."

He looked over at me and said, "Great. We need good bus drivers."

The food was delivered to the table, and when I reached for the ketch-up, I accidentally knocked the glass of water onto Mr. Hamilton's legs. I was very embarrassed and was pleading for his forgiveness when he said, "Boy, don't worry—accidents happen!"

He just cleaned up the mess. We ate and then he looked down at his watch. "Got to get back. Wouldn't want to miss the show!"

He put out his hand and asked, "What's your name?"

We shook hands and I said, "Don. Don Smith!"

And just like that, he was gone.

Mr. Hamilton's simple act of kindness helped me throughout my life in some very extraordinary situations, in ways that neither he nor that young Don Smith ever could have imagined.

SCHOOL

School was easy for me, not because I was smart or anything, but because I showed up for class. I never liked the idea of missing school, but I was also something of a class clown. I would put a thumbtack on the chair for the teacher to sit on, or when he turned to write on the blackboard, hit him in the back of the head with a spitball.

Spitballs were easy to make—just get two pieces of toilet paper or a paper cloth, and spit in it. Roll it up and you had a spitball. The class would laugh as the teacher turned around and asked,

"Who threw that?"

I would turn and look out the window like I didn't even hear him.

In school, I remembered everything the teachers said in class. When I took tests and got the results, I'd see a big fat A. I seemed to acquire knowledge by osmosis. Whatever was presented, I sucked up like a sponge.

For elementary school, I attended PS 11, which was about three blocks from my house. It wasn't a bad school, but I didn't like it. Other kids were taken to school by bus or driven in personal cars. I was confused by the differences between my family and the families of the kids around me. I walked to school alone, even though I was only eight. I thought that all the other kids were happier than I was. I refused to cooperate with the teachers and began to find myself losing interest in the whole system. I developed a speech impediment and the only one in the world who understood me was my sister, Beverley.

My mother decided that maybe a new environment could kick-start me back into reality. I was sent to PS 9, which was about a mile away. I didn't like this school either. There was no cafeteria, so lots of us kids would go to a local donut shop and gorge ourselves on glazed sugar donuts. Then we would share a quart of milk to chase the donuts down. That was where my lunch money went. I didn't eat breakfast, so that was basically my source of nourishment until supper.

My teacher, Mr. Silverman, noticed that something was "wrong" with me because he couldn't understand one word I said.

My sister had to be called for all translations. This caused a big problem, so the authorities at PS 9 decided to send me across the street to a "six hundred school," which was an alternative school designed for retarded kids, emotionally troubled youth, and the handicapped.

My day consisted of working with clay. When I made something out of a mold, the teacher would compliment me in simple English, like, "Way to go!" as if I were an imbecile.

A speech therapist came twice a week. I met with a psychologist once a month. They would try to converse with me, get frustrated, and then call Beverley.

She would arrive and ask, "What's the problem, Poochie?"

I responded, "I udda gos suvies."

My sister would turn to the "experts" and say, "He says that he wants to go to the movies."

Then they would all act like they had known what I had wanted the whole time.

When all was said and done, I was labeled a "troubled youth." I thought, "If these experts had gone through what I have, they'd be troubled too!"

The kids in the school felt that the experts were completely ignorant about who we were and the core issues of our problems. I thought, "I have some problems, yeah, and I might be a 'troubled youth,' but I'm not stupid," which is how they treated me.

Many of my friends ended up with either the school psychologist or detention authorities trying to figure them out. Most were either given up on or misdiagnosed. What did these "experts" know about me and my friends and our struggles? What did experts understand about the nicknames we gave one another and the pressures even the nicknames caused? Like "Headquarters," the nickname for a youth who suffered from hydrocephalus and had a head two sizes bigger than normal. My cousin had a growth on her face and was nicknamed "Suede Face." Did the experts know how difficult it was to live with such afflictions and show courage without the slightest complaint?

Most of my friends just needed somebody to listen to them who would give them regular attention and feedback. The "experts" were being paid to apply what they thought they knew about human nature and societal norms to help us out of the messes we were in, but they lacked firsthand understanding of our experiences. As a result, we rarely respected them and certainly didn't cooperate. Instead, we preferred the bitter enjoyment we got out of showing that they couldn't help us.

LIFESTYLES

———————

In 1960, Nikita Khrushchev took off his shoe in front of the United Nations General Assembly and yelled, "We will bury you!" I honestly thought that he was talking about burying Bedford-Stuyvesant, my family, and all my friends. That particular white man really scared me. On a local level, though, most whites I encountered were friendly with me, such as the few white business owners in the neighborhood and my mother's boyfriend, Jess.

The prejudice I did feel was prompted by media exposure to the world outside my neighborhood. I wondered, "Why are there so few blacks in the major leagues?" and "Why was Nat King Cole the only black entertainer that I see regularly on TV?" I had friends who used terms like "whitey," "honky," and "redneck," but I did my best to overlook these stereotypes and I tried to not use disrespectful language toward anyone.

When I was about twelve, lots of black entertainers had conks—straightened, wavy, shiny black hair. I wanted to process my hair and bought the Conkolene Straightening Cream.

My friend Adam asked, "Are you ready?" as he twisted off the top of the processing cream jar. He had already prepared my hair for the event with an application of grease.

After reading the back of the jar, Adam warned me that I might feel some burning. He took out a hunk of the white cream using a long metal fork. I squinted my eyes in an attempt to read the back label, and got more nervous when I saw a skull and crossbones and the red caption that read,

"Warning: Contains lye. Avoid contact with eyes."

The burning didn't start immediately, but about two minutes later I

I idolized the look and sound of Doo Wop singers like The Drifters, right down to their straightened ("conked") hair.

could hardly keep my eyes open.

Adam said, "You might have some burning soon, but that only means it's working!" I looked at Adam's head, which was as nappy and woolly as could be.

I thought, "He's conking my hair, and he seems to be an authority on the subject, but his hair is not conked." I was suddenly sorry about my decision, and as the pain began, I could not reason anymore! It felt like someone had taken a razor blade and was cutting my scalp into tiny pieces. I screamed at Adam, "Time to rinse!"

Adam got a bucket, took me to the kitchen, filled the bucket, and submerged my head under the faucet. He poured the bucket of water on my head and then turned on the tap for more water. It was a relief, but I still felt the pain. I went over to the mirror to look, and saw that I had a process.

"Mission accomplished," I said.

"It sure looks nice!" Adam said.

The idea of getting the process originated straight from my passion for singing at that time. It was from the Doo Wop performers I idolized, like The Cleftones, The Flamingos, and The Heartbeats. I wondered if they had suffered the same pain that I had.

That conk worked just like I wanted it to! To my mind, it seemed like I could sing better and that the girls were noticing me more!

PRODIGY

In the *Random House College Thesaurus*, a prodigy is defined as a "gifted child, great talent, whiz kid, phenomenon, rare occurrence, or rarity."

When I look back at my childhood, I recall that I was always quicker and faster than other kids. When I ran I never broke a sweat or was ever exhausted. But I honestly never thought my abilities made me special compared to my friends.

I remember a fire escape ladder near Schreder's that I had been trying to jump and touch for months. It must have been nine feet high and I kept trying and trying. One day I focused, took three giant steps, and ran as fast as I could. I leaped and touched the ladder with inches to spare. I was only ten!

I had an inner energy that I can only describe as wanting to jump out of my skin. I knew something was different about me, and it scared me at first. I didn't want to really stand out from the crowd—I just wanted to be a normal kid.

Most games kids my age played just weren't challenging to me. Often, I would rather work on some personal goal than play a game with the rest of the gang. Part of me wanted to hang around with these kids, who seemed to be having so much fun together, but mostly I was a loner and I learned to live that way. Most people notice the special skills of a prodigy and appreciate the positive aspects of these gifts. But they don't always see how challenging and isolating it can be for such kids to be so different from their peers.

Bert would tell me that when I was born, he couldn't believe my physical coordination as an infant. And indeed, I began to run around the house as an eight-month-old, a gigantic baby athlete. The amazing thing is that I remember some interactions I had with other infants as if it were yesterday. I would pass by my one-year-old counterparts and read their infant minds— not really with language, but through intuition.

"What gives him the right to walk, run, and play faster than us?"

I would think, "I really don't know! I just can!"

At four I was jumping rope with the girls (they let me because I was cute) and chalking the street for hopscotch games. I can't remember too much about when I was five or six, but I do remember running my first mile around Prospect Park. Right after I finished that mile, I ran to the track at Bishop Laughlin High School and sprinted two 2:20s.

Bert also told me over and over again that I was a good athlete—better than other kids. I didn't pay too much attention to Bert's enthusiasm because I knew that he tended to exaggerate. I thought, "All dads tell their kids that!" But then it was confirmed by other people in my family. And I began to feel that maybe his observations held a grain of truth as I discovered that I had perfect timing, both in athletics and singing.

At age nine I remember joining a baseball team. I got hit in the face with the ball and bled profusely. I actually remember that I was relieved. I thought, "Hey, I am normal. I got hit!'

I came back the next day with the right side of my face bruised and very swollen. I was playing first base when a ball was hit to me. I went to second, quickly ran to first, and caught the return throw for a double play.

"Shucks," I thought, "not again!" But my natural athletic gifts weren't really suited to baseball. I switched to basketball and found that I could do lay-ups perfectly after only the first day of practice. Although I was a bit awkward since my body was growing so fast, my shot was good and I could do strenuous athletic exercises with ease.

Bert had played basketball at City College. He saw my athletic potential, and he signed me up at the Bedford YMCA. The coach was a police officer who knew Bert and he was happy to have me on his team. Gene Smith was an excellent coach, one of the best I have ever had. He was a disciplinarian, but he was also fair and caring.

I remember Coach Smith once gave our team subway tokens to an away game. At the Franklin Avenue station, I jumped the turnstile, thinking that I could save my token for another time. Wrong! Coach Smith caught me and admonished me. I did not play that night. This was a lesson I would always remember.

At the age of twenty-two with my first basketball coach, Gene Smith.

The Bedford YMCA produced some wonderful and gifted athletes; Lenny Wilkens, Connie Hawkins, and Michael Davis all played there. Of course, none of us thought that we would be legends who would be talked about for years to come. Of all the great players, I probably was the least destined for such an accolade. Little was mentioned about me in the playgrounds compared to Connie Hawkins or across-town legend Roger Brown. I was a tall, lanky kid coming into puberty, who was extremely shy and didn't like to brag or blow

A young Michael Davis. My YMCA teammate went on to play professionally for the Baltimore Bullets.

my own horn. I had very few friends and enjoyed being by myself. People picked up on this and they thought I was pretty strange. Little did they know that I was struggling to survive.

No one knew my experiences because I kept them to myself. For example, there was the time I came home and found the neighborhood kids in my hallway shooting up heroin. They asked, "Do you want some?" I immediately recognized the danger and responded, "Sure, but my mother's calling me now, and I'll be right back!" I then began plotting my excuse for the future when the same situation presented itself, making a mental note of my next survival excuse or option.

My grandmother surely knew about my abilities! After the Coney Island "spanking" she apologized in the way that only grandmothers do. She made me a gigantic sweet potato pie! She also surprised me by putting whipped cream on the top. I was eating this favorite dessert of mine when she came over and whispered words I would never forget.

She said, "Poochie, there is something special about you, I can see it!"

As time went on, I began to see that my grandmother's words were right on target. Besides my natural athletic gifts, there were other differences between me and my friends. I observed things and situations in my head, and then they would happen, sort of extreme déjà vu.

For instance, I once observed a man from a distance and thought, "When that man gets close to me he will say, 'Those Dodgers lost a heartbreaker last night!' "

When he approached, I asked, "How ya doing, sir?" Then just like I had predicted, he uttered, "Those Dodgers lost a heartbreaker last night!"

These premonitions began to happen all the time in different situations, and with each new experience, they became more troubling and baffling to me.

CONFLICTS

As a kid I had very few role models. Bert used to take me to Ebbets Field to see the Dodgers. I wanted to be Pee Wee Reese or Carl Furillo. They were my favorites! Pee Wee was lightening-quick and Furillo had a cannon for an arm. I never thought of what race they were. I just felt awe! I would save up Elsie the Cow ice cream wrappers and after getting about twenty of them was eligible for two free tickets. Bert and I would sit in the bleachers and he bought me hot dogs, peanuts, and a program.

On one of these outings, he showed me how to officially score a baseball game. It was hard! Each player had a number that corresponded with the position he played on the field, and you had to explain what every player's part was in each play. If an error was made, that also was recorded. Bert was a master at scoring. A fly ball would be hit to right field, and he would have everything down in seconds. "Incredible," I thought.

That day I noticed something for the first time. It happened after the seventh inning stretch as "Take Me Out to the Ball Game" was being sung. I looked over to the Dodger dugout where Campanella was taking off his catcher's gear and realized that he was about my complexion. That same inning I was more surprised when the great Jackie Robinson batted, and I realized that he was a black man or, as we were called then, a "Negro." I then scanned the field and counted three more blacks! All the rest were white, even the umpires. The Dodgers won that game and Bert and I were happy as we headed out of Ebbets.

Bert dropped me off at my house, where I said goodbye and ran up the steps to my apartment. In taking off my pants for bed I heard the crumpling of paper. I put my hand in my pocket and pulled out an Elsie wrapper that I had forgotten. I don't know why, but for the first time I realized that Elsie the Cow was also of color! That was the first time I remember noticing how few public figures were black.

When one comes from a broken home, one tends to notice permanence and order in every other place but his own. In going to my friends' homes, I was happy to be invited but shocked to see how orderly things were. A father, a mother, and children sitting down at the dinner table talking about what transpired in each of their worlds on that particular day bewildered me. After dinner, dad would help the children with homework while mom would tidy up. In my head a picture of my mother would flash and then suddenly disappear.

On some of these occasions I would get mad at my own father. I would think, "Bert, you never prepared me for this. You never told me there were two worlds, white and black. You never told me how to survive peer pressure and suggestions. You never taught me how to study, or for that matter, why to study. Doggone it! You never told me about the divorce!"

Then I would snap out of this downward mental spiral by thinking, "Hey, I have a basketball game tonight!"

⫸⫷

I used to wonder a lot about things that confused me. About one block away from my house on Clinton Avenue were very beautiful mansions and expensive cars. When I was about twelve, I had a summer job at a grocery store, and I used to bring groceries to this area. I marveled at the attire the white people wore: fur coats and expensive leathers in the winter and silks in the summer. I prayed to be fortunate enough to bring groceries to that section of town because they gave five-dollar tips.

When I did get the chance to deliver there, I was shocked upon entering the houses. I noticed high cathedral ceilings and the natural shine of the dark wood. The heavy curtains hung luxuriantly and the furniture was elegant. Very few blacks lived in this private hideaway, and I could never figure out why. Then one day I began to put the whole thing in perspective. It happened one day as I was sitting in a theater.

The movie *Gone with the Wind* was very popular then, as it still is today. I was watching the movie and saw how the slaves lived separately from their slave owners. There was the big mansion for the owner and his family, and the crude shacks for the slaves and their families. The slaves worked very hard in the mansion, only to return to their shacks.

Then I realized the setup! At my house, I had to go outside our apartment to our hall to use the toilet. "Could it be?" I thought. Was there somehow a well-devised plan to emulate the same living conditions that were prevalent in the South?

"Impossible," I thought. "But why not?" I reasoned. If we blacks became a threat, the way to control us was to create the same conditions slaves lived under.

Then I began to see the matchbox we were living in and the structure of our neighborhood: a liquor store on every five blocks and a storefront church on every two. If you were lucky you could somehow miss the dope man who would try to convince you that he had something that could make things better. The whites on Clinton Avenue during those times knew how to stay immune from such temptations. The mystery to me was how did they escape and we didn't?

When one comes from a broken home, one craves permanence. Being around permanence was like being wrapped in a gigantic warm blanket on a cold and wintry day. At 454 Vanderbilt, I never felt steady or secure.

For one thing, I was very fearful of ever letting my few friends know that I lived over a soul food restaurant and that I had to pee in the hall toilet. That was another reason I didn't make many friends. I could just imagine bringing someone to my house for dinner. He'd ask to use the facilities and I'd say, "Just open that door and you'll see our bathroom just to the right!" No way! Or I telling a girlfriend that she had to go outside into a freezing hallway to use the toilet.

My grandmother tried her best. My mother appeared to live in a different world. Bert was an enigma. So with whom could I discuss these inner conflicts? Two outings a month with Bert was just not enough.

I was also an extremely sensitive child. Sometimes my friends would go to the pier and fish. We bought bloodworms for bait. One particular day when I was nine, we were cutting our bait with a knife, and as I pulled the worm out, it ripped into little pieces. When I saw what I had done, I began to feel enormous sympathy for the poor worm. It was like I felt his pain. My friends began teasing me, calling me a wimp.

That night when I was in bed, I thought about the pain that was inflicted on the whole worm population. I then began to cry, "Oh God I'm sorry, please forgive me!" That was the beginning of the shyness and humility that has followed me most of my life.

✦

I was trying to do my best in school and spending more of my after-school time at the YMCA, following Coach Smith's orders. My basketball skills were improving at an unbelievable rate. I was now dunking a volleyball, which was not bad for a kid of my age and height. My teammate Michael Davis was also improving very quickly, and Coach Smith was the main factor. Our team started to beat all the others, and Brooklyn began to talk about us.

About that time, I met Roy Killens. He had an enormous love for the game of basketball, and he became a positive force in my life. Roy had a very strong work ethic and was the type of guy who would try hard. His natural physical abilities were limited, but with his enormous drive and innate wisdom, he wreaked havoc for his opponents. We used to meet at the Y, where he would encourage me to lift weights and run around the track above the basketball court with him.

Roy worked just as hard on his grades and seemed to understand the importance of knowledge. He was my encouragement during those years and being with him protected me from hanging out with those who could do me harm or block me from my destiny. With a little luck, Roy could have been a very good college player. He played for a while at North Carolina College, but fate took him in a different direction. He served in Vietnam and upon his return became a police officer in Philadelphia.

Not everyone on our team found a healthy life for themselves. Take Stanley and Butch, for example. They were wonderful kids who did the little things on our team, like diving for loose balls and doing whatever else Coach Smith asked of them. They were fancy dressers, and when the Latin craze hit, they were very good at a style that was popular then—the Palladium.

I was a horrible dancer and at that age I thought the whole concept of dancing was weird. Get up and make funny movements, spin the girl around, work up a sweat, and then the song was over. Wait a few minutes and another song would be played and the same thing would happen again. "Nonsense," I thought as Stanley and Butch danced with their girls.

Then just before I was to go to Sands Junior High School, I started noticing that both Stanley and Butch had begun skipping Y practices. A few years

My friend Roy Killens.

later, I saw them uptown on Fulton Street and where their destiny had taken them. It had led them to heroin addiction and a life of pure hell.

God's plan for me took me in a completely different direction.

ADOLESCENCE

SURVIVAL

_____

I got through grammar school in good fashion, since I was hardly ever absent and I got really good grades. My speech impediment just disappeared, as I knew it would. I was about six foot three but still lanky. The fact that I ate only doughnuts until evening everyday back at PS 9 had a lot to do with my not having much meat on my bones. In my first year at Sands Junior High I was happy, because they had a cafeteria. In fact, I was generally happier than I had been at PS 9.

Sands Junior High School 265 was located right in front of the Brooklyn Naval Base. You could walk outside and see huge ships and freighters coming and going from all over the world, and soldiers kissing their wives and hugging their children for the last time before they headed out to sea and service.

As a Bishop, I worried about my safety, because I was smack-dab in the middle of Chaplain territory. For backup, I decided to take a friend to school with me; that friend was a long fork that my grandmother used to turn over her roasts. I never planned to use it, but I just wanted to prove a point if any Chaplains had the thought of harming me. I kept the fork in the sleeve of my leather coat, which I never took off.

One day I got sidetracked and accidentally dropped the fork during our free period. The dean of students, Mr. Chance, was told, and I ended up having my parents come in for a consultation. They both showed up, and that was the first time I could remember our ever being together as father, mother, and child. It seemed very strange! It got stranger when I again saw that they would not look in each other's direction, nor would they speak to each other.

Mr. Chance saw the problem and quickly put me on probation. I was told never to return again hiding a weapon. I agreed and the whole thing was over. My mother left and Bert took me to a side room and said, "You know, Pooch, you have your whole life ahead of you. Don't mess it up by doing things like what I heard you did with the fork."

I really didn't have anything to say. I wanted to tell him about the Chaplains and the possibility of getting my a_ _ kicked or my life taken, but I didn't think he could understand. I just nodded my head in agreement. He left and I went home to make a decision. With the decision made, I went to sleep and the next day returned to Sands Junior High with another fork—a longer one!

Once in a while, Coach Smith would come to my house to check up on me. I would see him on his beat and thought how different he looked when he was in a police uniform and not in his coach's attire. Of course he knew about Bert's criminal problems, but we never discussed them. Bert, on the other hand, pretended no one knew, but everybody did.

Then one day I fell in love! Her name was Dolores and I don't know if she was as beautiful to others as she was to me, but I fell hard. At Sands, she did just about everything. She was the lead singer in our upcoming play *Oklahoma* and she was the school's vice president.

She was also Hebrew's girlfriend. Hebrew was one of the leaders of the Chaplains. When he found out that Dolores and I were speaking to each other, he became enraged, and one day a group of about ten Chaplains was waiting for me. I went outside and they moved in on me. I pulled out the long fork and they ran. Mr. Chance found out and this time my parents were not informed. I was simply suspended.

About a week later, Mr. Chance called and invited me back to school. He said that he had heard about the problems between the two rival gangs and that in this instance it sounded like I was threatened. I was grateful that someone finally understood.

BASKETBALL—THE LIFESAVER

"Pooch, pick up, it's Bert!" my sister Beverley yelled, as I was in the kitchen eating a bowl of Wheaties.

The previous week a small mouse had gnawed its way through the cardboard and cellophane wrapping of the cereal box, even though the top of the box wasn't yet opened. As I tried to separate the cellophane, he bit me. He was just swinging there on my finger before I realized what I had to do. I grabbed him with my right hand and squeezed as hard as I could to make him let go of my finger. The mouse screeched and fell to the ground. He limped back into his hole as though he were inebriated or suffering from a debilitating disease.

I walked to the back and picked up the phone.

"Hello," Bert responded, "Pooch, I have tickets to the Knicks game tonight. You want to go?"

Of course I wanted to go. What kind of question was that?

"What time?" I asked.

"I'll pick you up at six. The game starts at seven," he said and then hung up quickly.

I became excited as I thought about the matchups and stars I would be seeing that night. Wilt Chamberlain versus Bill Russell. Elgin Baylor versus Oscar Robertson. My friend Roy and I always discussed Wilt versus Russell and who was the best big man. We came to the conclusion that Russell had better support from his teammates but that Wilt was the better athlete of the two. Russell just kept winning championships! Elgin was a pleasure to watch, as he would dribble the ball with his head twitching back and forth.

I used to wonder if his head moved like that when he wasn't playing. Oscar Robertson was my favorite and I could see why they called him the "Big O." What an incredible athlete! He was virtually impossible to stop!

Bert arrived right at six. I was excited to go, but as I stepped into his car, I felt sorry for my sister Beverley. I was always the one Bert was interested in, never her.

Beverley June Smith was born on May 28, 1942. The fondest memories I have of her are captured in a picture we once had of her sitting slightly

turned at a piano. Like me, my sister was out of the house most of the time. She married early, began having children, and moved out when I entered my first year at John Jay High School. We used to discuss Bert, our father, but with a sort of fake positive attitude. Beverley never said any-

My sister Beverley and me.

thing negative about him, but I could sense that she felt that he could show more concern for her.

On this evening, as we headed for the Knicks game, like so many times before, I thought, "She'll be fine. If anybody in this world can move on, it's my sister Beverley." I opened the car door.

Bert asked, "How are things going?"

"Okay," I said, and slid onto the front seat.

We headed for the Brooklyn Bridge, and then I remembered something as we crossed. The year before, Bert had called and said that he wanted to take me to Delancey Street to buy some shoes. I was very happy because I was growing, and a new pair of shoes could come in handy.

We entered a shoe shop and I began looking at shoes. Then Bert took me to an area of the store where they had larger sizes. I found a pair that I liked, but Bert picked up a pair of clodhoppers, like something Herman

Munster would wear. When I saw them, the first thing I thought was, "Oh no, I wouldn't be caught dead in those!" Bert disagreed. He went into the back room with the salesman and I could hear him bargaining to get the price down. Once the deal was sealed, I was pretty much forced to get them. The salesman wrapped them up and we headed home via the Brooklyn Bridge. Bert dropped me off and when his car was no longer visible, I walked over to a trashcan and threw the shoes in!

A year had passed and Bert never noticed that I hadn't ever worn those clodhoppers. We arrived at 8th Avenue and 50th Street, the site of Madison Square Garden. This was *the* arena for all basketball players. It had a delightful vibe, and the lighting was dim, but adequate. There was as much activity outside the Garden as inside. Scalpers were always trying to get the best price for the tickets that they had purchased months before. The smell of popcorn and beer perfumed the air. Vendors yelled, "Programs! Programs! Get your NBA programs!"

Bert bought a program and handed it to me. We headed for our seats and I was very excited. We sat down, and I realized that our seats were pretty good. Then I thought of my sister Beverley and what she was doing. I knew she liked basketball, too. I began looking through the program and at the NBA player pictures. I began reading about how basketball was invented by placing a peach basket high above the ground. Shots were taken, and then a player would climb up to retrieve the ball. Then I laughed as I thought how ingenious it was for someone to cut a hole in the bottom of the peach basket—it was like inventing the wheel!

The players came out for lay-ups and shooting, and I was in awe. We were fortunate, because that night it was a triple-header, and three games would be played.

Wilt and Russell were playing right before my eyes, and I noticed that Russell was a lot shorter than Wilt. I liked the Celtic green. I thought about the history of the players, including Heinson, Bob Cousy, and the Jones boys. I remembered the incredible defense of Satch Sanders, who played based on how his skills could help the team, never worrying about being a superstar. He knew that's how championships were won—by the unselfish play of individuals for the sake of their team. Red Auerbach knew it too and was a master at getting the right combinations. It was a good game. Wilt dominated, but the Celtics won.

That was also the first night I ever saw Oscar Robertson play in person.

"Wow!" I thought.

The O did everything that night, winding up with thirty-five points, twelve rebounds, and fifteen assists. Elgin ended with forty points. I felt blessed to see possibly the four best players of all time on the same night. I was so entranced that I forgot that Bert was sitting right next to me.

"What great games. Those Celtics are too much!" he said.

I nodded my head in agreement. Upon exiting the Garden, Bert looked at me and asked, "What do you think?"

I don't know why he asked that question. But I looked at Bert right in the eyes and said with seriousness and total conviction, "I'm going to play in the NBA one day!" Little did I know that one day I would be on the same team as the Big O.

⋙⋘

I did not make the junior high school team that year. Daydreaming about Dolores may have had a lot to do with it. Hebrew had dumped her, but I had become more practical. I thought it would be wiser to drop the whole idea to save my skin.

My grades were good and I had to decide about the high school that I wanted to attend. I thought about Boys High but felt that I wasn't talented enough to make that team and, believe me, you needed talent. I considered John Jay High in South Brooklyn. It was only about fifteen minutes from my house by bus or a half-hour jog. They already had two very good players, Curly Matthews and Rudy Walker. I really was sold on the idea when my buddy Roy Killens told me that he was going there too.

John Jay High School

John Jay was just west of Prospect Park and not far from my old grammar school PS 9. The school was right in the middle of the Italian neighborhood, where the graffiti letters "SBB" could be seen everywhere. SBB stood for South Brooklyn Boys. Bruno, the rider of the bike who had challenged my gang when I was younger, was a member of that gang.

The ethnic makeup of the school probably was 80 percent Italian and 20 percent other. Like at Sands, I knew I had to be careful. The year before a brother was stomped to death right outside the school grounds, and the SBB were suspected. A few days later I had to rethink my decision of not taking the fork to school.

I don't know how it happened, but it did! I was in the school gym playing basketball when the guy I was guarding went in for a lay-up and we made contact. I pushed him and he shoved me right back. After shouting profanities at each other, I made a major mistake by shouting, "White boy, meet me outside after school!"

Here I was, a first-year freshman in a predominantly Italian school, selling wolf tickets to an Italian! As the day progressed, I forgot all about my invitation. The school bell rang at 2:15, and I grabbed my books to head home. I opened the door of the school to exit when I noticed a wave of Italians in front of me. Thinking that an Italian bazaar was in progress, I was suddenly brought back to reality as the wave parted, and the guy I had fought with in the gym moved toward me with fists raised.

I raised mine, but sensing that I would be pulled into the crowd and possibly stomped to death, I ran for my life. Jesse Owens could not have caught me. My heart was beating like never before, and the fear of imminent death ran through every sinew and cell of my long and lean quivering body! I headed south with about fifteen Italians close on my heels.

I dashed into the Methodist Hospital emergency room and pleaded with the medical staff for safety. I looked outside the window, where the Italians were still visible, and I could hear them shouting at me to come out. Utter fear consumed me, a fear that I had never known before. I waited, and when I became calmer, began praying to God for protection. I waited and waited. Then I looked out and saw that only about five Italians remained. I waited another hour and left out the back door.

I was not about to go back to that school! I was scared. My grandmother admonished me by saying, "Boy, you can't hang out here; you better go and get your education!" The next week I returned to John Jay—petrified. I asked some Italian students about the whereabouts of the guy I fought with. I was told that his name was Tony and that he would be in the lunchroom during the third period. In class, I planned my earnest apology.

During third period I went to the lunchroom, found Tony, and apologized.

"No problem," said Tony as he bit into a hamburger. "Just don't let it happen again."

He put out his right hand to shake mine. I clutched it.

"I won't," I solemnly promised.

As the bell rang for the fourth period, a small mixed group gathered around me. One Puerto Rican came forward and looked right into my eyes as he said, "Do you know who Tony is?"

I shrugged and shook my head.

"Tony Bananas. His grandfather is Joseph Bananas, the head of the Brooklyn Mafia."

This information was frightening, but I still felt relieved. I had made peace in a situation that could have cost me my life.

BRUCE

Destiny put us together! Bruce was the biggest guy in the school. He stood six foot six and by his admission weighed in at three hundred pounds. Quite frankly, I thought he was fifty pounds heavier and two inches taller, but I never really knew for sure. The whole school knew him and gravitated toward him. He had the gift of gab and could talk anyone under the table.

I first met him in the cafeteria. I sat down next to him just as he was finishing a meal. He got up, put his empty tray on the conveyor belt, and then returned for another meal. He gobbled that one up before heading back for a third meal.

I was impressed. "Hungry, huh?"

"Starving!" he said, as he chomped down on a tuna fish sandwich.

That fall, Bruce tried out for the John Jay basketball team but didn't make it. The coach of the team was Robert Sears. He was a tough coach, who told Bruce that the major reason he didn't make the team was his weight. But on the court, Bruce could hold his own with the players of the day. He had a soft touch and was very light on his feet, despite his knock-knees and obesity. He moved with the grace and motion of a huge porpoise. He had the heart of a lion, and if we got behind in three-on-three games, he was our biggest cheerleader, urging me, him, and our other teammate not to give up. Bruce taught me how to be fearless. He could have been a very good college player, but it didn't work out that way.

Bruce and I used to travel all over the city playing basketball. At that time, I was just a couple inches shorter than Bruce and we made a good combination. We would get up early and head to the most competitive courts such as Ruckers, Riis Beach, or Greenwich Village.

Basketball was taken very seriously. Players would frequent a certain playground and then await the top players in the city. There would be twenty-five to thirty kids all ready to play five-on-five full court, but only ten could play. Everyone in the park instinctively knew who the strongest players were, and the best two would be chosen. Then the selection began.

"I'll take him!" the first player would say.

"I'll take him!" the second would say. They both picked four, and then we were ready to play.

If during the game it was discovered that a player chosen was not good—or as we called it, "a player"—that person would be boycotted for the next game—or forever. If a lay-up was missed or a pass dropped, the other team members would curse you, yelling and screaming. No nets were used, and arguments ensued about whether a shot went through or if it was an air ball. Sometimes knives were pulled, and the guys in the park would work out the problems among themselves, to the delight of the onlookers who had gathered to watch.

One incident that stands out in my mind happened when I was playing ball at PS 20, and I went in for a lay-up. A dirty player by the name of Chico flagrantly fouled me by literally punching me in the mouth. My tongue split down the middle, causing a wound about an inch long and an eighth of an inch deep. I suffered the entire ten days as my tongue healed. It seemed like everything I tried to eat contained salt, only adding to my pain and misery. I could do nothing during those ten days, not even sleep. I was in total hell.

When Bruce and I returned to PS 20, Chico and the rest of the players had forgotten the incident, but that pain was still fresh in my mind. We were on defense when I suddenly stole a pass, headed down the cement playground court, took the customary two steps, and prepared for the third. Taking the third step I exploded skyward, palming the basketball in my right hand. I saw Chico's face through the circular steel rim from above. I took aim and pushed the ball through the rim, making flush contact with

Chico's face, then shoved down as hard as I could, causing Chico's body to plummet to the ground headfirst. The back of his head turned pure red as blood gushed everywhere.

Bruce and I quickly left the playground without saying a word.

≫≪

Those New York City basketball games were dangerous. Thinking back on them reminds me of those old Westerns I watched as a child. A retired gunslinger (trying to be a good guy) comes to town and is confronted by an unruly mob (the bad guys). The good guy doesn't want trouble, but the bad guys continue to bully. Finally the good guy is forced to act, with detrimental consequences for the bad guys. That was basketball in New York in those days. Serious and harsh!

Another incident took place that was comical, but alarming, too. It was rumored that a Knick was playing a pickup game at the West Fourth Street playground in Greenwich Village. He had fouled one of the players who happened to be a local wino. The wino became angry and picked up a wine bottle, which he smashed on the cement table that was used for checkers and chess games. He immediately went after the Knick with the sharp and jagged edge of the remaining half of the bottle. The Knick ran out of the park and down Sixth Avenue with the wino running after him, screaming, "M_ _ _ _ _f_ _ _ _ _, you might be a Knick at Madison Square Garden, but you're just another nigger here in the Village!"

Many more rumors circulated throughout New York in those days. Things were said about players and no one knew the exact story, but everybody claimed to be an eyewitness.

One story is probably the most famous of any. It involved Jackie Jackson, the great leaper and former Harlem Globetrotter. If everybody who claimed they saw this was telling the truth, then about one million people would have been at the playground the day it happened! Some said a young Wilt Chamberlain was involved, others say it was someone else. Bruce and

I even used to tell people that we were there when it happened, but we also just got caught up in the hype.

The story goes like this: Jackie was playing in a game against Wilt Chamberlain, and in the second half, Jackie came down on a fast break. Wilt was right in front of him, the only obstacle in Jackie's path. Jackie went up and dunked right in Wilt's face. The dunk was so powerful that the people who had witnessed it slapped high-fives for about ten minutes in astonishment. Wilt was totally embarrassed. After the game, Wilt went over to Jackie to ask him his name and where he was from.

Jackie answered, "My name is Jackie and I'm from Brooklyn!"

Wilt then asked, "How high can you jump?"

Jackie proudly replied, "I can touch the top of the backboard!"

Wilt couldn't believe it and replied, "I believe your name is Jackie and you are from Brooklyn, but you can't touch the top of the backboard!"

Jackie insisted that he could, and sensing a showdown, the crowd focused on the two players, filled with anticipation.

Wilt climbed up on the fence, reached out, and placed a dollar bill on the top of the backboard. Then he descended and said to Jackie,

"Go ahead, show me!"

Jackie, it is reported, walked to the free-throw line, where he took three or four deep breaths and then shot off like a high jumper, calculating each step. The last step sent him straight up. The crowd gasped in unison as Jackie touched the top of the backboard.

Wilt was shocked. He climbed the fence, attached himself to the basket, and reached out to retrieve his dollar. He looked on top and was amazed to see two quarters and five dimes that Jackie had left for change.

If you ask about this story in New York, most would say that they were there—just like everybody claimed they saw Bobby Thompson's home run, or how they remembered seeing Babe Ruth point to where his home run would be hit. All I know is that I wasn't there and neither was Bruce!

≫≪

Sometimes students from John Jay would meet at Bruce's house. It was an honor to be chosen because Bruce didn't trust everybody. My friend Roy Killens and I would go over and find about six people there. Bruce would play "Sketches in Spain" by Miles Davis and Latin songs by Tito Puente. Some danced but I just watched. Killens was an excellent dancer, making me marvel as he swung a girl around and around. At times Bruce would try, and his body would load up to move his gigantic mass. After about two hours everyone would be gone and Bruce and I would play chess. He beat the tar out of me because I hardly knew anything about the game. I just wanted to talk to Bruce about life and possibly the conflicts I was going through.

However, I would reconsider after sensing Bruce's vibe—a vibe that made me feel that if I did tell him about my problems, he would not understand, because he wasn't the one experiencing them. I felt that Bruce might think that I was feeling sorry for myself. So even though Bruce was a good friend, we could not converse about some of the things that best friends shared.

Bruce got himself into some comical situations. I have never laughed so hard as when I visited Bruce right after he got married. He gave me the directions to his new two-bedroom apartment. I drove there and knocked on the door, and then heard a huge bark that made my body turn cold. I knocked again and heard an even louder bark. The door opened, and I saw Bruce holding on to a huge Saint Bernard. That dog must have weighed two-hundred-fifty pounds. As Bruce yelled, "Hold boy, hold!" I looked on the floor and saw an enormous bone. I looked into the apartment and spotted where the dog had destroyed the door to the bathroom. Jokingly, I thought, "Big man needs a big doggie. I bet Bruce calls him Tiny."

In Bedford-Stuyvesant, we were taught that if a fight broke out and you were outnumbered, the best thing to do is run. Not Bruce! One night Bruce and I were buying a pizza to take back to his house. At the pizza parlor, Bruce got into an argument with five Puerto Ricans. Pretty soon a fight developed. Assuming that Bruce also lived by the Bedford-Stuyvesant philosophy, I took off, thinking Bruce was right next to me. I looked back and saw Bruce fighting them all! I felt guilty, but Bruce never mentioned anything about it. Then I realized that Bruce was from the Park Slope area and had never been in a gang. He operated on a completely different philosophy regarding fights.

Besides the humor and social interaction that being around Bruce afforded, I also learned two valuable lessons during those days. The first was the importance of sharing the ball on the court. One Saturday morning, Bruce and I met and took the train to Sheepshead Bay to play an official game against the "White Boys," as we called them. The neighborhood was primarily Jewish, with a sprinkling of Italians.

Bruce and I would be on the same team and would have to pick three players. We usually picked the same players every time, and the White Boys would beat us every time—we never even came close to winning. We could not figure out the reason we always lost, and we would discuss it over chess games. How could we lose? We devised different strategies and tried them out, but they all failed. We lost game after game to the White Boys.

Then one day I got the stat sheet after a game and really took a good look. I was the high scorer and Bruce was second. Nobody else on our team had more than four points. Then I looked at the White Boys' stat sheet. Each player had double figures and their bench contributed twenty points. It was a team effort. This was a lesson that improved my game and affected the way I played from then on. A team is a team, and all must share the ball!

The second important lesson happened spontaneously when Bruce and I were heading home after playing ball the entire day. We stopped by a store to buy orange juice and coffeecakes like we always did; then we caught the train back to Brooklyn. During that train ride, Bruce told me something that lives with me to this day. He was never one to compliment a player on his game (and neither was I). You just did not do that in those days, or the word might get out that you were soft. But on this day, Bruce painted the picture and I got the message.

We had won all our games at the Riis Beach playground. Bruce seemed to be deep in thought. Then he moved in closer and said,

"The game is close and we are down by three points—10 to 7. And then you hit four deep jump shots in a row to put us up by one. The opposition throws the ball in, and you steal it. You dribble the length of the court and dunk backwards on Lew Alcindor. I don't believe it!"

Bruce sat back, shaking his head and smiling to himself as if he were envisioning it again.

The train pulled into the Sterling Street station and we exited. I had no idea why Bruce seemed so excited. Then I realized he was just talking about something that I tended to forget—that I possessed a skill that was natural and easy for me, but not for others. To Bruce, what I did that day was as amazing as if we had just watched Bobby Fischer checkmate in six.

LEW AND THE GREATS

I first saw Kareem Abdul-Jabbar when he was Lew Alcindor and I was Don Smith. We were both teenagers. It was at the 52nd Street station near Central Park on the A train route. He was being followed by a mob of spectators who were pointing at him and saying, "My gosh, look at that guy!"

What they were shocked about was his height—seven foot one—and they let it be known to him. Lew seemed very annoyed by the attention and motioned to his friend George to shoo them away. They moved about twenty feet or so, when another mob that was descending from an escalator did the same thing—pointing in awe.

I thought to myself, "I bet that guy gets that on a daily basis." I felt sorry for him.

I had felt the same way when I had visited Coney Island's freak shows. I walked through the show and saw the fat woman who must have weighed eight hundred pounds. The performers were in eight-by-eight-foot cubicles with signs on the outside of the doors that listed who they were and a short history. "Siamese twins joined since birth!" a sign read. Another described a man with warts all over his body. This grotesque show brought tears to my eyes! These people toured with the show and were paid to be gawked at and ridiculed. For a few extra dollars, they would sign autographs for you. I spoke to many of them, and they were really caring and kind individuals. However, some spectators laughed and made fun of these performers.

Seeing Lew and how people stared and pointed at him brought back those same Coney Island memories. I ended up in the same car as Lew and George. At that age, I was "only" six foot three and I realized I was about ten inches shorter than Lew. George stood at about Lew's waist. I was shocked. The train came and Lew had to bend over to get off. I just ducked! Amazingly, I ran into George many years later when he coached my son, Yusef, in college. We had some great laughs remembering those times!

The people on the train noticed Lew and the same looking and pointing began, just like at the 52nd Street station. I sat across from Lew and George, observing them unobtrusively. I noticed Lew's eyes, which were bigger than the average black man's. I looked at his hair, which was a little straighter than the average woolly black hair. Later I learned that Lew, like me, was of West Indian origin. His family was from Trinidad and Tobago, while my father was from Barbados.

We rode the train all the way to 155th Street, got off, and headed to the same playground—Ruckers. All the "legends" played here. Some might not have been great shooters, but they did the intangibles like assists, defense, or shot blocking. These players were on local teams with the greats who went on to NBA fame, but many of them never became as well known themselves.

Ed Simmons, who played with the legendary Connie Hawkins, was the one responsible for getting the ball to the "Hawk" at Boy's High School. Without Ed "The Czar" Simmons's great passing and court decisions, the "Hawk" might have just been a pigeon. I would not have progressed in my skills without playing against and with players like Michael Davis, Rudy Walker, Roy Killens, and Bruce Stewart. We were all pretty much joined at the hip by pushing each other day in and day out to help our teams and grow as basketball players.

Few went on to play beyond the local courts, so many did not fulfill their basketball dreams. One was the late Tony

One of the great coaches—
Zeke Clement.

Legendary coach Howie Jones.

Jackson. Tony probably was the Bernard King of his day. The only difference was that in those days one didn't put up quite so many forty-point games. Tony could run like a deer and had the incredible court awareness reserved for the gifted. He played for St. John's University during the days of the basketball scandals. During halftime at one of the games, a reporter asked Tony if he had ever been approached by anyone to fix a game. Tony remembered that a gentleman did ask him one time, and Tony said, "I'm not going to do that. Get away from me!"

Tony was only trying to be honest. Then at the end of the game, federal agents entered the locker room and asked Tony who the man was and why hadn't he told the authorities? Then as quick as you could say "Pete Rose," Tony Jackson's career was over—squashed forever.

I met Tony only once, but after I heard what happened to him, he remained in my heart and soul throughout my career. During my collegiate career, I wore a piece of tape on my right wrist. Psychologically it served two purposes for me. It helped me monitor my touch, and it served as remembrance of my Bedford-Stuyvesant friends—Tony Jackson included.

The great players would not have been legends without the great coaches such as Zeke Clement, Howie Jones, Mickey Fisher, and my YMCA coach, Gene Smith. Without them, Brooklyn would not have been known for basketball.

Peer Pressure

When I wasn't at Bruce's house or on the playground, I could be found on Bergen Street and Classon Avenue, even though Bert and Coach Smith advised me to keep away from these areas and to avoid the influence of the guys in the gang who hung out there. At sixteen, I thought I was in control and could not possibly slip or make a bad decision.

The news of weekend parties spread like wildfire. In New York during those times, we didn't go to a party until 1 A.M., and just about every party developed as if it were staged according to a preplanned script. First, things would be going fine, with kids dancing and having fun. Then almost like clockwork, someone outside the party would throw a garbage can through the front window, shouting,

"Nigger! That's my woman you're dancing with!"

Then he'd climb through the window. Switchblades were pulled and bottles were broken to use as weapons.

Girls would scream and urge the intruder to "cool out," but he would just tackle the guy he claimed was dancing with his "lady."

Then the crowd would pull the two guys apart, and order would be restored. The girl would then embrace the guy who had come to claim her like he were some movie hero. If it was summertime, they would go to a park and have sexual relations. If it was winter, they would do it in the elevator or right in the hallway.

I don't remember anyone getting killed in those dramas, but stabbings were quite common. The next week it was another apartment, a different garbage can, and a different lady, but the basic script was always the same. It seemed like we were all actors in a huge game called life.

I thought I could participate in all this and stay out of trouble, but I was fooling myself.

≫≪

The so-called traumatic experience is not an accident, but the opportunity for which the child has been patiently waiting—had it not occurred, it would have found another, equally trivial—in order to find a necessity and direction for its existence, in order that its life may become a serious matter.

—W. H. Auden

THE ARREST

Jimmy was a cat burglar, Linwood was a comic, and I was a gifted athlete.

When Linwood first introduced me to Jimmy, I saw a large head with sinister-looking eyes. Linwood was fun to be around, but I felt that Jimmy could be abusive if left unguarded. I didn't trust him from the beginning, but I thought I could handle anything, so I dismissed my gut feelings.

Our friendship began pretty innocently. We chipped in and Linwood took the money to a liquor store. He returned with a fifth of Twister wine, which we took turns guzzling as we walked around the neighborhood. We noticed a *New York News* delivery truck at a red light. I jumped up on the back and passed a bundle of newspapers to Linwood, who passed it on to Jimmy. We were laughing the whole time. I had the bundle on my shoulders as we walked to the entrance to the subway station. Then we split our spoils into thirds. A bundle contained about a hundred newspapers, so we all ended up with thirty-three apiece. Linwood and Jimmy gave me the remaining papers, since I was the one who had gotten them off the truck. Was I proud!

At the Borough Hall station, we went our separate ways, and I boarded the train. I began in the first car and worked my way back, selling the newspapers for six cents a piece. Many gave me a quarter and told me to keep the change. This money went a long way in satisfying my ravenous appetite at the John Jay High School lunch line.

Linwood and I both had rap sheets, but it was all for petty crimes, such as breaking into parking meters and stealing papers. I knew Linwood well, but I barely knew Jimmy. I continued to ignore my intuition to stay away from this guy.

We had hung out together just a couple of times when we decided to go to Coney Island. We got off the subway in the Flatbush area, about six stops before the Coney Island stop. We didn't have much money, so Jimmy looked for a place to burglarize. Linwood and I weren't interested in burglarizing anyone, and we didn't think that we could possibly be implicated in anything Jimmy did. We had no idea what it meant to be an accomplice to a crime. It was Jimmy who was robbing folks, not us, we reasoned. On the other hand, we sure liked the idea of having some money to spend at Coney Island.

Jimmy was looking up, casing the fire escapes. We didn't know what he was looking for, but once he found it he disappeared, leaving us outside waiting. He showed up an hour later with a handful of cash—just like magic! Jimmy gave Linwood ten dollars and me the same. We went to Coney Island. When our tens ran out, Jimmy gave us more. We ate hot dogs, cotton candy, and peanuts. We went on the Wild Mouse and Cyclone rides. We hit baseballs in the batting cage and rode miniature live ponies. We had a ball, all at someone else's expense. Linwood and I didn't see the big picture, only the ten apiece and nothing more. This worked out fine twice, but the third time everything changed.

The night was August 2, 1962. We took the train and got off at our usual stop. Jimmy climbed the fire escape, and we waited and waited. After about an hour, Jimmy returned. He had a weird expression in his eyes, an evil look. Linwood and I glanced at each other as Jimmy left.

I yelled, "Where are you going? Come back!" but Jimmy had already disappeared into the night. Figuring he would return, like he always had before, we waited again.

Then we heard sirens and saw that the area was flooded with police vehicles. We were standing about half a block away.

I innocently said to Linwood, "Let's see what happened to Jimmy!"

Linwood said, "Let's get the hell out of here!"

We took off running. Then, from about twenty feet behind us, I heard the command, "Halt! Halt or I'll shoot. Stop! Stop now!"

I fell to the ground, trembling. I had no idea where Linwood had gone. A police officer approached cautiously, and I was handcuffed and taken to the building. A detective met the police officer at the entrance, and I was led to the second floor to the scene of the crime.

I looked and saw blood everywhere. I smelled blood and sensed that a struggle had taken place. I was speechless.

"Do you know anything about this?" asked a burly detective.

"No, I swear!!"

"Well somebody does!" he uttered.

"Not me!" I declared.

This "cops and robbers" chess game went on for an hour. Then more officers and detectives arrived, and one had Linwood in handcuffs. I looked at Linwood's face and saw that he had been beaten. Our eyes met and if they could talk, they would have said, "Don't say a word!"

They separated us, and for three hours, I was interrogated.

"What's your name?" a detective asked.

"Donald Smith," I replied.

"Where ya from?"

"Brooklyn," I said.

"What are ya doing in this neighborhood?"

I felt like responding to his racial reference with a smart-aleck remark like "To buy a watermelon" or "To buy some chitlins." I laughed in my mind. But then I looked around, saw the seriousness of the situation I was in, and said, "We were going to Coney Island to...."

A detective right behind me suddenly interrupted me.

"Linwood said that you hit her."

"Hit who?" I asked.

"The old lady. You know she might die? She's at the hospital in critical condition."

Before the detective could say anything, I interrupted.

"I don't know anything about a lady. I was waiting downstairs with Linwood and we didn't do anything!"

We were then beaten, handcuffed, and put in a back room. Two hours later we were taken to the 71st Precinct on Empire Boulevard by paddy wagon.

We were fingerprinted, photographed for mug shots, and booked. The detectives then put us in a cell on the ground floor and took turns monitoring us.

Linwood tried to apologize for squealing, but I said, "Hey—don't apologize. I was telling them everything I knew, too."

Exhausted, I collapsed and slept.

I woke up when I heard a commotion outside of the cell we were in. I saw flashbulbs flickering and then people jostling for position. I spotted press ID passes on suit lapels, and then realized that they were reporters looking for a story.

One asked, "Who are you going to have represent you?"

Another asked Linwood, "Did you hit the woman?"

I did not know what to do or how to reply. The detectives quickly cleared the reporters away from our cell door. Our cell was then opened and we were taken to the basement to the same paddy wagon that had brought us there. We didn't have any idea where we were going. Like sheep to slaughter, we were headed to the Brooklyn House of Detention for Men at 275 Atlantic Avenue.

This detention facility was built in 1957. It was a newer jail than the Tombs, but it was well known that the place was overcrowded. By the time I arrived, there were 1,012 inmates. I was number 1,013.

Bert had been imprisoned three years earlier at the Tombs. Now here I was, Donald Alfred Smith, at the Brooklyn House of Detention.

SIX LOWER B FOUR

I was all ears as my cellmate was giving me the facts—his facts. After having been interrogated and beaten, I was terrified.

I thought, "What if the old lady dies! Would they send a sixteen-year-old to the electric chair?" Or would I spend the rest of my days making license plates for the state of New York?

Horace, my cellmate, was a Mike Tyson look-a-like who had been arrested for vehicular theft. His description of the crime was, "I liked the Chevy, so I hot-wired it and took it for a spin!"

It was his matter-of-fact attitude that worried me.

I thought, "So you take someone else's possession like it's your own." I didn't understand at the time that my petty thefts were really just the same thing on a much smaller scale.

Horace was a Golden Gloves boxer and feared throughout the jail. I was very fortunate to share the same cell with him because he was twenty or twenty-one, and he looked out for me like a big brother. Other felons might have tried to take my manhood if I was alone.

Just then I heard a loud yell that startled me. Horace remained calm and said, "It's the count!"

About three times a day, guards would walk the outside tiers and count how many inmates were in each cell. When the words "On the count!" were yelled, all the inmates had to put their hands outside of the bars to be counted. Horace and I were doing that very thing. The guards yelled "Sims! Smith!" We both said, "Yes!" They they declared, "Lower B Four is account-ed for," and moved along until all the cells on our floor were counted. They climbed the next flight of stairs and did the same for the upper tiers.

Horace looked at me and remembered that we had been talking.

"If you get Judge Mann at your hearing, you can pretty much turn around and kiss your a_ _ goodbye. He hates black people!" he said.

"I didn't do it. I'm only sixteen!" I said defensively.

"Don't matter. Judge Mann is no joke. Like the devil himself!" Horace's voice was filled with persuasion.

I was horrified as my eyes filled with tears.

"No sense crying. What's done is done!" Horace continued. "Maybe you'll do forty or fifty and that's if she doesn't die. If she croaks, Mann wouldn't bat an eye in giving you the death penalty. He's a beast like that!"

I began shaking. I thought as I looked around, "I'd rather be dead and in my grave before doin' forty or fifty years in a place like this!"

From the depths of my soul, I prayed, "Oh God, please help me. I believe in You and You alone!"

People throughout Brooklyn, criminals and noncriminals alike, knew about Judge Mann. I had heard of him from members of my gang. He was the senior judge in the Kings County Supreme Court. Rumor had it that a black man had raped one of his daughters, and when blacks came before him, it reminded him of his heartache.

Then I told Horace what I had heard regarding Mann. Horace said, "That's right, his daughter was raped by a brother!"

My mouth fell open as Horace continued.

"What I heard was that one time a brother went before Mann on a manslaughter beef, and Mann said right before sentencing him, 'You know, I'm feeling pretty good today. I'm feeling so good that I have good news and bad news for you.' The defendant's lawyer said, 'What's that, Your Honor?' whereupon Judge Mann said to the bailiff, 'Make him stand up for his sentencing!' The bailiff went over to the black defendant and told him to rise. Judge Mann then said, 'You have been found guilty of the crime of manslaughter in the second degree. Then he slammed down his gavel and screamed, 'Ninety-nine years in the state penitentiary. Get this scum out of my courtroom!' The bailiff handcuffed the horrified defendant, who then asked Judge Mann about the good news that was promised. Mann peered over his bifocals and said calmly, 'I could have given you life!'"

Now I was totally horrified because my trial was to be in the same courtroom, with Judge Mann presiding. I waited for the trial for three months.

During that period, I became good at card games like dirty hearts, spades, and whist. We used to gamble for food. We would play for our dinners and I won 75 percent of the time.

One night I won three liver dinners gambling. The losers didn't mind—they hated liver. I still love liver! Even the kind of liver they served, with a rubber band around it. I could never figure that out! Dinners were served on metal trays. No knives or forks were provided, so you had to grab your liver with your hands or try to cut it crudely with your spoon. I did the latter. A cup of stale coffee was provided, along with a chunk of hard bread, a lump of butter, and a lump of jam. Also on the side was usually a small portion of fruit cocktail or pineapple. I ate everything. I grew and grew.

I was given the job of folding inmate sweat socks. Folding sweat socks was easy. You grab the toe part of one sock and twisted it into the opened part of the other. The secret was in how you twisted your hands. I became pretty good at it and made five dollars per week. It was the first real job I had ever had. One day, while folding, I thought of a way to escape. I began to take socks back to my cell. Even Horace didn't know my plan.

After a while I had about half a dozen. I tied them together to make a rope. My plan was to tie the top of my rope to the first horizontal bar on the iron cell door and hang myself. My grandfather had hanged himself, and my sister told me that

The Brooklyn House of Detention. I was confined in this building in Six Lower B Four, on August 3, 1962.

Bert had mentioned something about having a cyanide pill when she visited him in the Tombs. It seemed like this was the natural thing to do. I wanted to execute my plan in the worst way, but couldn't. I got it all set up, had it around my neck, but I just couldn't make myself jump. I tried, but I couldn't.

※ ※

The play area was on the roof in a tightly fenced zone. I could see the Williamsburgh Clock, and if I looked intently, I could see my house at 454 Vanderbilt Avenue. I loved to play basketball even more in jail than on the outside. It provided a complete distraction from my fears. When I first arrived, I was six foot three and good at basketball. Within four weeks I had grown an inch. My game had improved dramatically and was the talk of the sixth floor.

The sixth floor housed inmates who had committed property crimes, like Horace, or young first-timers like myself—kids like me who could be taken advantage of if they were on the upper floors with the hardened murderers, sociopaths, and rapists. I heard that Jimmy was on one of these upper floors, and I was glad we were separated. I had been incarcerated for nearly three months. The old lady pulled through, thank God, and my bail was dropped to twenty-five thousand dollars. I was there so long that jail life was becoming normal.

One day I was eating in the cafeteria when my name was called. I froze, thinking that it was Judge Mann coming after me.

The guard shouted, "Smith, Donald Smith!"

I said, "Yes?"

He continued, "You've been bailed out. Collect your things and be ready at your cell!"

I was totally awed! After three months, I was finally leaving.

I was taken back to my cell to await discharge. Horace didn't know I was leaving because he had missed lunch while he was in a meeting with his attorney.

When I came back, Horace said, "Whatever you do, don't sign a Y.O."

I was baffled and asked, "What's a Y.O.?"

Horace said, "Y.O. stands for 'youthful offender' and it is an agreement for a youth that grants a maximum of three years for any offense!"

I then asked, "Why shouldn't I sign one?"

He said, "Because you'll never be able to use it the next time you get busted!"

I thought, "That sounds logical." Then, like a ton of bricks, the situation hit me, and I said to Horace, "You might get busted again but I will never ever come to a place like this again." And then I told Horace that I had been bailed out.

It was a November afternoon when I got my freedom and walked out of jail. I could not wait to get back to John Jay High. The next morning Bert and I were at my attorney Leonard Kaplan's office at nine. I signed the Y.O. paperwork, and Kaplan assured me that the charges would possibly be dropped and that I would most likely get probation with no criminal record.

God had heard my prayer and answered it! Even though the Y.O. was signed, I feared going before Judge Mann for sentencing. He might find some technicality and throw the book at me.

My sentencing was set for December 20, 1962, at two in the afternoon. I got there at noon. I waited and prayed, and when my case number was called, something happened that increased my understanding of prayer.

The bailiff addressed the court: "Ladies and gentleman, Judge Mann is ill and will not be in this morning. The presiding judge will be Judge McDonald."

My deliverance came in the form of Judge Mann's absence. I was sentenced to three years on Riker's Island, but Judge McDonald remanded my case over to the probation department.

I was so happy to see everybody, and they welcomed me back. My grandmother cooked a turkey and stuffing just like I knew she would. Coach Smith was jubilant but careful not to show any favoritism toward me in front of the team. And at John Jay, Bruce and Killens were also happy.

Then I wondered if they even knew about my arrest. The case made the headlines of many newspapers. However, New York City newspaper employees were on strike during that period. As a result there was limited circulation. Bert told me that the newspaper strike was my saving grace. If the story had been publicized under normal conditions, there would have been enormous political pressure to put away three black teens who had allegedly beaten up a white lady.

Instead, few read about what took place on August 2, and now I was wondering, "Did my friends?" I knew I was innocent of that awful crime, although I was guilty of choosing bad friends. I had an explanation ready for anyone who asked—but no one did.

CHANGE

I hated math! Social sciences were my thing, not rounding numbers off to the nearest whatever. I was more interested in subjects like why slavery existed, or why the American Indians lost their land, or why Jews were persecuted in Germany during World War II—not how many apples were in a bushel. I was a feeling-type person. My math teachers were boring—they seemed like closed souls who lacked understanding of the real world. To me, the ability to appreciate a rainbow or the crying of a baby was more important than mathematical formulae.

At John Jay, I became a very good student. I had a plan to change my behavior, and it began to work like a charm. I missed no classes and began to soak up knowledge like a sponge. Even so, I slipped into bad habits once in a while.

Once, during a test, I asked a student who was sitting next to me for the answer to a science question. I remember whispering in a very low voice, "What's the answer to number 6?"

The student looked around nervously and said, "It's C!"

I felt guilty, but then I invented a rationale for my cheating and thought, "I only did it once," or "At least I'm not like Chan, who does it all the time."

Chan's cheating puzzled me. He was an immigrant with physicians as parents, and I couldn't possibly see why he did it. I didn't know much about Asian cultures, but I respected what little I knew. Chinese family life seemed very orderly, where children showed tremendous respect to their parents. Much later I understood that Chan had to become a doctor. Nothing else would be accepted or tolerated. If he failed, he would lose face among his family and culture.

I realized that Chan had a hard time just being a normal kid, a stress-free kid. So Chan would cheat. A grade of B was not good enough. It had to be an A at any cost. I understood that even though Chan was a good student and from an educated and balanced family, the enormous pressure to succeed in school placed terrible strain on him. At least I wasn't stressed out so much that I was terrified to fail!

I realized that within every family—even families that seemed more successful than mine—kids could feel negative effects.

JAZZ

I was a young, just-released-from-jail sixteen-year-old who wanted to make something of myself. I didn't know what I wanted to become.

But I tried a few alternatives. I applied for a job as a messenger in Lower Manhattan. I didn't get that position, but I did get a job pushing expensive fur coats around on a dolly. I loaded the coats onto trucks, and then the coats would be delivered to famous department stores such as Macy's or Barney's.

On Fridays I was paid and would travel to Greenwich Village to treat myself to an Italian dinner or possibly a movie. I still loved being alone, and after Linwood and Jimmy, crowds bothered me. I never wanted to make a wrong decision like that again, so I leaned toward solitude. It was safer that way.

One night I decided to go to the Village Gate to hear some jazz. The Ahmad Jamal Trio was performing, and I had never heard a name like that before. I thought Mr. Jamal was from Ghana or something. It never dawned on me that he was an American.

He played his hit "Poinciana," and I was hooked. He then went into "Billie Boy," and at that moment I realized that all my Doo Wop interest had suddenly transferred to jazz. Every weekend after that I was in Manhattan going to shows. I loved the piano and had the privilege of seeing the greatest piano players live.

I saw Thelonious Monk, Horace Silver, and Bill Evans. Like Billie Holiday's voice, Bill Evans's music touched me and eased my pain. When he played, I knew what he meant in his ballads.

Bill Evans and Billie Holiday (although I never saw her perform live) were the jazz musicians who helped shape my temperament and outlook on life. What Billie Holiday experienced and had to endure was clear in the lyrics that she sang:

♪

Southern trees bear strange fruit,
Blood on the leaves and blood at the root,
Black bodies swinging in the southern breeze,
Strange fruit hanging from the poplar trees.

Pastoral scene of the gallant south,
The bulging eyes and the twisted mouth,
Scent of magnolias, sweet and fresh,
Then the sudden smell of burning flesh.

Here is fruit for the crows to pluck,
For the rain to gather, for the wind to suck,
For the sun to rot, for the trees to drop,
Here is a strange and bitter crop.

—"Strange Fruit," written by Abel Meeropol and sung by Billie Holiday

Club owners would ask Billie not to sing "Strange Fruit," but on most occasions she did.

She later died of a heroin overdose and possibly a broken heart. Bill Evans also struggled with addiction during most of his adult life. He was born on August 16, 1929, and died on September 15, 1980, of a bleeding ulcer, cirrhosis of the liver, and bronchial pneumonia.

Besides the piano, I also loved the saxophone and would go to see Dexter Gordon, Rahsan Roland Kirk, and Gene Ammons. I learned the names of the top clubs, like Slug's, The Five Spot, and, of course, The Village Gate. I was only sixteen, so I pulled hairs off my head and pasted them on my chin

Strange fruit: Two men are lynched in Marion, Indiana. After being accused of murdering Claude Deeter, twenty-three, and assaulting his girfriend Mary Bail, nineteen, two young African-American men are taken from the Grand County Jail and lynched in the public square. Photo taken on August 9, 1930.

and lip to look eighteen. It worked!

I was mesmerized when I learned that John Coltrane, Miles Davis, and Bill Evans were in the same band! I truly appreciated these fantastic musicians. Outside of being naturally gifted like Ahmad Jamal, Sarah Vaughan, or Louis Armstrong, the only other way to achieve greatness was to pay your dues. You had to play with the greats, travel with them, and think like them.

I would get into an argument if I heard someone slander a great jazz musician. When Eddie Harris and Miles Davis experimented with electric sounds, I was angry, thinking that they were selling out. At times friends would compare the great legends of the day to less-gifted musicians and that would infuriate me. I deemed myself jazz's self-appointed sixteen-year-old bodyguard and was proud of it.

I remember a joke I heard recently: A man had traveled to New York on business. He decides to take in some famous sights and goes sightseeing at the Empire State Building. On leaving, he takes the elevator down but gets stuck on the 35th floor. It was a Friday afternoon around five, and the poor gentleman was trapped. After a while he began yelling, "I can't take this, get me out!" On Saturday his yelling became more serious: "Please, I can't take this get me out of here, I can't take any more!" On Sunday the man was crying, and totally mad, yelling, "Help, somebody help, make it stop. Stop! Please stop!"

On Monday two workers heard the man and one said to the other, "My God, that poor man has been stuck in that elevator all weekend. Let's let him out." The other worker put his key in the emergency lock and turned it. The elevator descended to the lobby and, as the man walked past, the workers asked, "Are you okay, sir?"

The poor man who had been in the elevator for three frightening days responded by grabbing his head and saying, "I'm fine, but please, no more Kenny G. *No more Kenny G!*"

Don't get me wrong. Kenny G is talented, but he is not John Coltrane, Miles Davis, Bill Evans, or Ahmad Jamal.

MAKING THE TEAMS

After I got out of jail, the basketball season was already underway. I thought I was big enough to play, but Coach Sears at John Jay thought otherwise. He saw me as a "project," which he verbalized to his two stars, Rudy Walker and Curly Matthews. Both tried to get me on the team, but Sears thought I was too weak.

With Curly and Rudy, John Jay High had one of the top teams in Brooklyn. Curly was a great offensive player who was smart and patient. Rudy was chiseled like a Mr. T character, could rebound with the best of them, and was a tenacious defensive player.

I didn't make the team that year and had to wait until the next. During the summer I learned that I had a problem with my eyesight. I suffered from astigmatism, so when the ball was thrown to me, I fumbled around. I got glasses and started to eat better, and in no time my basketball game improved. I was wiry but strong.

My senior year, I played center. We had good ball players on the team and knocked off some top teams that season. Bert used to come to the games and would yell at Coach Sears about his erratic substitutions. Coach Sears would tell Bert to "shut up!" which prompted Bert to move to the other side of the gym. We were a very talented group. We beat two top teams that year, New Utrecht and Sheepshead Bay. While I was playing at John Jay High, I continued to play at the Bedford YMCA.

Coach Smith was not one to compliment players, but I would see pleasure in his eyes when I made a great play, like the time I was thrown an alley-oop pass and dunked the ball backwards over everybody.

Hank Whitney, the basketball player who recommended me to Iowa State University.

One day Coach Smith told me that he wanted to talk with me about something. We went to a fast-food restaurant and he began, "Don, you are some player and have enormous potential. You are a pleasure to coach, and I would like you to go on in basketball. I want you to come to the Y on Friday and play against Hank Whitney. Hank played for Iowa State University. If you do well, we think you might be able to go to school there."

I really appreciated these compliments from Coach Smith, and knowing him, knew that it came from his heart. I asked, "What time will Hank be there?"

Coach Smith said, "7 P.M."

I said, "It's on!" and we left the restaurant.

For four days I worried about going up against the Big Eight Conference standout Hank Whitney. I began doubting myself. "You're not that good. People are just pumping up your head with nonsense!" Then I thought, "Coach Smith would never lie to me. I can play!"

Friday arrived and at exactly 7 P.M., we were ready to play one-on-one. I glanced at Hank, who looked very intimidating. He stood about six foot seven, with a corn-fed physique. He didn't smile as Coach Smith introduced us.

We played for about half an hour and I didn't know what to say after we finished. Then I saw it! Hank had a big smile on his face, and he seemed more sociable. Coach Smith and Hank spoke for a few minutes and then both approached me.

Hank put out his hand and said, "I have never met anyone who could jump higher than me. I will call Iowa State University and see what we can do about helping you go to school there." I looked over at Coach Smith and realized that he was smiling at me for the first time in my relationship with him.

So the idea of going to Iowa State was planted in my mind, and I wanted it to happen. While I waited to hear from the school, all kinds of doubts clouded my mind. I was concerned. Maybe Hank was just trying to be kind in saying goodbye after our game. I did think that my vertical jump was incredible. My jump shot was deadly and soft as I shot it off the backboard, and I rarely missed. But those doubts kept coming back to me. What was wrong with me?

About a month after meeting Hank at the Y, I got the news that I had been accepted at Iowa State University of Science and Technology in Ames, Iowa. God again had answered my innermost prayers.

⁂

I was on cloud nine for days. My grandmother tried not to show her emotions and spent more time in the kitchen, cooking. I went through the community telling people goodbye.

If Bert or Coach Smith knew that I had gone to Bergen and Classon to say *adios* to my gang friends, they would have both had babies. Later I went back home to follow the orders of my mother: Go get a haircut; see your probation officer; call the airport and confirm the reservation.

I had no problem with the first two, but the airport part concerned me. I simply could not understand how a gigantic plane could lift off the ground and rise high into the skies. The idea of something so big traveling over five hundred miles per hour was overwhelming, and now I wondered if I had the courage to go.

Some years earlier, a plane had crashed about a block away from Bruce's house on Sterling Place, right off Flatbush Avenue. It was wintertime, and I went over to see the wreck. The plane's wing stuck up higher than any of the buildings in the area. It was a United Airlines flight, and there had been only one survivor, 11-year-old Stephen Baltz. So I thought that if the flight I was to take to Iowa crashed, at least I had a chance to be the one lucky survivor.

I walked into the barbershop to get that haircut. The place was crowded as I saw four barbers working on four heads. I was met with the usual greeting.

"Where you been at, kid? If you guys keep growing those Afros we all will be out of business!"

I chuckled as I laid eyes on my barber, Shorty. I had been getting haircuts here so long that Shorty was like family to me.

"I've been around but have been focusing on my grades. I got a scholarship to college to play basketball," I volunteered.

"Well that's great, Pooch. You're a very smart kid and you have feelings for people. You'll go far in this life if you just keep your head on your shoulders."

After Shorty finished cutting the hair of the person he was working on, he motioned to me and said, "Hop up and let me cut your hair for the last time!"

I didn't know what he meant. Why had he said those words, I wondered. Would the plane I was taking crash like I had thought? Would I never return to Brooklyn, and if not, why?

Shorty finished and I tipped him. When I said goodbye, I felt that it really was for the last time.

I then went downtown to see my probation officer, Martin Tausner. Mr. Tausner had been in my corner since I was thirteen years old. He was very tough on me but fair. He had also given me a very good reference letter to help raise my bail. Mr. Tausner was a huge man with a very thick Brooklyn accent, who had seen some kids make it and others destroy themselves on drugs and alcohol.

I told him that I was going to school in Iowa, and all he could say was, "That's a miracle! I can't believe it!" Knowing what I had been through as a youth, neither could I. He embraced me and said, "Take care of yourself and study hard!" I left his office and headed home.

In going back to my apartment, I almost forgot my third and final assignment—to reconfirm my reservation. I called Delta and asked the ticket agent, "Could you please let me know the status of a Mr. Donald Smith leaving on Flight 231 on March 12, New York to Chicago, Chicago to Des Moines?"

I waited a few minutes and the agent said that everything was confirmed. My tasks were complete, so like any growing teenage boy, I fell asleep.

Leaving Brooklyn

———

"Hurry up, Poochie! You're going to miss the plane. We must go!"

My mother was very anxious as she urged me to hurry. I don't like ties and never have, but I figured the thin one hanging from my neck served a purpose. My mother had bought me new shoes, clothes, and toiletries.

I was starting to get nostalgic and, quite frankly, scared. I thought, "This is March and I will be turning eighteen years old, and I'm going to college." The only person in my family who had ever gone to college was Bert, who attended City College. Now here I was, doing the same thing.

My grandmother yelled from the kitchen, "Make sure you have clean underwear on!" I could not understand why grandmothers said that kind of stuff. If the plane crashed, who would care?

My sister Beverley seemed to be dealing well with the idea of me leaving, but my young half-brother Duane seemed as confused as I was. I completed all the goodbye formalities with my family, and then called Coach Smith to say farewell.

My mother was radiant. She was shining as only mothers can when they are proud of their children. I went to the kitchen, got my mayonnaise jar, poured milk into it, and dumped in three scoops of Hershey's chocolate. I went over to the stove and picked up three of Grandma's biscuits and began eating and drinking. I yelled, "No one can cook like you, Gran!" as I wiped a tear from my eye.

A few minutes later a horn sounded outside. It was the taxi, my ride to the airport.

The trip took forty minutes on a good day, but if the turnpike was busy, sometimes it could double that time. The driver said that if necessary, he could take side streets. I glanced over at my mother, who looked like a cross between Lena Horne and Dorothy Dandridge. She was beautiful.

I then began to reflect. A year and a half ago I had been arrested for first-degree assault, burglary, and a Sullivan Law violation. A kid who stole from parking meters, grocery stores, and newspaper delivery trucks! A young wine-drinking, marijuana-smoking, Doo-Wop-singing kid!

Then I somehow caught ahold of my emotions.

"No," I said to myself, "I am not all those negative things. I am a product of my society, I am a child of the world, and I am fallible like anyone. Those bad acts were not me but a dark and shadowy replica of me."

I glanced out the taxi window and saw a sign that said "Airport—5 Miles." I became afraid and prematurely homesick. I thought, "I don't want to go, maybe next year. Maybe the SAT test was wrong and I didn't pass! That would be more logical. A black kid from Bedford-Stuyvesant going to college! No way!"

As we pulled up to the airport drop-off area, my mother suddenly said, "Study hard, I'm late, I have to go!"

I looked at the taxi as it sped off and yelled at my mother, "I love you!" In the back taxi window I could see my mother mouth the words "I love you too" as she put up her right hand and blew me two imaginary kisses. I felt pretty good because that was the first time my mother had ever said she loved me.

I grabbed my two new suitcases and entered the terminal. I walked to the ticket counter and was greeted by my father, who was standing at the check-in counter. I walked toward him and he began to lecture.

"This is a chance for you to make something out of yourself. Be careful who you hang out with and keep your mind on your studies!" I nodded my head on his every admonition.

He continued, "Let your past problems be a lesson for you!"

"Yes. Okay!" I replied, slightly annoyed.

I looked over to my right and saw the destination sign—Delta Flight 231 to Chicago was now boarding.

I hesitantly embraced my father and then I entered the plane.

I had fought through my fears and now I was more curious than scared. It was a beautiful spring morning with sunny skies, and I was paying attention to every minute detail as Flight 231 took off with grace and precision. Then, like a flash, we were landing at O'Hare International Airport.

I was proud of myself. I had handled my first flight with maturity. O'Hare was bustling with thousands of people running in every direction. The public address system gave flight information and I heard mine: "Flight 101 leaving for Des Moines, Iowa, gate number two." I went to the TV monitor to confirm it, walked to the gate, and boarded the flight.

We took off quickly. "Too quickly," I thought. I was sitting in a window seat, and about twenty minutes into the flight, my Doo Wop brain began scanning the lyrics I knew. Like a movie, I began seeing the great singers I had idolized: Stevie Wonder, The Righteous Brothers, Little Anthony and The Imperials, Curtis Mayfield. My mind focused harder. It was as if I were turning binoculars to get a better focus.

Then I saw the vision in my mind. First it was a picture, and as my mind relaxed, it turned into a news article. The face was that of Buddy Holly! The article read: "February 3, 1959—Buddy Holly, Ritchie Valens, and The Big Bopper were killed today in a plane crash over the snow-covered cornfields of Mason City, Iowa!"

I froze. "Plane, please don't crash now. I am only seventeen!" I thought as I looked out the window. As we started our final approach, I saw row after row of corn. I then recalled some lyrics I once sang at Sands Junior High School: *The corn is as high as an elephant's eye and it looks like it's climbing right up to the sky / Oh what a beautiful morning, oh what a beautiful day.*

Things were not so beautiful for me at this moment. I became very attentive from that point on. I started to look at the flight attendants after hearing every noise or feeling sudden movements of the plane to try to ascertain if they were normal. The flight attendants smiled, but I didn't believe their smiles. The pilot then made the final approach announcement, but I didn't believe that either. My young mind insisted, "We're lost!"

Then, like a normal plane making a normal descent, we made a very smooth landing. I heard, "Ladies and gentlemen, welcome to the Des Moines International Airport. The present time is 2:30 Central time. I hope you enjoyed your flight and thank you for flying Delta."

I put down the airplane Bible I was clutching to my chest and gasped a sigh of relief. "Thank God!" I thought.

When the door opened, I was the first one off—running! I looked around and saw something unnatural. I couldn't put my finger on it, but for some reason I suddenly felt like a Martian or an alien. Then I realized the problem. There were no black faces to be seen.

"Where on earth am I?" my mind whispered. I walked to the baggage area and noticed a black skycap. I felt elated as I walked toward him.

"What's up, bro?" I asked.

"Hi there," he responded in perfect Iowan English.

I knew then that I was in trouble! I looked around and saw that everyone was white—Iowan white! That even included the skycaps! I was instantly homesick. I knew that the planned itinerary was to meet Coach Glen Anderson at the arriving baggage area, but I couldn't tell one white face from another. I was fearful that one of the faces might have a hood over it, and then I would really be in trouble.

A few minutes later, a tall, pigeon-toed gentleman approached, put out his hand, and said, "Donald Smith? Hi. I'm Coach Anderson, ISU."

I tried to be cordial, but I was nervous.

"How was your flight?" asked the coach.

"Good," I said.

"Do you have any luggage?" Mr. Anderson asked.

"Yes," I replied in another monosyllable. I went over and took a bag off the conveyor belt and Coach Anderson took the other. We walked to the loading area outside where we met another man. He put out his hand and welcomed me to Iowa. Both bags were placed in the trunk of a silver Buick. Then as quick as one could say "Jackie Robinson," we were off on the forty-five-minute ride north, to Ames.

The driver, whose name I cannot recall, was very informative. He told me about how the corn was harvested. He described the pig and cow populations. He then went on to discuss the snow and the unpredictability of Iowa winters. To this day I really think that gentleman was preparing me for a cultural shock. As we drove, I noticed that the rows of corn went on endlessly. The driver kept talking.

"Ames is about forty miles north of Des Moines. Do you drive?"

"No," I said. I stared out at the corn.

He then began to tell me about Cyclone basketball and how the other sports teams were doing. Coach Anderson, who had been silent up to this point, began discussing the same. "ISU is in the Big Eight conference. Wilt Chamberlain went to Kansas and we had Gary Thompson."

I continued to stare at the corn like I was counting every stalk. Then the driver asked me if I wanted to listen to the radio. I really didn't, but neither did I want to be rude, so I answered in the affirmative.

The radio was turned on, and I heard the song "Sugar Shack." *"There's a crazy little shack across the track. ..."*

I tried not to let the driver and Coach Anderson know that the music being played had nothing to do with my experiences or me. So in my mind, I substituted Motown songs I liked for every one that was playing on the car radio.

Before I knew it, we were entering the campus of Iowa State University.

IOWA STATE
UNIVERSITY

GETTING STARTED

_____

Near the crossroads of the nation, where I-35 and I-80 intersect, Ames is cen-
trally located to all points. Interstate road systems place Ames less than a day's
drive from Minneapolis, Kansas City, Omaha, Chicago, St. Louis, and Milwau-
kee. Average winter temperature: 20.8°F. Average summer temperature: 71.8°F.
Average annual snowfall: 30.1 inches. Population: 27,003. Population by race:
Caucasian 26,694, Asian 151, Black 116, Other 42.

I was taken to the Memorial Union, which is a central gathering place on
campus that includes a hotel. Coach Anderson filled me in about the following day's itinerary. I was really tired and could hardly lift the suitcase out of
the car trunk. Coach Anderson took my other bag, and we rode the elevator
to the third floor. As I entered my room, I said goodbye to Coach Anderson
and thanked him.

I lay down on the king-sized bed for a few minutes and then I went
over and turned on the television. I saw Sammy Davis Junior, Frank Sinatra,
and Dean Martin in a movie. I wondered if Dean and Frank really liked
Sammy as much they appeared to. Then I fell asleep.

The next morning I was awakened by the worst recitation of the English language I had ever heard. It was coming from the television that I had
left on all night. I looked closely and saw men wearing big cowboy hats and
the biggest pants that I had ever seen. It was an animal auction! The man
talking seemed like he was selling hogs.

I could make out some of the gibberish as the cowboy spoke. "Do I
hear 20? Do I hear 25? Now 20…now 25…?" I didn't know what in the

The Fountain of the Four Seasons, in front of the Memorial Union at Iowa State University.

world the man was talking about. Iowa seemed the complete opposite of Brooklyn.

I decided to call my mother, thinking that I could get her before she left for work. I called and got my grandmother, who said that my mother had left an hour earlier. I realized that the time difference of an hour had thrown me off.

Then my grandmother said, "Pooch, Shorty the barber died last night. They said that he just collapsed. They don't know why!"

I had known instinctively something was wrong when I was in his shop. Just before we hung up, I told my grandmother that I loved her. That was the last time I ever spoke to her.

Coach Anderson had said that he would come by at ten that morning to take me to campus for registration. I showered and went down to the restaurant for breakfast. The Union was very busy as students rushed about, preparing for the upcoming spring quarter. As I ate, I thought about how the courses would be at a college level. I knew that I wanted to major in something where I could make a difference. My plan was to go back to

Brooklyn after graduation and help out in my community.

It was now eight in the morning, and I decided to take a look around the town. I exited the Memorial Union and headed outside. After walking about two blocks, I saw a street sign that said Lincoln Way. I continued on and passed a pharmacy, then a bookstore. I then saw a theater and a few blocks further, a pizza place. I noticed that all the people on the street were rushing to their destinations, and that everyone was white.

Even though school wouldn't start for a week, the campus was already crowded. I saw wave after wave of white faces. I decided to walk back to the Union and, lo and behold, right across from the pizza place, I saw a black-faced man heading my way. I smiled and prepared what I was going to say, like, "What's up, bro?" or "Hey brother, where's the brothers?"

As I approached, I tried to make eye contact, but he dropped his gaze. I went over to him to try to start a conversation, but he wouldn't speak to me. I looked into his very, very black face and realized that he looked like no brother I had ever seen before. Then I looked at his upper right chest and saw a badge with his picture that read "Congo." He was a foreign exchange student! I headed back to the Union.

Coach Anderson arrived right on time. We headed over to Beardshear Hall for registration, where I went to a small office and met an older lady who had some mannerisms that reminded me of my grandmother. She introduced herself as Dorothy Erskine. Coach Anderson told her that I was from New York, and she asked me if I knew Hank Whitney. I told her that he was the person responsible for getting me to ISU. She seemed pleased.

Mrs. Erskine asked what I wanted to major in and how many credits I wanted to take. She handed me a course book and I began to read. The more I read, the more confused I became. Mrs. Erskine saw the difficulty I was having and said that she would help me.

She advised me to take fifteen credits a quarter, saying, "Donald, if you do this, you'll graduate on time. No more, no less!" I believed her and said that I would. I selected fifteen credits, mixing the more challenging classes with the easier courses. Later I really appreciated her advice because I had friends who had taken all the easier courses in the beginning and then had to take all the difficult classes at the end. Many athletes flunked out for this very reason.

Coach Anderson and I then went to his office, where he introduced me to his staff. There I met Vinnie Brewer who had been on the basketball team and was also from New York. Vinnie and I went to the gym, where he introduced me to the members of the team. Vinnie and I decided to shoot.

Vinnie had been a very good player for the Cyclones. As he was shooting, I was impressed with his overall skill level. He gave me some pointers on my shot and discussed the Big Eight Conference. After the workout, he dropped me off at my new dormitory residence at Friley Hall.

EPPIE

All the students in Friley Hall were really curious if Richard Kimble, the main character of the popular TV show *The Fugitive,* could find the one-armed man. Like most of America, I knew Kimble was innocent. He was a doctor, accused of a crime that he didn't commit. Now he was a fugitive, running from the law, trying to prove his innocence. Eppie Barney was the only other student in the TV day room besides me who wasn't white. Eppie was a very muscular man, but the thing that stood out the most was his politeness. During a commercial, I worked up the courage to approach him, and I extended my right hand.

"I'm Don Smith," I uttered.

Eppie responded almost in relief, "Eppie, Eppie Barney from Cleveland, Ohio!"

We looked back at the TV and it appeared that Dr. Kimble was caught, but every week we knew that somehow he would get away. Sure enough, a police officer who had put the doctor in the police car forgot to secure a door, and Dr. Kimble once again escaped.

"How boring!" I thought.

A young pizza delivery guy entered the TV room, holding three pizzas high above his head with his right hand and a large plastic zipped cash wallet in the other.

"Two pepperonis and one large mushroom!" he shouted.

Two football players paid for a pepperoni and the mushroom, and a bespectacled student who looked very much like Buddy Holly paid for the last pepperoni.

I looked at Eppie, and it seemed that we had the same thought: "I'm not that crazy about pizza!" I was never a fast-food person, and I could tell from Eppie's physique that he wasn't either. He stated that he was a tight end and was looking forward to spring practices. As we spoke, I felt less stressed. Talking to each other was easy because we shared cultural common ground.

The TV room was usually full of about twenty white males who seemed to all have Beatles-style haircuts. I found during the very short time that I had been in Ames that my conversations with many of them were superficial. My interest in jazz might have made me a bit more mature than the students that Eppie and I were now surrounded by, or maybe it was my fast upbringing in the tough streets of Brooklyn, but I knew that something was missing. Not so much racially but culturally!

I thought that Eppie felt the same way. Then almost in desperation I asked, "Do you have a roommate?"

He said, "No."

Then we both uttered in complete unison, "Do you want to be my roommate?" And we both said, "Yes!"

That's how I became roommates with the talented future Cleveland Browns star, the late Eppie Barney.

Then almost like a miracle, we looked at the TV screen and saw Bill Cosby in *I Spy*, and for some reason that I could not explain, I knew that everything was going to be all right.

ENGLISH 101

The Iowa State University campus is one of the most beautiful campuses in the Midwest, or for that matter, in the country. As I walked to class, I noticed that the trees seemed to outnumber the students. The grass had awakened after a brutal winter. As a robin landed on a Beardshear Hall concrete step, I thought, "The groundhog has definitely not seen his shadow!" I looked over to the left and saw the pale pink building that was my destination—the English Department.

When I first saw Mr. Rogel, I didn't know whether to laugh or cry. He was a Mr. Rogers clone with glasses. He wore a gray sweater, a white shirt, and a green tie. His pants didn't quite make it down to his feet, so I could see a pair of yellow dotted socks and a slightly polished pair of loafers. I thought, "They sure don't dress like that in Brooklyn!" I wanted to laugh, but caught ahold of myself as I looked around the classroom. I noticed that the other students were staring at me, just as I was observing Mr. Rogel.

I looked around again and realized that out of approximately twenty students, I was the only person in the class who wasn't white. I had been mentally preparing myself for that challenge, so I wasn't bothered too much. Even so, I remember that moment well.

The man in the gray sweater began his diatribe. "This is English 101. If you are not signed up for this class, you are obviously in the wrong room! My name is Mr. Rogel—R-O-G-E-L." He said it as if he were trying to prove a point.

"Please take a look at your course outline."

I looked around and saw twenty white faces suddenly look down at three white pages. My brown face did the same.

"Look at my grading system on the first page," he said.

His next sentences sent shivers down my spine.

"I am a very tough teacher and you, as students, should learn to use English well. There will be no excuses in my class."

I didn't know how the other twenty students felt, but I was becoming pretty intimidated.

"You will write five themes this quarter and each of you is allowed only five mechanical errors per five hundred words."

I didn't know what in the world he was talking about.

He continued, "Our first theme will be written on Monday. Bring at least three blue theme books. Any questions?"

I was nervous, but I put up my hand and was acknowledged.

"Mr. Rogel, what's a theme?" I asked in my Brooklyn accent.

No one laughed, thank God, but Mr. Rogel's neck became blood-red as he responded, "See me after class!" He continued with the rest of the lecture that hour, and when class was over and the other students had left the room, I just sat there.

Mr. Rogel came over and asked, "Where did you go to high school?"

I responded proudly, "Brooklyn, New York."

He asked, "Did you take English in high school?"

That statement offended me because up to that moment, I thought I was a pretty good student.

He then asked, "What were your classes like?"

I began to realize what he was getting at and replied, "They were good. I was a B student!"

Then for some reason I thought that I would try to impress him because I felt that he was trying to demean both my educational background and me.

"A verb is an action word, like 'run'!"

I moved my hands to mime running.

He looked at me with both eyebrows raised.

I went on, "A noun is a person, place, or thing—like a house." I tried to show him how really smart I was. "An adjective is...."

He interrupted me angrily as he asked, "What's a theme?"

Since I didn't know what the word really meant, I spelled out T-H-E-M-E.

"No!" he said. "Not the letters. The process!"

I was stumped. I didn't know what to do or say. I walked toward the exit and said, "Thank you for the advice. I'll see you on Monday."

On Monday, I went to the campus bookstore and bought three blue theme books. They cost about ten cents apiece. Each book contained about ten lined pages. I still had no idea what a theme was or how to write one. I walked to class and sat in the first row.

Mr. Rogel arrived and said, "On the blackboard, please notice the topics that can be chosen for your five-hundred-word themes. Pick one topic and good luck!"

The infamous college theme blue book, an object of fear and loathing.

I looked at the board and saw the topics: *Oedipus Rex, Moby Dick, The Iliad, The Catcher in the Rye,* or *Uncle Tom's Cabin.* I had heard of *The Catcher in the Rye* while in high school but was totally lost with the others. As I sat there while other students began writing, I started to get really angry. It was clear to me that this was a different culture, based on an educational system that was denied me in Brooklyn. The rules were different, and, most alarmingly—I didn't know how to write a theme! I knew how to answer multiple-choice questions about verbs, nouns, and adjectives, but I had no idea how to arrange them in a theme to express my ideas. I had to choke back tears.

Mr. Rogel saw that I was not writing and came over to assist. I told him that I hadn't studied any of the topics on the board.

He then said, "Write a theme on being a freshman."

Relieved, I said "Sure!" and began writing. It was hard, but I thought I did a fair job. I handed in my paper and left the room.

On Wednesday I went to class early to get the results of the test. I expected at least a C, and if lucky, a B minus. The papers were on Mr. Rogel's desk. I sifted through them and found mine. It was covered with red corrections!

Mr. Rogel came over and whispered, "You have more mechanical errors than allowed in the entire quarter in this course. You'd better drop out of the class."

"No," I thought, "I can do this. I'll stay in class and do my best." I didn't understand that I had already failed the class on that first theme. I flunked, just as Mr. Rogel had predicted, and I felt like an idiot.

I learned from that firsthand experience that public education systems are not equal. On that day and in that classroom, I made a personal decision to help change that policy in my lifetime.

THE 1960S

Neither time nor space will ever replicate the impact of the 1960s. Events unraveled with such fury and unpredictability. From civil unrest to political instability to landing on the moon, our nation underwent a total transformation.

The change forced many not to measure time by months or weeks, but by minutes, seconds. Time during this period became dearer and more precious because many people were faced with their own mortality. For many, minutes and seconds were all that remained.

This decade seemed to take on a human form, and we were asking it—no begging it—to stop! Like a bully, it had no conscience, no empathy. Our nation was in trouble on all fronts. In the midst of this turmoil, Cassius Clay, who later changed his name to Muhammad Ali, showed up on the national scene.

≈≈

It seemed like we were all awaiting him, both black and white.

Sonny Liston was the scariest and meanest boxer alive at that time. Cassius Clay seemed like a brash loudmouth who was extremely stuck on himself. Clay was from Louisville, Kentucky, and claimed he became a boxer because someone stole his bicycle when he was a child. I jokingly thought, "Did Sonny Liston take it?" However, the more I heard young Clay speak, the more I heard a real commitment and a real belief that he could win.

One night Clay went to Liston's home and yelled, "You ugly bear, I'm gonna kick you're a__!" At the weigh-in, which was televised, I could see that Liston seemed scared and worried. Then, just like Clay had predicted, he beat Liston. The fight ended in the sixth round when Liston wouldn't come out for the seventh; Clay won on a technical knockout. The world was shocked, but I wasn't. I was proud of this great black role model. Of course, when he switched his name to Muhammad Ali, I was confused. I was also very worried for him.

❧

The Vietnam War was escalating. With the troops of South Vietnam and its West-ern allies occupying Vietnam after the end of World War II, the independent Viet Minh, under the guide of Ho Chi Minh and General Vo Nguyen Giap, clashed fiercely with the French forces. The defeat of the French led to the creation of a demilitarized zone on the 17th parallel to separate North and South Vietnam.

By the 1960s the majority of the allied occupation of Vietnam consisted of American forces. America's longest war began with a formal attack on North Vietnam in 1964, based on misinformation that North Vietnamese troops had attacked two U.S. warships. Young men were drafted from all over the country. The average age of a soldier was nineteen.

❧

When the draft letter arrived at the dorms, I thought it was just an ROTC flyer. But when I read it, I turned numb. I was scheduled to take a physical, and it said I had to be there two weeks from the date the letter was mailed.

I went to the physical scared to death! Had I escaped Brooklyn only to die in the rice paddies of a country on the other side of the globe? I was asked by the doctor to lie face-down on a long table. At first I thought it was a rectal exam and cringed, but when I saw the physician grab a tape measure, I knew that he was trying to determine my height. I was too tall to be measured on a standard scale. He began counting "six feet … six foot two … six four … six foot six."

And then it seemed like the doctor didn't say anything for a couple of years. Then I heard "six foot six and a half," and I yelled "Yeee–es!" Anyone over six foot six could not be drafted. I got an automatic "4F" (shorthand for medical exclusion from the draft).

Muhammad Ali was not as fortunate. He refused to be inducted and was pretty much "white-balled" for three of his prime boxing years. He proudly stated, "I don't have anything against my yellow brothers in Vietnam. I won't go!"

That was a courageous statement to make in the early sixties. Decades later, when the world witnessed Muhammad Ali shaking with Parkinson's disease as he lit the torch at the Atlanta opening ceremonies of the Olympic Games in 1996, we saw how heroes can disagree with but still love their country. I then realized how America, despite its continuing inconsistencies and blemishes, had progressed in some ways.

THE OLD GYM

When I was not in class, I was at the old gym, playing basketball. In the spring, the gym was packed with basketball players and athletes from every other sport. The track above the court teemed with all types of people jogging, jocks and nonjocks alike.

The track coach, Bob Larson, asked me if I wanted to be on the track team as a high jumper, and I agreed. He told me that he had watched me in some pickup games and could not believe my vertical jump. We met one day as planned and I tried jumping, but I had problems when I got up to the bar. He tried to explain that it was quite normal to have lift-off problems in the beginning, but after I did it a few times, that it would be easy. I tried again but lost interest and told him so.

At the old gym, we played three-on-three games. I met some amazing people there. Two regulars were the Strand brothers, Eli and Ron, from upstate New York. I met Eli first.

We would start the game as best of friends, then before you knew it we would be arguing and talking trash. We never did anything harmful like throwing elbows, but all six players just hustled and scrapped to win. If we played against one another, whoever lost wouldn't talk to the others for days until we met again in the old gym. Whoever had won would egg on the loser.

"Homeboy—how have you been?"

If I had lost, I would say something like, "Eli, you're not from my home and are not my homeboy. You're a farm boy from Tuckahoe, New York. I'm from Brooklyn!"

Another funny athlete, Joe Beauchamp, was one of the main players who would either be on my side or one of the Strand brother's sides. His attitude added to the merriment and fun of growing up. Everyone liked Joe. A defensive back on the football team, he was from Milwaukee, Wisconsin. He later went on to have a successful career with the San Diego Chargers. He was a very hard tackler and thought that he was macho. We used to wrestle, but I never let him know my complete strength. I used to just keep him at bay and sort of toyed with him.

I think he knew I was stronger than I let on, but he didn't know why I didn't use all my strength. The main reason was the fact that I never let anyone know just how strong I was. Call it a Brooklyn thing, but I always tried to cover my back by not letting people know too much about me. It was safer, and you lived longer that way.

One day Joe and I went to a store on West Street to buy some groceries. Joe went over to the freezer and got what he called "Big Hot Dogs." When he showed them to me, I recognized them as knockwursts.

Joe began laughing and said "Knockwurst" in a belittling tone.

I said, "Yeah, they're called knockwursts!"

Joe said, "You're stupid if you think that's the name of those big hot dogs!"

I said, "Well, if you think so!"

Many, many years passed when I saw Joe in his hometown of Milwaukee. He apologized and said, "You were right. Those big hot dogs are called knockwurst!"

I replied, "Knockwursts!" and we both started laughing.

⫸⫷

Across the street was the new gym. I could never figure that one out because the old gym looked newer than the new gym. That was where we lifted weights and played racquetball, badminton, and squash. I was never one to lift heavy weights. I believed that it could be harmful in that it could impede the natural flexibility of my tendons and muscles. Having macro-muscles is dangerous if the micro-muscles have not been properly built up first. The person that lifts weights to exhaustion has to prepare or "load up" to move on the court, in effect, telegraphing to others what he's going to do. Thus I was most successful against ballplayers that were "buffed" to the max.

So when I was in the gym lifting a mere fifty pounds in twenty-rep sets, some athletes couldn't figure it out because they were straining to bench-press two-hundred-fifty pounds. I found that in this instance, less was more. I lifted light weights, which developed muscle firing speed. This method of training combined with my natural sense of timing resulted in extreme power.

My freshman teammates could see this formula working for me, and soon the Big Eight Conference would see it.

Freshman Year

When I realized that core courses were required for graduation, it made it easier to structure my time. I labeled core courses "difficult" and electives "easy." I don't know if Mrs. Erskine, the wonderful woman I first met at the registration office meant it like that, but that was how I used her advice and it helped.

She was a great person. She not only helped me with registration but also often invited me to dinner at her house, and she was one of the few white adults I felt I could really trust. She gave me a sense of family away from home. As a matter of fact, I called her my "Mom in Ames."

I guess it was due to flunking English 101 that I decided to become a physical education major. I thought if college was as difficult as that English course, there was no way I would pass any subject. Taking physical education classes was a safeguard for me until I could get my confidence back. I was not on a full scholarship but on probation until the university was sure I could do the work. I was worried that there was a possibility that I would be sent home. I decided to stay at ISU for summer school to make up for the failure. Little did I know that I would get in trouble again!

When I saw the bicycles in front of the classrooms and students getting off and on them, I decided

Dorothy Erskine, my "Mom in Ames."

that I would do the same. I thought the bikes belonged to the university and it was pretty much "go for yourself." So coming back from psychology class one day, I jumped on a Schwinn and headed back to Friley Hall for lunch. I rode up to the bike rack and was greeted by an Ames police officer. The officer was accompanied by the bike's owner, who was yelling, "That's him, officer—that's the guy who took my bike!"

I was astonished. This guy was acting like a little kid whose bike had been grabbed by a bully. I thought, "What in the world would I want with your stupid bicycle?"

I thought the whole thing was ridiculous but the police officer didn't think so, and he took me down to the police station for questioning. I couldn't believe it! They asked me where I was from and my whole name, including my mother's maiden name. I thought the whole thing was crazy, but I cooperated and was honest. I told them that I was from Brooklyn, New York, and my mother's maiden name was Coombs. I told the officers that I thought the bikes were a convenience for all students to use to get around campus.

One officer said, "You've got to be kidding me!"

Then I was asked, "Do you play sports?"

I said, "Yes. I will be on the freshmen team this fall." The officer then said something that made me very nervous: "I'll have to call the Athletic Department and let them know that one of their players is a thief."

I thought, "Well that's it! I'll be on the next bird out of here."

I dreaded arriving in Brooklyn to face my mother, grandmother, my father, and "the whole world" as a failure.

"Please don't," I pleaded, but the officer picked up the phone and began dialing.

"You've got to be kidding me!" Coach Anderson echoed as I later tried to explain my rationale. "Those bikes belong to the people riding them—the students!"

I looked around Coach Anderson's office and saw pictures of Big Eight legends—Wilt Chamberlain, Clyde Lovellette, and Bill Bridges. I looked to my right and saw a large portrait of Cyclone All-American Gary Thompson. I petitioned, "Please don't send me back to Brooklyn. I want to stay here!"

Coach Anderson looked at the wall and glanced at the same portraits and pictures. He looked at me sternly and said, "Please, just stay out of trouble."

≫≪

That summer I worked very hard and got passing grades. I began to see how classes were structured and what I had to do with my time to be a successful student. That fall I found out that the English Department had released Mr. Rogel. The rumor was that too many students were failing his class, and there were many complaints that his grading system was too punitive.

"I could have told you that!" I thought.

People began talking about how good I was. I didn't feel that I was better than anyone else. I just liked to play basketball. People would come and watch. The word began to circulate that the freshman team was better than the varsity. Then I began to notice something strange. When I would dunk the ball people would go crazy, and that was just at practice. I didn't think I had jumped that high, but onlookers thought I did. One day after a scrimmage a student came up to me and asked, "How did you do that?"

"What?" I asked the student.

"You don't know?"

"Know what?" I asked in bewilderment. The student looked down at a notebook and glanced back at me. "You hit all thirteen of your jump shots!"

I never kept stats like that. I felt that the student keeping the stats was prying or doing something illegal. Then I slowly started to comprehend. I didn't understand or even recognize the skills I had. I could do things with ease that were very difficult or impossible for others. Rather than feeling proud of my skills, I had that sinking feeling again that I was completely different from anybody else. What made matters worse was that I was still incredibly shy and a loner. That made some people think I was aloof, but solitude was something I enjoyed almost as if it were a hobby.

TOUCHING THE BOLT

The varsity team defeated our freshman team that year, but it was a good game. Our team would be together for four years and would only improve. I visualized winning a Big Eight championship and going on to an NCAA berth. I was getting along with all my teammates, even though I was never invited out with them. They hung out together and since I liked my solitude, I didn't mind at all.

There was very little to do in Ames in those days. Buying a pizza or taking in a movie at the local Ames Theater were the favorite activities. I remember seeing a James Bond film there for the first time, but generally I didn't go out. I figured that students were at school to study and learn, so being in the dorm on a Saturday night never fazed me at all. I counted my blessings, as my grandmother had taught me. I was grateful for some of the most basic things. I remember thinking to myself, "At least I get three good meals a day and a bathroom that's warm!"

My first year, I began to grow from the six-foot-six-and-a-half measuring experience on the doctor's table to a six-foot-eight frame. The food served in Iowa was the best in the world. The corn is a hundred percent fresh, of course, as well as the other vegetables grown there. The meat was raised on local farms. Nothing was imported. My weight rose from two hundred and five to two hundred and twenty-seven pounds, and with no police sirens or the normal Brooklyn drama to disrupt my nights, I was sleeping well. I even started to look like an athlete.

Our freshman team went undefeated that year. I shot 53.7 percent from the field and 73.9 percent from the free-throw line. I pulled down eleven rebounds a game. My high in points was 37, and I ended the short freshmen eight-game season with 24.3 points-per-game average. With John McGonigle, a deadeye player from Moline, Illinois, we were expected to bring success to Cyclone basketball for years to come. John and I had no doubt we would.

It was in that season that I did something that told me that I was not an average athlete. One Friday after practicing at the old gym, I decided to do some extra shooting. I was the only one in the gym when it happened. I really don't know what even made me think of doing it, but I just got an urge—like when you need to scratch your back or when you get a sweet tooth. I looked up at the backboard and saw two black bolts that were about four to six inches from the top of the backboard. I focused on the one on the right and wondered if I could touch it. It then became just me and the bolt. I walked to half court and focused. I took about twelve long measured steps and exploded on the thirteenth. I flew to a place I had never been before. It was beautiful! I put my right hand out and touched the six-sided black bolt. I came down and landed perfectly. I took a deep breath and exited the building. I was only eighteen years old when that happened, and I never told a soul.

The 1964–65 Varsity Cyclone basketball team had a mediocre season. Everyone was talking about the young freshmen team and its phenomenal Don Smith. I still didn't get it. If you had asked me, I would have said that I was worried about even making the team. I was now nearly six foot nine and weighed two hundred and thirty pounds. There wasn't an ounce of unwanted fat on my body. People told me that I had the perfect basketball physique. My legs were long relative to my torso. One student said that when I jumped, I almost looked like a kangaroo. That's how I was given the name "Kangaroo." I was given other names such as "Sky" and "Great One."

My game and jumping in particular were natural gifts, and it never occurred to me to take credit for them. That attitude kept my ego from getting out of control. If other people wanted to give me nicknames, that was fine

The freshman Cyclone basketball team at Iowa State University, 1964. I'm not hard to spot.

with me. I really never paid much attention. The only label I was worried about was being called a nigger.

That possibility crossed my mind after Eppie moved off campus, and I began rooming with a farm boy from a small Iowa town. He would go back to the farm on weekends to be with his family. Before leaving he would put small notes all over the room, telling me things like "don't sit on my bed" or "don't touch my razor." I felt he thought my color might rub off on him. What if he went home one weekend looking like me? Once he was gone for a weekend, and as I was getting something from our shared closet, I stepped on a piece of paper. I read some of it, just to find out what it was. The first sentence I read was, "How are you getting along with the Negro?" I realized it was a letter from my roommates' parents.

I thought, "If they would ask, I'd be proud to tell them that my name was Donald." I never spoke to him about the notes or the letter. That entire year, he kept writing the notes and I kept to myself. He wasted a lot of energy worrying about the fact that I was not white.

Many black students discussed racial issues among themselves. They felt excluded from campus activities, but I never really cared because I was a loner anyway. I guess some players and other black students began questioning my "blackness," but I was totally innocent of all charges. On weekends I would just stay in the dorms and do my homework or go to the TV room and watch Sonny and Cher or *The Carol Burnett Show*. (Cosby on *I Spy* was one of the only black actors on any show at that time.)

Many black students went to Des Moines on the weekend, and I went with a group a couple of times. One time I met a girl in Des Moines in my sophomore year who baked me pies and cakes. I guess she believed that the fastest way to a man's affection was through his stomach. She tried her best, but by that time I had seen plenty of students become parents accidentally, and I backed off.

What really cracked me up was the way the white students spoke. It took me a couple of months to pick up on their slang. A "bod" was a girl's body! I thought they were talking about a plant pod or seed—pretty much like "weed" was used to describe marijuana. I heard "that sucks," and while I thought that it had a sexual connotation, even to this day no one can explain what it really signifies. Then the guys' favorite—"beaver"! When I heard that one I really thought a beaver had run up a girl's dress. I found the term totally childish and distasteful, but it was really funny to them! All I know is that we didn't talk like that in Brooklyn, not even close. We had other nonsense.

Another thing that I just could not understand was the music. I was used to the Motown sound. The Temptations, Four Tops, and Otis Redding gave me a message. Not only that, it was like these performers were my friends. When things got me down, I would put a record on and instantly feel relief. It was cathartic.

Then I would hear the music played by the Iowa State students. The songs "Henry the Eighth," "Mr. Tambourine Man," and, worst of all, "Devil With A Blue Dress On" were played constantly. Don't get me wrong. I loved the Beatles, the Stones, and Bob Dylan, but sometimes, especially if I was having a bad day, I could not relate. I needed Motown! It seemed like it worked the same way for the white students on campus. When I was playing Stevie Wonder, The Supremes, and Mary Wells in my dorm room, I would see smirks and displeasure on the faces of students as they headed to class. I guess it all boils down to where you're from and what you're used to. Who said that integration would be easy?

Mono

The fall of 1965 was not an easy one for me. When I got the phone call from my sister that our beloved grandmother had passed away, I was in a state of shock and disbelief. I was totally devastated. Her first stroke had disabled her so she limped, but the second had taken her life. Overcome by homesickness, I thought more about my surroundings. I missed my family, my friends, and my culture.

I was also having identity problems. I'd had a great freshman season and our basketball team was the talk of Ames. People began saying that we had a dynasty and I was the main reason. I began to feel the pressure but didn't know how to deal with the acclaim. My roots were in Brooklyn with my people, not in Ames with farmers. My mind began playing tricks on me as it told me, "You're a sellout! You've gone to Ames and you will lose every iota of your culture. You don't care about the brothers you grew up with."

One week I took a trip back to New York to be with my brothers. I went right back to Bergen Street and Classon Avenue and met with the guys I grew up with. I was totally shocked when I realized that there was now a difference between us. I had grown intellectually and socially. The things that I had done as a kid held different meaning now, and my relationships with the guys I knew were not the same.

Of course I loved them and wanted the best for them, but I had to fulfill my destiny. When the wine bottle was passed, I had to say "No!" But the response from Lefty, my long-time friend, hurt deep to the core.

"So ya go to college and now you're better than us, huh?"

I tried to explain that I had stopped drinking a long time ago but to no avail.

He continued, "Nigga, I knew you when yo' a_ _ was stealin' and runnin' the street with yo' nose drippin'!"

I was quiet as I began walking back to my house.

Then Lefty shouted at the top of his lungs, "Don't ever bring yo' sorry a_ _ 'round here again!"

I left, devastated. I hadn't had a drink in a long time, but I was so depressed that I slipped back into that old habit. I went to the Village Vanguard and had a few beers. I began reflecting on what Lefty had said earlier in the day. Maybe he was right; maybe I was a sellout and a turncoat. But as I listened to Bill Evans play I began to understand. I had been given the gift of basketball and I had to do something with that gift. If it collided with the views of people like Lefty, so be it.

When I left the Vanguard I walked over to Greenwich Village Park. It was very rainy and cold, but I sat down on a park bench and before I knew it, I had dozed off to sleep. About an hour later I awoke and began to cough. That whole week I coughed and coughed and began to feel very feverish. I decided to see a doctor. He told me that I had pneumonia and would have to take antibiotics and rest. I had to be back in Ames in two days.

Upon returning to Ames, I tried to get over my sickness, but I was tired all the time. It was late August, and I knew that I had to start training for the season. My exhaustion continued, so I decided to see a doctor. He ordered a blood test and found that I was suffering from mononucleosis. He prescribed some medications and told me to rest for a month.

"A month!" I thought, "I'll miss the season!" I was very worried.

We had the nucleus of a great team. We had Raul Duarte from Peru who, at six foot ten, could give us a solid backup at center. Dave Fleming at six foot five was our "Moose" on the boards, and our great shooter, John McGonigle, would be vying for a starting role against two very talented players, Don Ziegler and Dave Hartman.

I followed the doctor's orders and just like he said, I started to feel better in a month. Even though I started out slow, I somehow managed to average eighteen points and thirteen rebounds. I shot 51 percent from the field. My season high was thirty, and I was voted Sophomore of the Year. However, I felt that we were a better team than our record showed. Maybe my illness had something to do with it, so I vowed to have a better 1965–66 season.

≫≪

That summer I met Marilyn. She was about five foot nine, with blonde hair and blue eyes. We met at the Memorial Union and somehow we were attracted to each other. She became my best friend. We would go out on dates and do the things couples did. Of course some people would stare and grimace, but that didn't bother us. In general, the fact that I was "Don Smith" made my color neutral. I was well known all over town, so I got away with behavior that would have caused a less recognizable black man all kinds of trouble.

In comparing notes with other black students, they were having problems too. But what was one to do? I didn't feel like I could change the world. I was just trying to live my life. Marilyn and I ate popcorn at the theater and went dancing. We shared our problems and thoughts just as other couples did. If racism did exist in Ames, we could not have cared less. We were happy!

≫≪

Call it confidence or wishful thinking, but when I read the upcoming basketball schedule, I didn't see a loss.

An athlete must think like that. Playing against Ohio State, Minnesota, and the University of Southern California might have been intimidating to some, but not to me. I felt we would win and go on to a national title. The team name or the individual players on that team didn't faze me in the least. My attitude was that we were Iowa State and we would prevail.

Around the fifth game of the season, something peculiar happened. It first began in a home Ohio State game, and then it happened the rest of my collegiate career. Whenever it did occur, I wanted to hide myself or run away. It reminded me of my Doo Wop years and my intense shyness in front of an audience. When the announcer said, "Starting at center, number 35—Don Smith," the people stood up and clapped, and they clapped and they clapped. It seemed like an hour. I thought I was dreaming.

"Who were they clapping for?" I wondered. Then I realized it was for me! They were giving me a standing ovation even before the game started. I stood at courtside, shocked. I looked around and saw seven thousand people, and they all were clapping for me.

"Wow!" I thought. At that moment I decided that I would always do my utmost to reward the wonderful people of Ames for their appreciation of my skills.

We lost the Ohio State game 79 to 77 at the buzzer on a forty-foot shot. I had twenty-seven points in the tough loss. Our team didn't feel sorry for themselves. We didn't have time. The University of Minnesota game was next.

Our team wanted to make up for the Ohio State heartbreaker. We got off to a very quick start and blew out Minnesota 87 to 69. I ended the game with thirty-six points, going fourteen for eighteen with sixteen rebounds. Any time I exited the game, I noticed that all the Iowa State fans were cheering and clapping. This was a gesture that I would receive at all the home Cyclone games throughout my career.

Our town was ecstatic, and my teammates were confident. Not since the 1956–57 season and Cyclone All-American Gary Thompson had Ames been so excited. I was playing great and so were John McGonigle and Dave Fleming. Our bench contributed by adding good defense and quality minutes. The town was abuzz.

We traveled to Wisconsin and there we lost 80 to 73. In that loss I had twenty-five points and John McGonigle twenty-seven. Then we began

This page and opposite: My halcyon days as an Iowa State Cyclone. I was double- and triple-teamed most of my career.

a five-game winning streak, which started at home against Drake. At that game McGonigle had twenty-five points. I had twenty-nine with seventeen rebounds in the win.

Traveling to Arizona for the Sun Devil Classic Tournament, we were a

confident bunch. Our first opponent was the
University of Southern California. In that
game I broke a school record by scoring for-
ty-one points and adding eighteen rebounds.
Teammates McGonigle, Duarte, and Fleming also had good games. The championship
game was against Texas, and we won in a
blowout, 101 to 87. I sprained an ankle but
managed twenty-four points after leaving

*With my teammate,
John McGonigle.*

the game with seven minutes to play. I was later selected tournament MVP,
but it was really a team effort all the way. The USC game gave our team
national exposure.

The Big Eight season opened, and we found our record at 4 to 1 and in
first place. Then just like a battery failing, we went dead. We lost four games
in a row and were knocked out of the national ranking. We won our next
two but lost the next three and ended the season a mere 13 to 12. Throughout it all, I averaged 24.3 points and 13.4 rebounds a game.

Despite these losses, Ames
was proud of us and thought that
we had accomplished something
or reached heights that were un-
attainable. John McGonigle and
I thought otherwise—something
was wrong. Then little by little, I
began to put the pieces together.
As a program, we at Iowa State
lacked structure, with no training table like the big schools. We
would meet for pregame meals,
but we really did not have general concern for one another.

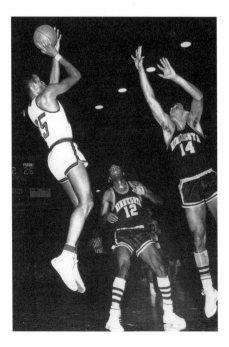

Dave Fleming and Coach Anderson.

The only time I would see my teammates was at practice or in classes.

As a team we would lose by slight margins, which I thought was because we were not close or bonded. Coach Anderson seemed hard to communicate with—not in the sense that he was mean or anything, but coaches did not become friends with players in those days. I longed for the day when Coach Anderson would say, "Don, you're a great player, take us to an NCAA title!" Or just "Don, what about lunch today?" But it never happened. That lack of communication led to mediocrity and a losing season.

I was to blame as well. My shyness didn't allow me to be the leader that our team needed. McGonigle tried, but that resulted in verbal clashes with Coach Anderson. John saw that we had one of the best rebounders in the nation—me. Coach Anderson preferred a controlled, slower game, which John realized didn't make sense with the specific talents of our team. We were a running team, and Dave Fleming or I could pick up any missed shots in a faster game. John could see it, but Anderson was determined to stick with his strategy.

During our junior year, John was sent back to second string.

"What's going on?" I asked him. "You obviously play as well as you did last year!"

John just said something like, "You know how coaches can be." John had tried once again to convince Coach Anderson that we needed to play a faster game if we wanted to win. That disagreement had escalated into an argument, and McGonigle had slammed a ball into the wall and walked off the court. I had no idea this had taken place since neither John or Coach Anderson told me about it, but moving John to second string made no sense to me. I told Coach Anderson that I wouldn't play unless he put McGonigle back in the game. As a result, Anderson reconsidered the lineup and John was made first string again.

McGonigle explained this episode to me many years later, when he expressed appreciation that I had stood up for him. He was later selected for the Chicago Bulls, but during our senior year he broke his foot and didn't finish out the season. That was a great loss for our team, and it ruined his chances for a career in the pros.

"MOOSE"

Dave Fleming was our "Moose." He was not very quick, but he took up a lot of space at six foot five and two hundred and thirty pounds.

We were at practice when I heard a greeting from my right:

"What's up Don?"

I looked and was staring straight in the eyes of the "Moose."

"Hi Dave," I answered.

"Your hair looks nice!" he joked.

"Thanks to you," I replied.

The day before Dave had given me a ride to a barbershop in Des Moines. This was the first time I had ever done anything with a teammate. After we climbed into his Chevy, we had talked. I could feel that Dave respected me, not just as an athlete, but off the court as well. We discussed the war in Vietnam and music. The Beatles classic "A Hard Day's Night" was playing on the radio.

Dave asked, "You like the Beatles?"

"The Beatles are great!" I replied. I began scanning Beatles hits in my mind like a jukebox machine.

"They're from England," he said.

I thought, "I probably know more about the Beatles than Dave, but he sure is nice to educate me."

I asked him if he knew about The Temptations. Dave began clapping his right hand on the dashboard and started singing "My Girl."

I joined in and before you knew it, we were at the barbershop.

We went in, and Dave's was the only white face in the whole place. He looked around inquisitively. Our eyes met and he seemed to say, "Help, I'm uncomfortable!" I looked back and my eyes tried to relate to him that all was okay. These were just different colored faces.

I hopped up into the barber's chair with my usual greeting. "What's up, Smitty?" Smitty, the owner of the shop, was a tall, thin gentleman with a white mustache. He did not tolerate foul language on the premises, and I was thankful for that since this was a step out for Dave. Black barbershops are filled with gossip, rumors, and pure truth. The atmosphere all depended on the social dynamics of the people present. Things were not always what they appeared to be at Smitty's shop.

Dave "Moose" Fleming.

"Why don't you learn how to play defense?" Smitty whispered.

The previous week we had played on TV, and I had three blocks in the last two minutes, securing the win. Smitty was telling me in barbershop talk that I had played well, saying something bad to express a compliment.

"Yeah," I said, "we almost lost that game."

Smitty then began a long speech. "Lew Alcindor, Hayes, or Wes Unseld can't even carry your jock! You are probably the best player in America but how do you manage to be only a five-hundred ball club. I don't understand!" Smitty started to become more emotional. "It's the coaching—it has to be! I guarantee that if you were at UCLA or Kentucky, you'd be an NCAA contender. It's Anderson. It's got to be Anderson!"

I didn't want to say anything bad about my coach. Coach Anderson did things based on his understanding. I had heard this criticism before and said, "Anderson is Anderson."

Smitty became incensed. "That's what's wrong with you. You are too damned nice!" he muttered, opening and closing his scissors quickly.

I was shocked to hear the word "damn" come from a newly born-again Christian. I looked over and saw Dave trying to act as though he had not heard our conversation. He looked at the table in front of him that was covered with magazines and selected an outdated *Ebony*.

"Good luck," I thought.

There were about seven customers waiting. Smitty got my attention again.

"I worry about you—not too many Negroes up in Ames and these times are very confusing, lots of unrest."

I nodded, thinking how we were now called "black" and not "Negro" anymore.

Before Smitty could continue, one of the customers screamed, "That's crazy!"

"What?" asked Smitty.

The man handed Smitty the front page of the *Des Moines Register.*

Smitty peeped over his bifocals and said loudly, "See, *that's* what I mean. Here you are with a sprained ankle and you score nine points in the loss and Anderson says 'his pride was wounded.'"

Smitty again uttered, "Damn!" but this time, with more emphasis.

I hadn't seen the article, but I had heard about it. I had hurt my foot in practice coming off a pick and I wasn't at my top level. I gave it a go anyway, which resulted in a nine-point performance, the lowest of my NCAA career. What Anderson was reported to have said didn't bother me. I rarely read the newspaper articles where I was mentioned. Why should I? To be elated if we won and depressed if we lost? I didn't need the mania. I could smell the talcum powder and knew that I was finished. Dave put the *Ebony* down with a puzzled look on his face.

Using a comb, Smitty gestured that Dave was next up for a cut. Dave looked around at every customer nervously. Then Smitty said something to Dave that made all of us laugh.

"We cut white hair too!"

Dave waited a few seconds, and then realized that Smitty was making a joke. Dave relaxed and joined all of us in laughter.

I paid for my haircut, and Dave and I left the barbershop. We got back into Dave's Chevy. Dave then asked a question that no one had ever asked me.

"Don, how do you people keep such positive attitudes under so much persecution?" When Dave asked that, I reflected on the racial turmoil in the U.S., the Jim Crow laws in the South, the beatings and lynchings, and the "white only" signs. I realized that Dave was visualizing the same horrific events.

I replied, "I don't know Dave. We just do."

When we arrived back on campus, Dave dropped me off. It was some thirty years later that I learned that my friend and teammate had committed suicide. Dave was born into the white majority, but he struggled with the negative aspects of society.

I wish I could have given Dave, my friend and my teammate, a better answer on the drive back to Ames from Smitty's barbershop.

WILLIE

The summer after my junior year was a very difficult one. I was lonely and homesick, although I knew home wasn't really there for me anymore. I had just come off a season where I had averaged nearly twenty-five points per game and fourteen rebounds. Schools had double- and triple-teamed me, and that still hadn't stopped me. The standing ovations I received when my name was announced at the start of home games or when I exited didn't inflate my ego. I still felt more surprised or embarrassed than anything else. I was a walking legend in Iowa, but I felt detached from the accolades, as if they belonged to an acquaintance that walked around with me.

During this period, Oklahoma State's coach, the renowned Henry Iba, designed a special defense to contain me. After one game against his team, in which I managed to dunk a ball regardless of his defense strategy, he protested to the refs that my dunk was really offensive goaltending. The refs disagreed, but Iba was angry. I was by no means the only one dunking in our conference, but it was right after that game that Iba took his complaint to the NCAA National Rules Committee. By the next year, dunking was banned from NCAA games. My guess is that if that if he'd had a black, high-flying dunker like me on his team, Iba would not have done this.

Once I couldn't dunk, I had to adapt to the new rule, and my shooting percentage plummeted to 41 percent for awhile. Lew Alcindor (later Kareem), playing for UCLA in the Pac 10 Conference, developed his devastating "sky-hook" during the period of the ban. He spoke out against the rule and said that it was clearly racist, since more black players than white players were adept at dunking.

Reporters asked me whether I agreed with Lew's opinion. I felt that his comment had a lot of merit. But I answered that I thought the new rule was more a direct effort at stopping me than all black dunkers. I wasn't thinking about the big picture the way Lew was. At the time, I didn't realize the broad effect the ban would have on the whole game. I took it personally, because I was in the same division as Iba's team, Oklahoma State. In hindsight, the question I should have asked was, "If I had been white, would Iba have banned the dunk?"

The rule lasted for nine years until it was finally repealed in 1976.

⇒⇐

The only time I discussed basketball was at practice or at games. Most of my time off the court was spent studying, playing the flute, or watching TV. I hardly interacted with other students, black or white. I was alone 90 percent of the time. The other 10 percent I spent with Marilyn. It seemed like I was walking a very complex and confusing line. From 1964 to 1968, I was probably the most recognized athlete in the state, but I felt isolated. I missed my own culture, but after my visit home, I knew that I didn't quite fit there either. I just played basketball and enjoyed it. My interest remained on my studies and the issues of the day.

Like most campuses in the 1960s, we had a Black Student Organization. Its president wore a big Afro and sunglasses pretty much like the black leader, H. Rap Brown. I could not accept many of the BSO's nationalistic views and I never joined the group. Because of that, I received negative vibes from some of its members. However, I never got bad vibes from Willie Muldrew. Willie was my friend.

I met Willie before he was active in the BSO, and his affiliation with this group never affected our friendship. We were roommates one summer quarter when we stayed in the old dorms.

Like everyone who saw him, the first thing I noticed about Willie was his gangster hat. He was not a gangster—not even close—but he liked that fedora. He wore baggy pants and sported a small goatee. He was chiseled like the great football player that he was, six foot two and two hundred sixty pounds, with incredible speed, potentially a first-round NFL draft pick. He was born on the South Side of Chicago and attended Tilden High School, an all-male trade school.

Everyone loved Willie! He was as social as they come. I remember him dancing around our dorm room one time holding a broom as if it were a girl and singing "Just My Imagination" by The Temptations. I would see him on campus and he would move his fingers as if he were going to poke me in my eyes. Then I would raise my hand vertically over my nose as if it were a defense for the move, and we would laugh out loud.

My dear friend Willie Muldrew.

Willie was the one I confided in when Marilyn and I broke up. He helped me get some perspective and my sense of humor back when I really needed it. I wish he had confided in me before he joined the BSO. He was a great friend, but he developed a lot of problems. Looking back, I wish I had been able to help him the way he helped me.

FACING UCLA

———————

It was right there in black and white on the Cyclone schedule: Iowa State versus UCLA at Pauley Pavilion. UCLA was the number-one team in the nation and we were going to play them in a nonconference game.

There was no doubt in my mind of our victory. We had added Bill Cain and Dave Collins to the team. At six foot seven, Cain had the heart of lion and the wingspan of an enormous eagle. We used to meet high above the rim as we divided rebounds between us. I noticed that he had great timing and played like a seven-footer. Collins was six foot two and could do it all. Bill and Dave were both from upstate New York. I felt that they would be vital in not only beating UCLA, but also in winning our first Big Eight championship.

Point guard Tom Goodman and I settled into our seats, and our plane took off like clockwork. I had been waiting for this day for three years. It was marked on my calendar and etched in my mind: Iowa State University versus UCLA at Pauley Pavilion. I began to think of the great players, Walt Hazzard (a.k.a. Mahdi Abdur-Rahman) and, in my opinion, the greatest college team of all time, the 1964 UCLA team. They featured Gail Goodrich, Fred Slaughter, and Keith Erickson, along with the fantastic Hazzard. They were led by the greatest coach of all time, John Wooden.

Walt Hazzard was an incredible player. He was a fantastic passer, a tenacious defender, and an amazing offensive player who led the feared UCLA full-court press. Teams could not even get the ball over half court against them. The amazing thing about this team was that its players were small. The tallest starter was Slaughter, at six foot six.

I always respected the little guy. To me, guards were the most important position on the court. A weapon I used was to turn into a guard during games. Don't get me wrong, ball handling was the weakest part of my game, but I knew if I passed to a guard and then made a diagonal cut, I would get the ball back. This moving-without-the-ball concept was crucial, but most players could not adapt to it. My formula was pass, move your body, get the ball back. That's one reason I was sitting next to Tom Goodman on the plane. We both understood this concept instinctively because it worked for us on the court; we didn't have to speak about it.

Tom had incredible court awareness, and we agreed in our overall approach toward the game. John McGonigle, our point guard, was a tremendous shooter, but ball handling was not his strong suit. That's how Tom Goodman, at only five foot ten, helped our team. He could penetrate and dish the ball off to me deep, to Bill Cain on the wing, or to McGonigle at the top of the key. Tom Goodman was my collegiate Spud Webb!

Most players on the team were excited about going to Disneyland and doing the Hollywood tour of the stars' homes. I was focused only on one thing—Lew Alcindor. Mentally I was preparing myself as I considered Lew's strengths and weaknesses. I knew if he got the ball deep, I was a dead duck. So I needed help from the weak side. That was where Bill Cain's skills came in; he could help me defend Lew.

We had an exhibition game against San Fernando Valley State College the night before we were scheduled to play UCLA. As I remember it, their tallest player was about five foot; they all wore Coke-bottle glasses, and their legs resembled tree trunks. Why this game had been scheduled was beyond me. Then the game began, and I immediately noticed that we had taken the game lightly. It seemed like we were mired in quicksand, and nothing we did worked. We had a case of severe "Hollywooditis" and were blown out.

Upon leaving the gym, which held about twenty fans, the people acted like they had won the Final Four. Some yelled at us, "Hey ISU! You can't beat San Fernando Valley! How are you going to beat the number-one team in the country?" I had tears in my eyes and really couldn't answer that question. Like Goliath, we had been slain.

Running out onto the floor at Pauley Pavilion, I was simultaneously embarrassed about our loss to San Fernando and proud to be playing against the much-talked-about UCLA Bruins. I knew we had taken the San Fernando game lightly because UCLA was the main reason we made the trip. I was totally focused and relaxed.

Our team ran by the Bruins, who were taking lay-ups. Lew and I made eye contact, and from his eyes I read, "Please don't embarrass me tonight!" Lew remembered me from Riis Beach and the Greenwich Village playgrounds. I thought, "Big fella, are you ready to run?" I felt my advantage was quickness.

Lew was extremely agile, but not as agile as I was. I would have him play me as a forward to bring him out. It was like a psychological chess match. The first half we were down double digits, but not so far that we couldn't have come back. At halftime, Coach Wooden made some offensive adjustments that significantly impeded our ability to stay in the game. Lucius Allen and Edgar Lacey proved the difference as we were blown out 121 to 80. Lew had forty-five points and I had thirty-three. We both had double-digit rebounds as well. We pretty much neutralized each other.

Upon our return to Ames, people were talking about the great game I had played, but I was very upset. We had not only lost back-to-back games, but how could I be complimented when I had allowed forty-five points to Lew? He shouldn't have been complimented either in allowing me thirty-three. Lousy defense, I thought, and I felt that Coach Wooden probably thought the same.

⇜⇝

I made second team All-American. I was praised and talked about not only for being a prolific scorer, but also a fantastic rebounder. Some said that I was the highest jumper that they had ever seen. I didn't feel anything! It was as if they were talking about someone else, a different Don Smith. Not the Don Smith who had survived a dysfunctional childhood and escaped a forty-five-year prison term. Not the boy who sold newspapers on subways, smoked marijuana, and guzzled down cheap synthetic wine.

The decade of the 1960s had not finished its assault on the nation. The newspaper headlines did not help my depression or the depression of the nation: "Twenty one dead in Los Angeles riots; hundreds hurt; 20,000 troops sent in; President condemns the violence."

I thought of all those who had been assassinated. President John F. Kennedy, Malcolm X, Dr. Martin Luther King. This menacing decade seemed to taunt and say; "I'm not finished yet!"

Then, as promised, the carnage continued.

Being honored on "Don Smith Night" with Coach Anderson at the microphone.

My friend Willie had joined the BSO and become its vice president. In the fall of 1968, he was kicked off the football team. Rumor had it that he was drinking a lot, but I had known Willie to drink only occasionally. There was also a rumor that he had dropped out of school, but I wasn't sure about what was really going on with him. Our paths had drifted apart.

I finally saw Willie again when I was high on his shoulder on Don Smith Night, when Iowa State played (and was defeated by) Kansas State. A staff writer for a Kansas City newspaper described the evening:

Smith Honored By His Own

By Dick Wade, *Kansas City Star,* March 6, 1968

… Then unfolded one of those moments those in intercollegiate athletics like to discuss. What could have been one of Iowa State's most frustrating hours was turned into one of its most creditable.

Those 7,000 people, 98 percent of whom were white, stayed to say, "Thank you," to Don Smith, Iowa State's Negro standout who played his last game in Ames.

There were speeches by the president of the university, Coach Glen Anderson, the president of the Cyclone Booster club, the president of the student body and the mayor of Ames. There were

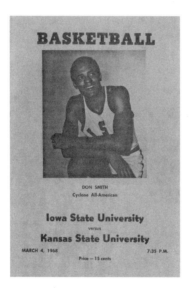

gifts, within the limits set by collegiate rules. And Smith's jersey was retired, only the second time in school history this has been done (the other was 1957, when Gary Thompson closed his career).

Smith thanked the crowd—and apologized for missing three free throws in the last six minutes. He forgot the records he set, the games he won. He remembered the championship he didn't win; this, he said, would have been the only way to thank Cyclone fans.

Then, his teammates carried him off the court. A late arrival would have been sure Iowa State won that night.

But there is more. Perhaps the most noteworthy item is the total sincerity on both sides. Iowa State likes Smith, and Smith likes Iowa State.

He is the poor boy from Brooklyn, one with boyhood friends who now are in prison. He might be in trouble today if it hadn't been for sports.

And he will be in a position that will enable him to help others stay out of trouble tomorrow. He will combine social work with pro-basketball after he is graduated from Iowa State—and he will be graduated.

When you think about it, Iowa State did win Monday night. So did a lot of people—white and black.

Then the Iowa State band began playing the ISU fight song, and the crowd started cheering. As I was lifted up after the ceremony, I looked down and saw a big hat. Willie! I hadn't seen him for months. He looked up at me, and I could see that he was grinning. Willie was happy because I was happy. Along with my teammates, he carried me off the Armory court for the last time.

In the commotion of the evening, Willie disappeared. That was the last time I saw him, the final time.

⊰⊱

On May 23, 1969, my friend Willie was shot. Some say that he was shot in the head. Others said he was shot in the heart.

It didn't matter to me! He was dead and I was angry—very angry!

As the news of Willie's death trickled in, I had many questions. Was Beth, Willie's girlfriend, okay? How was Willie's family taking it? Was anyone else hurt? In the confusion, my mind automatically went back to my childhood for some explanation as to how this could have happened.

My childhood hero—King Kong, rescuing Fay Wray.

The big brown gorilla is as clear to me now today as he was then! Lots of heroic characters populated my childhood—Rin Tin Tin, Lassie, Tarzan, Zorro—but my favorite was King Kong, the gigantic, kind soul, who was destroyed by a world that misunderstood and feared him.

When I heard that Willie had been shot, I worried about his girlfriend too, afraid that something may have happened to her as well. The scene in which Kong falls from the top of the Empire State Building, carefully protecting Fay Wray in his hand, rushed into my mind. That image was shattered as, little by little, rumors and newspaper articles revealed the story of that evening.

The newspapers reported that Beth had killed Willie. The story in the *Des Moines Register* said that Willie had pursued his girlfriend, who was trying to end their two-year relationship. It was alleged that Willie had abused Beth on numerous occasions. My only experience of their relationship was that Willie and Beth really cared for each other. She had visited his family in Chicago, and Willie had proudly shown me pictures of the visit. The allegations against him seemed completely contrary to what I had observed with my own eyes.

The article went on to say that Willie was "upset about being dropped from the football team," "depressed about the failure of the BSO," and "his life was in shambles." During his BSO days, Willie always seemed happy-go-lucky to me. I began to discount the news reports as purely negative propaganda. The situation was perfect fodder for a sensational press—a white girl and a black man had dared to be lovers, and the only view the press would support was that the white girl had no option but to kill him to get out of the relationship.

Even the pictures the editors ran with the story seemed chosen to slant public opinion against Willie. Beth looked as fragile as Twiggy, a popular waif-like model in the sixties. The paper placed one of Willie's football action pictures, in which he was grunting to look as intimidating as possible, right next to a picture in which Beth looked particularly fragile. I had seen them together, and it seemed like the media was making big-hearted Willie out to be a monster. I was enraged. The trial took place quickly, and Beth was acquitted of Willie's murder.

Willie Muldrew was a hero in my mind. He was an idealist who was concerned with the welfare of all people, and who became vice president of the BSO because he wanted to draw attention to the plight of the American blacks who were the victims of segregation, lynching, and racism throughout America. He had lived through his country's assassinations and civil unrest. He probably sacrificed an NFL career when he joined the BSO, but it was more important to him to correct the wrongs and draw attention to the problems of the day than make it to the NFL. That was the image I held of Willie for many years.

After Willie's murder, I shut down more than ever. And the pressures of the 1960s were too much for me to take. I felt tired and numb. If I were a druggie, I would have drugged; a drinker, I would have drunk. But I used neither, so I did what I did most of my life when I got confused—I secluded myself.

Some folks on the ISU athletic staff told me that I was a shoo-in to represent my country at the upcoming Olympic Games in Mexico City. I couldn't have cared less. When the offer came, I declined.

After the basketball season ended, I worked on the last requirements I needed for graduation and my degree in Sociology (I had changed from

Physical Education in my sophomore year), but I spoke little and was hardly seen.

As I closed out my career at Iowa State, I was averaging close to twenty-five points and fourteen-plus rebounds a game, which was an enormous success. But the emotional stress of Willie's death was taking a terrible toll. I was never one to get up and read the sports pages first thing in the morning, so friends would tell me when they saw articles about me.

One day, a friend sent me a copy of a letter that was printed in the *Ames Daily Tribune,* near the end of the season. I hadn't seen it before, and it came to me when I was feeling pretty low. It was written by a local basketball fan named Fred Wright. He was very generous in his comments about me, and although I don't consider myself a player who should share the limelight with Wilt Chamberlain or Bill Russell as this kind man did, it was still good to know that he enjoyed watching me play and appreciated my skill level. I still could not understand why people thought I was great, but it helped me get through this hard time to hear that what I did brought enjoyment to others.

Letters To the Editor: Praise for Smith
By Fred Wright, *Ames Daily Tribune*, March 4, 1968

To the Editor of the Tribune:

Although I surely share with all other Iowa State basketball fans the hope of a long-awaited Big Eight title and N.C.A.A. berth, I regret very much that we are now approaching the end of the great and exciting Don Smith era. I have seen many basketball games and have watched the performances of numerous stars such as Iowa State's All-American Gary Thompson, Wilt Chamberlain, Bill Russell, Elgin Baylor, Bob Pettit, George Yardley, and Wesley Unseld. Also, I have enjoyed talking basketball with former Iowa State center Bob Stoy, who is married to my niece Joanie. None of this qualifies me as a basketball expert, but it has helped me appreciate the outstanding play of Don Smith. It is my belief that Don is a real superstar who belongs in the class with Chamberlain, Pettit, and Russell, and I feel that his being overlooked on the A.P. and Look All-American teams is a great injustice. I hope that all those who share this belief with me will tonight, at Don's last home game, let him and everyone else around know in no uncertain terms how we feel. I now offer a few remarks, based mostly on my own observations and conversations with the experts, in support of my assertion that Iowa State's Don Smith is a superstar who should be on everybody's all-American first team.

One way, it seems to me, to determine a basketball player's true worth is to observe how much effort the opposing teams, especially those that know him well, exert in guarding him. I have never seen anyone, even Chamberlain and Pettit, who were guarded as tightly and roughly as Don is. In every Big Eight game of his that I have seen, and this includes all of his home games, the opposing team has used every device they could get away with to keep him from even touching the ball within ten feet of the Iowa State basket. Drake appeared to work harder in their games with Iowa State to stop Don than they did to stop Unseld in the recent Louisville game played at Des Moines. Bob Stoy has told me that although he was occasionally double-teamed he was never guarded in the rough and frequently illegal manner that Don is. This kind of treatment is reserved for a superstar whom you can't otherwise contain. Had the referees been more observant or courageous, Don's average points per games might well have been at least 10 to 15 higher.

Another test of a basketball player's worth is his defensive ability. Because of his great jumping and his fast reactions, Don Smith is frequently able to block close shots, and in this respect he is in the class with Russell, Chamberlain, and Alcindor. He is at least as good defensively as Hayes and is in my opinion far superior than

Unseld.

Finally, in judging a basketball player's worth one should, I believe, consider how much of a team player he is and also how much he contributes to his team's success. I assert that no one else is a better team player or contributes more to his team's success than does Don Smith. U.C.L.A. would be a great team without Alcindor, Houston would be a great team without Hayes, and Louisville would be an excellent team without Unseld. Don Smith could replace any of these men and put the corresponding team just about where it is now. Moreover, he'd be a sure all-American on any of these teams.

I urge the entire Iowa State team to play their hearts out in the last two games for the great prestige of a Big Eight title and to give Don Smith a real chance for the national recognition he so much deserves.

GOING
PROFESSIONAL

The National Basketball Association

My goal in life was not an NBA career, even though I had mentioned to Bert that I hoped to play in the NBA someday. I was a player who played very hard for me, the people I knew, and for Iowa State University. I played a total of eight freshman games and seventy-five varsity games. I was never hurt seriously and never missed a practice. Coach Anderson and I disagreed at times on strategy, but we never got into any altercations. I tried to lead by example and didn't get into anything negative with my teammates.

What did bother me was how mediocre our teams were. In those three varsity years, we were only a five-hundred-ball team. I felt I had accomplished nothing. I had made All-American for two years and was considered one of the best players to have come out of the Big Eight Conference, which included Wilt Chamberlain and Clyde Lovelette. I led the Big Eight in scoring for two years and rebounding for three, but we had never made it into the NCAA Tournament.

Except for individual achievements, I had done nothing worthwhile. People would say things like, "I feel so sorry for you because you came to ISU and did not go to Kansas or Louisville." My response was always, "Iowa State was just fine with me!"

The first player chosen in the 1968 NBA draft was Elvin Hayes from the University of Houston. Elvin Hayes, or The Big E, was a three-time All-American. He was the NCAA Player of the Year in 1968 after his team beat UCLA and broke the Bruins's forty-seven-game winning streak. They called this "The Game of the Century" because a crowd of 52,693 showed up at the Astrodome in Houston and also because this was the first collegiate game to be nationally televised. The Big E dominated, scoring thirty-nine points and hauling down fifteen rebounds. In this game, Lew Alcindor had fifteen points but suffered from an eye problem. Hayes was an NBA All-Star for much of his career and was later inducted into the NBA Hall of Fame.

The Baltimore Bullets drafted the next player, Wes Unseld, from the University of Louisville. Unseld was a rock of a man. He was only six foot seven, but he must have weighed three hundred pounds. For his size he was an extremely quick rebounder. He could get the ball out on an outlet pass before he hit the ground. In 1968 he was the Most Valuable Player and the Rookie of the Year. He was a team player par excellence.

The third player taken was Bob Kauffman who, like me, was from Brooklyn. He went to school at Guildford and broke many records there. The Seattle SuperSonics picked him.

Taken fourth was Tom Boerwinkle, seven foot tall and over two-hun-dred-seventy pounds. He was from the University of Tennessee and was taken by the Chicago Bulls.

I was taken fifth. I was shocked. I was taken by the Cincinnati Royals and was very pleased to team up with Oscar Robertson, or "The Big O." To me, Oscar was the greatest player ever, not so much because he averaged a triple double one year, but because he was even better on defense than on his amazing offense. He was one who didn't rest on the defensive end, but who worked over screens and around picks. He was a perfectionist who wanted his teammates to reach their greatest potential.

There were no million-dollar contracts in those days, and as a young man, I didn't care about money anyway. I signed a contract for $111,000 and got a signing bonus. I felt fortunate because I had read an article about Bill Russell wanting one more dollar than Wilt Chamberlain and agreeing to a $100,001 contract. I later found out that both Unseld and Hayes had tripled what I signed for, but I felt that I would prove myself and then ask for a better deal.

I was twenty-two and just happy to be in the league. At that time, I never thought about the business side of sports. The fans in Ames wished me luck, and I flew to Cincinnati to start my new NBA career.

≫≪

I moved to an apartment on Reading Road, not far from the Cincinnati Gardens. I had a week before training camp started, so I traveled around the city. I was shocked to learn just how small Cincinnati was. It had only two movie theaters, and the downtown area was very compact. It seemed similar to Ames.

Maybe I was expecting something different, but soon I felt uncomfortable. Cincinnati is very close to Kentucky, and it dawned on me that my new home had a Southern vibe. When meeting new people, I felt that they were not being rude or anything, but just indifferent. I tried to dismiss my intuition by thinking that I needed to give the whole situation more time. I would adjust, I reasoned.

Ed Jucker was the head coach of the Cincinnati Royals. As a college coach he had taken the University of Cincinnati to two NCAA titles in 1961 and 1962. He called me into his office on the first day of training camp and began telling me his plans for the upcoming season and my role on the team.

"Don, at Iowa State you were a great rebounder—almost fifteen a game for your career. That's what we want you to do here for the Royals. Rebound."

I had no problem with that. I enjoyed rebounding more than scoring anyway. I made up my mind that I would follow Coach Jucker's orders. Why not? With Oscar scoring thirty points a game and forward Jerry Lucas nearly twenty, it made sense to strengthen our overall team with rebounding. Coach Jucker said that we were "family," and I believed his every word. Little did I know that I would become the black sheep of a very dysfunctional family.

The guys on the team did not want to associate with me. I naturally gravitated to Pat Frink, who had played at the University of Colorado and who I had played against in the Big Eight Conference. The other rookie was Fred Foster from Miami of Ohio University. Both Pat and Fred were excellent players, and I wondered if Coach Jucker had also told them about their roles on the team. Then I began to see that the veterans were treating me differently from the other rookies and that they were very unfriendly. No one had welcomed me to the team. I also began to realize that they were very sociable amongst themselves but brash and negative towards me. I figured it had something to do with me being a rookie and decided to be patient.

The exhibition season opened, and we had eight games in eight different cities in eight consecutive nights. I hardly played. At home games, the crowd was sparse with few minorities. The weather was cold and so was my heart. I spoke to Coach Jucker and he told me to have patience.

"We're going to bring you along slowly," he told me.

I had no idea what "slowly" meant to him. I thought, "Why would they draft a two-time All-American and then tell him, "We're bringing you along slowly?" Wasn't I factored into the system before drafting me number-one? Then things became clearer. I looked at the roster and realized that most of the veterans were from Big Ten schools. They were all part of the same group, and here I was, an outsider, coming from the Big Eight Conference as the number-one draft pick for the Royals.

I also wondered if the fact that I had mentioned in a *Sports Illustrated* article that I smoked marijuana as a kid was a factor. Did the team think that I was an out-of-control drug addict? On road trips Ed Jucker socialized with starting center Connie Dierking, whom he had coached at the University of Cincinnati, as if they were the best of friends. What outright favoritism, I thought.

Jerry Lucas possessed a photographic memory, but he couldn't seem to remember that I even existed. He did not say one word to me during my entire stint. Forward Tom Van Arsdale treated me pretty much the same. Fred Foster and I discussed this pitiful state of affairs for hours. In practices,

I thought I was a better player than forward Jerry Lucas and a much better player than center Connie Dierking, who was thirtyish with waning skills, but that didn't seem to have an effect on how often I played.

Oscar was having problems of his own. The greatest athlete to ever play the game was in a town that showed no genuine interest in the game or him. Oscar was a human computer. He knew how much time remained on both the game clock and the twenty-four-second clock at any given time, and he also kept track of how many fouls were on all the players on the court—of both teams—at all times. He could run the court with cat-quick speed or slow it down to poetic beauty. Oscar was Oscar! He was the general on the court, and we were his soldiers. A championship was all that he wanted, and both Oscar and I could see that it wasn't going to happen that season in Cincinnati.

I knew that if they wanted a championship, they needed to free Don Smith and let him play. But when the regular season started, I was brought along so "slowly" that I lost confidence in my abilities and myself. As that happened, Oscar became more frustrated, not so much with me, but with the whole mess.

In practice, I made rookie mistakes that would be ridiculed, not only by Coach Jucker, but by many team members. That kind of stuff can go on in fun, but this was serious ridicule. I became a scapegoat. I was screamed at and even benched if I made any error. I tried to deal with it by thinking, "All rookies go through this!" But I was wrong. This didn't happen to every rookie. I had hoped to bring them a championship, but no one could see that possibility but me. When the regular season began, I got no playing time.

I was put in the game only if we were up by twenty or down by twenty or with two minutes to go. I felt more like a cheerleader or the team mascot than a player. I decided to work harder in practice in order not to go completely mad. I made up my mind to get my rest and eat better. I thought that if I took care of myself and Connie Dierking or any other player didn't,

I would be ready when the opportunity presented itself.

We were playing the great Boston Celtics in an exhibition game in Ohio. I was put into the game at "garbage time" as usual. A shot was taken, and when I went in to get the rebound, I heard someone say, "I got it Smitty." I let the person who spoke get the rebound, only to find out that it was Sam Jones of the Celtics, who calmly laid the ball in for two points. Coach Jucker was enraged and I was yanked. About a week later, I was called into Jucker's office and told that I was being traded for Fred Hetzel and cash.

From October until February, I had played a total of only 109 minutes.

What happened to me in Cincinnati shook me to the core. I felt like I was a failure, that all the honors I had received were bogus, and that I was a fraud. I felt that I owed an apology to every coach on the All-American selection committee. How could an overrated player like me have been selected for the Olympic team? I wanted to call John Wooden and ask him, "How could you have spoken of me in the same sentence with Elvin Hayes or Wes Unseld?" I wanted to tell him that I wasn't the same person he had seen playing against his team at Pauley Pavilion.

Then I thought of Oscar. I wanted to tell him that he had a right to be disappointed that the Royals had wasted a number-one pick on me, that he had a right to think, "What if we had Unseld or Hayes and not Smith? We would have had a championship!"

This devastation continued throughout my final days in Cincinnati before my departure. I had to answer insulting questions by reporters and the media. In college I was known for having a feathery touch, but in games prior to my release, people were yelling, "Hey Smith, Ray Charles can shoot better than you!" I was now a six-foot-nine human being trying to hide.

Tragedy tends to test what a person is made of. I began to reflect on slogans we used during my college days at Iowa State like Joseph P. Kennedy's "When the going gets tough, the tough get going!" Very gradually, I felt the pain lift.

Somehow, and somewhere deep inside, I found a spot where I was comfortable, a spot where I was me again. That spot was not very big, probably the size of a human cell, but it was more powerful than the confusion of the other trillion cells. I was content in that spark that this one positive cell could generate! The other cells began following its lead. Then, little by little, my mental depression abated. Objectivity and reason returned, and I began to devise a plan to deal with the wreckage.

I made a number of vows to myself. The first was to never forget what had happened, and to learn from the experiences of that season. The second was to show those in Cincinnati the real Don Smith and what he could do. I decided I would always be physically and mentally prepared for every game. I formed a mental file that stored all the information regarding Cincinnati, and labeled it "Rookie Year."

I would refer to that file frequently throughout my career.

"Milwaukee Bucks, That's the Name of Our Team"

On the plane to Milwaukee, I thought of how powerful the human mind is. When all is boiled down, that's all there is—the mind! This gray, wrinkled piece of meat can be an ally or a foe. The mind has raised many to the highest levels and dropped many to their lowest.

"What will happen to me?" I pondered my fate. Then, as if it were a sudden thought, I heard someone speaking.

"Don Smith, Iowa State?" The man next to me in seat 6B put out his hand in excitement. I extended mine in puzzlement.

"You are one of my favorite players!" he said. "I remember your performance at the Sun Devil Classic in Arizona. That was a game that I will never forget. You just destroyed Southern Cal!"

I didn't know what to say. I just sat there.

He continued, "When I heard you were coming to the Bucks, I was thrilled!"

I felt that I had to respond quickly or I might never get the chance. "Thank you," I said.

Immediately he handed me a paper and pencil. "Could you please sign this for me?"

Throughout my career, I always had a problem with signing autographs, because I didn't feel worthy of the honor. For someone to think that I was something special or important was foreign to me. The people who taught school, patrolled the streets, or fought four-alarm fires should be asked for their autographs, not me. I reluctantly took the paper and signed.

It seemed like he thanked me over a thousand times. Then he grabbed a book out of his attaché case and said, "You'll be interested in this!" I took the book and glanced at its title, *Milwaukee Bucks Media Guide*. I began skimming the small booklet.

> *… The National Basketball Association originally awarded the franchise to a Milwaukee group of investors—headed by Wesley D. Pavalon and Marvin L. Fishman—called Milwaukee Professional Sports and Services, Inc. on January 22, 1968. Pavalon and Fishman were named President and Executive Vice President, respectively, as the franchise was incorporated on February 5, 1968.*
>
> *An application from Milwaukee Pro was registered with the Wisconsin Department of Securities for the sale of 300,000 shares of common stock to Wisconsin residents at $5 per share. Because the issue caught public fancy, an additional 125,000 shares were offered when the stock opened on the over-the-counter market on April 24, 1968.…*

I turned a few pages and read more.

> *… Milwaukee's first professional major league basketball team was the Milwaukee Hawks, who played in the Milwaukee Arena from the 1951–52 season through the 1954–55 season before moving to St. Louis, where a fellow by the name of Bob Pettit led them to great prominence and an NBA championship in 1958.…*

I was amazed at how little I actually knew about NBA history. I continued to look through the guide and came across the 1968 team photo of the Bucks and thought, "What a young, promising collection of athletes!"

I returned the guidebook to the kind gentleman to my left as the pilot announced our arrival. Minutes later we landed at the Milwaukee airport.

"Good luck to you in your career. Maybe I'll see you at a game!" said the man in seat 6B.

"I'm going to need more than luck," I thought. "Divine intervention would be more like it." How true that thought would prove.

∌ξ

Ray Patterson was right where he said he would be. The general manager of the Bucks, Ray was a tall gentleman with a toupee that would wave in the breeze when he walked. Ray was a wonderful person, and I developed an enormous respect for him. He took me to the hotel and was very cordial and helpful. This was so different from Cincinnati, where I had not been met by anyone.

Ray said that he was happy to get me and knew that I was an excellent scorer and great rebounder. He said that my addition to the Bucks was pivotal for the franchise and that I could turn things around. I felt honored that Ray thought those things of me, and I made a promise to myself to live up to his expectations.

We went to meet Coach Larry Costello, whose office was a stone's throw from the hotel. Costello had played for the Philadelphia 76ers and was a no-nonsense type of coach. He was six foot two with a crewcut, styled pretty much like a Marine. He welcomed me to the Bucks organization and said that he was happy to have a rebounder of my stature on the team. But the first words he uttered made me squirm.

"We want you to focus on rebounding, because we have scorers."

I felt that old anxiety rise up again. I sent up a silent prayer: "Please, not the Royals all over again."

Then Costello said something that made Ray and me laugh.

"But if you have to shoot, just make sure you shoot like you did in Ames!"

That last comment was so unexpected and welcome. A wave of relief passed over me, as if a huge weight were suddenly lifted from my body. A coach was giving me a green light to play my game! As Coach Costello told me what time practice would be, he handed me a Milwaukee Bucks travel bag that was loaded with practice gear, a playbook, and all sorts of Bucks reading material. Ray then took me back to the hotel.

When I got back to the room, I opened the travel bag. Inside were sweat socks and green, white, and yellow Milwaukee Bucks pullover socks. There were five reversible practice jerseys and two pairs of size 15½ Adidas shoes. There were about two dozen sweatbands and five jockstraps.

Then I saw something that I had seen on the plane to Milwaukee. It was the same media guide the man in 6B had shown me.

I opened it up to the middle and read.

> ... More than 14,000 fans participated in a team-naming contest. According to the 1969–70 Milwaukee Bucks yearbook (which is now referred to as a media guide), R. D. Trebilcox of Whitefish Bay, Wisconsin, was one of 45 persons who suggested the name "Bucks." His reasoning: "Bucks are spirited, good jumpers, fast and agile."
>
> ... With a name for the franchise in hand, Bucks executives went to work on developing a logo and colors. The majority of the task fell to John Erickson, who commissioned Milwaukee commercial artist Matt Kastelic to develop the team's first logo. The original logo featured a caricature of a buck wearing a sweater emblazoned with the letter "B" and spinning a basketball on one hoof while sitting on top the words "Milwaukee Bucks."...

The team even had a fight song. *"Milwaukee Bucks! That's the name of our team and we will fight..."* Milwaukee had created a professional team and given it a college personality and essence. I thought that was a very clever idea.

Soon after my arrival in Milwaukee, I was asked to do something that I had never done during my entire stay in Cincinnati—I made a public appearance. It was at Bob's Big Boy, a popular hamburger restaurant. I signed autographs and gave out Bucks schedules and team photos to the fans.

My self-esteem was coming back. Milwaukee helped me climb out of the hole that Cincinnati had dug for me. I was part of a team that had a great nucleus of raw talent, and the city loved its young Bucks. Our fans knew we were young and they were happy to watch us come up.

⇜ ⇝

Guy Rodgers was a legendary guard. He could do anything with a basketball and was as quick a guard as you would ever see. He had the superhuman passing skills only the greats possess. Dick Cunningham was our backup center. He reminded me of Lurch from the Addams family—but a very talented Lurch. Jon McGlocklin was a great shooter from the University of Indiana. He was joined by Sam Williams, a huge talent out of the University of Iowa, who had shared numerous awards with me in that state. He was an aggressive player who took the ball to the basket with authority, but he clashed with Coach Costello and had a short career.

Bob Dandridge from Norfolk State was also a great player. Of a slender build, Bob could run like his nickname, "The Greyhound." He could shoot with the best of them and made the All-Star team some years later.

Greg Smith was a six-foot-four swingman. He wasn't a very good shooter, but he could play excellent defense against guys five or six inches taller than he was. With his ability, Greg could leap out of the gym.

Wayne Embry was our team leader. At six foot eight and nearly three hundred twenty-five pounds, he could set the best picks of anyone I had ever seen. He had loads of experience playing with the champion Boston Celtics and Bill Russell.

We were ten youngsters, with Embry to show the way and Rogers to show the how. We were a loose but talented bunch, laughing together and joking about one another with little conflict. Bob Dandridge served as the catalyst, an Eddie Murphy-type character from Norfolk, Virginia, with a very candid wit. We young Bucks knew that whatever you did, don't let Bob get wind of it, or he would hold court on you like Judge Judy.

I remember one time when we were staying in a hotel. Two-a-day workouts had just ended. A player on our team had his fiancée over for a little intimacy. However, he made a huge mistake: He left one of the Venetian blinds open. A few of our teammates saw what was happening in the room and called Judge Dandridge. The next day after practice, that player was indicted, tried, and sentenced by Judge Dandridge, which provided comic relief for the rest of us.

What fun we had! I had a knack for doing things explosively. A dunk, blocked shot, or snagged rebound were signature marks of mine. I did it in my own way—not to show off, but because those moves felt as natural as a Jerry West logo.

That's when Eddie Doucette, the Milwaukee announcer, coined my nickname, "Dynamite." He was in the same category as Bob Blackburn, Chick Hearn, and Kevin Calabro—a great announcer. Doucette could attract fan interest with his clever nicknames and imaginative narratives. The Bucks would not have been the Bucks without Eddie. He was our voice, our identity. It seemed like things were finally looking up for me.

But in 1968, the Milwaukee Bucks were a mere 27 to 55, resulting in the coin flip that brought Lew Alcindor to them. Unfortunately, that same coin flip brought disaster for me.

⊰⊱

Time has a unique way of humbling the mighty and giving strength and confidence to the shy. Time reveals things people try to hide and events long forgotten. Sometimes time becomes a friend and ally to those who try to understand its mysteries. As humans, we often cannot fathom why things happen. In our ignorance, we futilely attempt to change things to fit our own niche in history. We look back and reason, "It should have been like that!" or "It shouldn't have worked out like this!" The reality is that things always work out according to God's design.

We may think of miracles as gigantic events, like Moses splitting the sea or Jesus feeding the masses. However, miracles happen everyday and to all of

The 1969–70 Milwaukee Bucks team. Front row: Assistant Coach Tom Nissalke, Len Chappell, Don Smith, Lew Alcindor, Jon McGlocklin, Flynn Robinson, Head Coach Larry Costello. Middle row: Greg Smith, John Arthurs, Fred Crawford, Bob Dandridge, Sam Williams, Guy Rodgers. Top row: Trainer Arnie Garber, Jack Lutz, Rich Niemann, Dick Cunningham, Waymon Stewart, Bob Greacen.

us. The problem is that we are often too busy to recognize them. Sometimes miracles are delivered by a messenger who is unaware of the impact his delivery has on another. It happened to me.

Our team had only two possibilities. The most sought-after collegiate basketball player of all time was the first-draft choice that year. The Phoenix Suns picked heads and the Bucks chose tails. The Bucks won and drafted Lew Alcindor. I'm sure Lew favored going to Phoenix rather than having to leave sunny California for icy Wisconsin. Phoenix was only an hour-and-a-half plane ride to Los Angeles.

Neal Walk would always be mentioned as the "other option," as if he were a piece of meat without any real basketball talent, but believe me, he was a good player. But when Phoenix fans mention Neal Walk, they would always wonder, "We got this guy instead of Lew?" It was a no-win situation for Neal. So Lew Alcindor packed his bags and headed to the cheese belt of America.

In the summer of 1969, I was content being the power forward on a very talented Bucks team. I kept thinking of what Coach Costello said in the 1968 season: "Just rebound. We have scorers." I was running in the morning and lifting light weights at night. I was extremely confident. Playing alongside Lew Alcindor would be an honor: two high-flying All-Americans on the front lines.

"Wow!" I thought. "The opposition can forget about an easy bucket with two flyswatters on defense!"

A short time later, my Don Smith bubble gum trading card came out. The cartoon coach in the picture looked like Ed Jucker, and he looked like he was crying! That seemed ironic to me, because I was the one whose career was almost destroyed by lack of playing time when I was with the Royals. I had cried on many nights, but I never told anyone.

Milwaukee winters can be brutal. We would awaken to ten inches of snow and were urged to deal with it. Milwaukeeans knew how! They would pull on their gloves and tug their wool hats firmly over their heads in an attempt to seal them off from the slightest exposure to the frigid air. Some dashed into Bob's Big Boy to fill their thermoses with hot brewed coffee. Then they would quickly chug it down, awaiting the warm feeling of contentment it delivered.

As I scraped the ice off my Buick Electra 225 one winter day, I stopped and blew into my gloveless hands. "My God!" I thought, "Why did Coach Costello call for practice on a day like today!" Coach Costello was from the old school. He believed in a hard work ethic. It was his second season as coach, and a lot was expected of him with the addition of Lew. We were at least expected to make the playoffs and possibly win the whole thing.

I thought, "We'll make the playoffs—we have Lew! But why must I freeze to death in the attempt?"

The regular season was only a week away, and today would probably be our last two-a-day practice. With Coach Costello, a day off was like dessert.

Our practice was in the usual place, at Marquette University. (We practiced at the Milwaukee Arena only briefly. It was big and too hard to heat in the mornings, and Marquette had a smaller gym that was always warm.) I arrived at about 9:30 A.M. and saw Lew enter at 9:45. He was wearing what I thought was a Mexican poncho, but now I realize it was a Middle Eastern woolen garment. I went over to the basketball rack and Dandridge started ribbing me.

"You should go over there, Dynamite," said Bob, pointing to an imaginary ball rack. "The bricks you shoot are over there." He, Greg Smith, and Dick Cunningham began laughing.

I quickly turned to Greg and joked, "You can't shoot either!" Then I turned to center Dick Cunningham and said, "With Lew joining the team, you're probably out of here anyway." I pointed to Lew, who was heading our way. As Lew came closer, I could smell the patchouli that he always wore. We laughed, and for once I had the comic offensive.

The team honestly thought I could not shoot. They didn't know that I was honoring Coach Costello's request that I focus on rebounds. He had apparently never made that clear to the rest of the team. Little did I know that this "no shooter"' label would follow me throughout the 1969–70 season, and that I was innocently adopting a stigma that would later cost me dearly.

Lew came over and began stretching, then grabbed a ball from the rack. He slowly began shooting sky-hooks. As he became looser, he sped up his delivery.

"Poetry in motion!" I thought.

It was a short practice. We walked through plays, and then Coach Costello blew his whistle and practice was over. He shouted, "Tonight we practice at 7:00 P.M. at the Arena. Be on time!"

I looked over at Coach Costello and he waved me over. He asked, "Do you know Lew?"

"Since we were young teens." I said. "I also played against him in college."

That was the extent of my conversation with Coach that day, but it was cause for concern on my part. I hardly knew Lew at all. We had hardly ever spoken on the playgrounds of Riis Beach or Greenwich Village. I knew that he lived in New York, had attended Powell Memorial High School, and that he was an exceptional student. But that was it. As I left practice that day, I was hoping I wouldn't be the player assigned to welcome the most highly sought-after player of all time. I was still incredibly shy and having problems of my own. How could I assume this role?

≫≪

I had recently moved my mother to Milwaukee from Brooklyn. She had her own apartment in the Juneau Village apartment complex where I lived. Across the street was a disco and restaurant named Buddy's Steak Out. Before you could say "AA," my mother began drinking there like she had in Brooklyn. I felt that my troubled past was now following me as members of the Milwaukee Bucks organization told me, "Don, I was in Buddy's last night and I met a woman who said that she was your mother!"

Players and fans—even President Wes Pavalon and general manager Ray Patterson—everyone knew her! As time went on, my mother became as well known as the mascot. I was happy that my mother had come to Milwaukee to live and share my success with me. However, I was embarrassed about her hanging out in Buddy's Steak Out every night. Her routine was the same as it had been in Brooklyn; the only difference was the geography.

My teammates had mixed emotions about Lew joining the team. Our center Dick Cunningham said, "I'm not going to give him my spot easily!"

"Right," I thought.

Anything was possible. Lew might blow out a knee or get traded. Stranger things had happened in NBA history. It was a business.

"Championship!" said forward Greg Smith, with other players interjecting cheers.

"Not so fast," said Bob Greacen. Bob was the number-two pick taken by the Bucks that year, but in preseason he had a very severe ankle injury, which opened the door for Bob Dandridge. "We have a long season and we have done nothing so far!"

I totally agreed with Bob. It was dangerous to count our chickens before they hatched.

Wayne Embry became the Lew Alcindor concierge. I was relieved. I didn't want to show Lew how excited I was about him being on the team. We hardly ever spoke, but I was observing everything. Like me, Lew sported a medium-sized Afro. Through his body language, I could see that Lew was not happy in Milwaukee. I guessed it wasn't the people or the city so much as the cold. Here was a college player leaving California for a brutal winter.

I began to feel enormous compassion for Lew. I thought about the pressure that he was under, how he had to produce night in and night out. No excuses. The media would not allow it. I began to see how the really famous stars actually live a very lonely existence.

It helped me appreciate my own situation. "Being Don Smith is not that bad after all!" I decided. One morning, I was leaving Juneau Village when I saw Lew on the elevator. He said that he had moved into Juneau and lived on the twelfth floor. As time went on, we would meet in the building either on our way to practice or to eat at Buddy's Steak Out. Our conversations focused primarily on the weather, but one day I was in the lobby, and Lew seemed more animated.

"I met a lady across the street who said that she was your mom, a Mrs. Smith!" I was happy that they had met, but I wondered if she was drinking or had for the first time gotten out of control.

During the holidays, my mother would invite Bucks players to her apartment for dinner. She would make ham, baked macaroni, and cornbread. Lew came a few times, and when he did, he never ate the meat. I noticed that and remembered that he was a Muslim.

During the 1969–70 season, I continued to observe Lew with interest. On the bus he would read book after book, article after article. Some players on the team welcomed him, while others were more cautious.

I was watching, listening, and taking in everything. I also read a lot. On the weekends I had no problem staying home, reading. My grandmother had long ago called me "a young old man." Of course, my teammates could not understand. Bob Dandridge would laugh and say, "Dynamite, what are you, some type of a hermit or something?"

The team would laugh with delight. I just heard a different drummer. Lew and I had many things in common—our hometown, our inclination toward study and solitude, and, eventually, our faith—but we never became really close friends.

When we were young, we had played against each other at Rucker's and at Riis Beach. The street talk then was always about Lew. I would hold my own against him, and people would point to me and say, "Lew's team won, but this guy is a great player too!" So I was prepared for the same thing with the Bucks and willing to do whatever was necessary for a winning team and an eventual championship.

≫≪

At the end of the 1960s, the decade seemed to say, "It's now time for me to leave. Let the rollercoaster ride of civil unrest and confusion cease. I have done enough. I must report back to my creator for an accounting. I leave everything to my successor, the 1970s."

≫≪

In the spring I moved out of Juneau Village and to the East Side. I really don't know why I did it, but in retrospect it could have been because of my mother's drinking and her constant presence in that bar. The East Side of Milwaukee was beautiful. I moved near the music conservatory and close to a park. In typical 1970s style, my apartment had a big beanbag in the living room, and a large strobe light flashed off and on. I would listen to "Eli's Comin'" by the Fifth Dimension, and the room flickered as the notes rang out. The neighborhood reminded me of a small Central Park. I often played my flute outside and read in the park.

One day I met a hippie-type guy who strikingly resembled the singer Lionel Ritchie. We ran into each other from time to time and became acquainted. One Friday night he rang my doorbell, and I invited him in. Dressed in a colorful dashiki with brown beads around his neck, he took out a bag and asked, "Do you want some?"

I answered, "What?"

He whispered in a low voice, like someone might hear, "Mescaline."

I had heard of the hallucinogen but never thought that I would come face to face with it. It was like encountering a grizzly bear up close and personal.

He passed me a small pill that was divided into quarter sections.

He said, "Let's drop it!"

I was going to swallow the whole thing when he stopped me by saying, "Cut it in quarters and take just one!"

Since I didn't know anything about drugs, I did what my acquaintance suggested. I don't know why I took the drug. I knew better.

He said, "You're lucky you didn't drop that whole thing. You would have been in trouble!"

I arrogantly said, "Sure," comparing the small pill to my enormous size. How could such a small pill do anything to a body like mine?

We left the apartment and drove downtown to a disco. I was watching the crowd dancing to "Proud Mary" by Tina Turner when suddenly everything began moving faster and faster. With the combination of the lights and the drug, people seemed to be jerking and spinning like Charlie Chaplin or poorly made cartoon characters. I went outside to regain my sanity and noticed all the light poles were moving and swaying. To my amazement, the traffic signal lights were flickering pretty much like the strobe light back in my apartment.

Then for some reason I began jogging, then running, and then sprinting through downtown Milwaukee. My heart was pounding almost out of control, and it seemed like everyone else was also sprinting.

I dashed the half-mile back to my apartment and was met by my acquaintance, who yelled, "Good trip, huh?"

I was too anxiety-ridden to answer. I thought, "Oh God, please help me!" We both ran back outside and headed down Prospect Avenue. We looked into the street and saw a mixed crowd holding up signs. They were yelling profanities and slogans. I could not tell if what I was experiencing was the mescaline trip or reality. I heard police sirens and saw more flickering red lights, this time from police cars. The police were mobilized en masse, and an unruly mob of demonstrators was growing. I was caught in the middle.

Just then a wild-looking bearded guy yelled, "Down with the pigs!" and hurled a Pepsi bottle toward the officers. Like dominoes falling, the police converged on the thrower and began striking him with what appeared to be miniature billy clubs.

The perpetrators were yelling, "F___ you pigs! Power to the people!"

Then, like a dream, everything receded to a nonviolent college protest, which seemed to just fade away. As I wandered back to my apartment, I reflected on the summer of 1968 when John Carlos and Tommie Smith, two African-American track-and-field medalists, raised their black-gloved fists on the Olympic Games podium in Mexico City.

They were protesting the problems that we, as blacks, were facing in this country. I was torn. I loved my country; however, racism was not right and had to be addressed. That is what I thought Carlos and Smith were trying to say. To me, they were courageous African-Americans who spoke out against injustice, regardless of the consequences. I was trying to understand how my destiny fit in with all that was going on in the world around me.

A More Logical Choice

After joining the Bucks from Cincinnati, I had revenge on my mind. I wanted to show everyone who Don Smith was, especially the Royals. I took care of myself and worked hard. I dove for loose balls and rebounded with the NBA greats, often outplaying them.

In Cincinnati I had played a total of 109 minutes in four months, or the equivalent of about two-and-a-half NBA games. Now I was playing forty minutes a night and loving it. The fans loved me, too. They loved our whole team. Ironically, all I could think about was the injustice I had experienced while playing for the Cincinnati Royals. I went through sleepless nights, and revenge was becoming an obsession. Like a heavyweight fighter, I wanted a rematch.

On March 6, 1969, Cincinnati came to Milwaukee to play us high-flying Bucks. We lost the game when Oscar took over down the stretch, but I turned heads with seventeen rebounds and ten points.

I would have to wait until the 1970 season to get total respect. It was almost a year to the day of my trade to the Bucks that we played Cincinnati again. The game took place at the scene of the crime, the Cincinnati Gardens.

꿍꿍

We were a very talented bunch. Lew dominated, but we could hurt the opposition from all positions.

We had the great shooter Flynn Robinson. Guard Freddie Crawford was a tenacious defender who had a great concept of how the game of basketball should be played. Jon McGlocklin was a fantastic shooter who could not be left unguarded. Of course, there was Bob Dandridge, who would run the living daylights out of you and drain twenty-footers with incredible accuracy. Greg Smith took on the tough assignments and usually held down the opposition's top scorers. Dick Cunningham spotted Lew at center and was extremely physical on the defensive end.

We had Guy Rodgers, Len Chappell, Sam Williams, and Bob Greacen as reserves who would have been starters on any other NBA team. I was a fixture and did what Coach Costello and Assistant Coach Tom Nissalke ordered, and that was rebounding. The fans in Milwaukee realized that we had a dynasty as we began beating teams both in the Eastern and Western divisions.

We won our division, going on to defeat the Philadelphia 76ers in the first round of the playoffs. Our next opponents were the legendary New York Knicks. I had no doubt we would beat the Knicks, but I wasn't receiving the playing time that I had been getting during the regular season. I guess Coach Costello thought Len Chappell's shooting could get us past the Knicks. That decision of substituting shooting for rebounding cost us a championship that year, as we lost to the Knicks in the Eastern Division finals, 4 to 1.

We had a great season, but we didn't get as far as many thought we should have. I again heard the "nonshooter" label applied to Greg Smith and me. Greg was not much of a shooter anyhow, but I considered myself a sharpshooter.

I now understand something that I didn't at that time. I was considered one of the highest jumpers in the NBA. My jumping ability was talked about the most, so people defined me in that light. It was very unusual for a player to have a forty-two-inch vertical leap and shoot eighteen-foot jump shots like a guard, but I could do both.

This is what Coach Costello could not visualize and what cost us a championship against the Knicks that year.

Lew won the Most Valuable Player award, averaging 28.3 points per game. The Bucks players were household names in Wisconsin. Like the Green Bay Packers, we were loved and followed. Little did I know that the greatest gift in life would be presented to me on the court, but it wouldn't be about basketball. This gift was given just before we made the playoffs. It happened at practice on a cold, stormy day in December of 1969.

Some practices were very difficult, so when they ended, we would run out of the gym for showers and then head for home. On this day, that didn't happen. I went to the free-throw line to take some extra shots and Lew came over.

Pointing to a cross I was wearing around my neck, he asked me in a very questioning manner, "What's that?"

I said, "It's my cross!"

Lew said, "Oh," and left.

I just stood there and forgot to take the shots I had planned to. I looked down at my cross. That question made me realize that I wore a religious symbol as an ornament and knew little about it. Lew had no idea how strongly his question impacted me.

I was a Christian and proud of it. I considered myself a good religious man who made mistakes, then corrected them. My whole family was Christian, too, but only by name. We never went to church. We rarely read the Bible and if we did, it was at funerals. Prayer was not practiced in my house; we played the numbers and never questioned whether it was right to do so. As "Christians," we followed no dietary religious laws. We drank alcohol and ate whatever we wanted, including lots of pork products like pig's feet, pork chops, and welfare hog headcheese.

The question Lew asked stuck with me the entire week. I made up my mind to find the truth. I began my search at the downtown Milwaukee Library.

My experience of religion up to that point was not spirituality, but a sense that narrow-mindedness, prejudice, and ignorance prevailed. During my search, I realized that others had also considered conversion. Many are born into a specific religion and later need to redefine themselves within the tenets of that system. Others remain in it, despite observing faults and contradictions, often for a lifetime. Any person who moves from one religion to another realizes that such a transition requires courage, commitment, and faith. The one leaving often has to vow to stay the course, even though society, friends, and family may disapprove.

In my search and eventual conversion, I applied a logical approach.

I first became aware of this idea in high school but became more interested in it during my junior year at Iowa State University. I was taking a geology course, which I hated. The professor was very enthusiastic as he addressed our class, "Look at the rock specimens on the table. Can anyone tell me if they are metamorphic, igneous, or sedimentary?"

I thought, "How in the world can anyone determine the name of a billion-year-old rock!"

The professor took a saw, cut the rock down the middle, and said, "Look at the sedimentary lines. See how they are arranged." As he spoke, I thought, "This is why geology bores me. At least in biology, dissecting a frog had more meaning and significance than cutting up a lifeless, dumb, inanimate rock."

I stared at the rock and then thought of the more logical way to gather information.

1. Take the information to the laboratory.
2. Dissect and examine the information.
3. Make a hypothesis and conclusion based on the facts.
4. Finally, and most importantly, be objective.

In doing this, I could see how a rock could be defined and named. When observing something with questions in mind, objectivity is critical.

Having been born a Catholic, I had many questions when I was a kid.

Sometimes I would ask the priest and found that he couldn't, or wouldn't, answer them. "You just have to believe," he would say.

I felt, "Belief cannot be blind!" I needed answers that somehow made some sense. I also asked him about the Trinity—how could there be three entities and still be only one God? He really didn't take my questions seriously, which left me increasingly doubtful about the Catholic religion.

I ate the communion wafer ("flesh of Christ") and drank the wine ("blood of Christ") on the rare occasions that we did go to church, and I had some serious misgivings about that whole process too. When I was in confession after doing something wrong, like stealing, my conscience told me to be careful and not get too close to the priest (who seemed pretty weird to me anyway).

My grandmother would always preach the need to follow your "gut feelings." Looking back now, I can see that if I hadn't taken her advice, I would have become a wino, drug addict, or worse, the "priest's friend." So, in 1969, the Milwaukee downtown library and my apartment became my laboratory, and the Bible, Qur'an, Torah, and Bhagavad Gita became my tools. I studied them objectively. It would take me four years to come to a final decision.

≫≪

Changes were also taking place in the Bucks lineup. Oscar was brought in from the Royals, and with the acquisition of Lew, I was expendable. Some said that Oscar engineered it; some said it was Lew; others said it was a combination of both. All I know is that I was traded on September 17, 1970, to the Seattle SuperSonics for Lucius Allen and Bob Boozer. Maybe Oscar wanted his close friend Boozer on the team, or maybe Lew wanted Allen, his former Bruin teammate, to join him. I thought about both possibilities.

These days, it is a running joke between Oscar and me about whether he influenced the deal. But at that time, I was incredibly disappointed. For the first time, I was playing on an NBA team and enjoying it. I had moved my mother to Milwaukee based on verbal promises the Bucks had made to me about being a "fixture." I was still only twenty-three, and I was just beginning to realize that the whole thing was just a business based on a group of men running up and down a court wearing shorts and playing a child's game—nothing more, nothing less. There was no true loyalty, and management promises were made and broken regularly.

I felt that I was being wronged, and refused to go to Seattle. I was seriously thinking about fighting the trade, even if I had to go all the way to the Supreme Court like Curt Flood had.

Smith May Sue Bucks, NBA
Bob Wolf, *Milwaukee Journal Sentinel*, September 22, 1970

Don Smith may sue the Milwaukee Bucks and the National Basketball Association because of the trade in which the Bucks sent him to the Seattle Supersonics, Atty. Lloyd Barbee said Tuesday. . . .

. . . "We're considering a lawsuit," Barbee said. "The trade poses the serious question of whether a human being can be made a pawn, a piece of property to be sent anywhere a club says he must go."

Asked if the suit would be filed on antitrust grounds, such as that brought by Curt Flood against baseball, Barbee said, "We will have to do some research on that. We will have to divide it up and do what we call creative legal research. There is a precedent for this in the Flood case, which I hope will be appealed."

Flood lost his suit, but has said he plans to appeal.

Smith based his objection to the trade on the fact that he was tired of moving his family—his mother and brother live in Milwaukee and he had planned to bring his sister and her four children here—plus certain "ambiguities" in his contract. He has one year remaining on the three year contract he signed with the Cincinnati Royals after they had made him their No. 1 draft choice two years ago. . . .

But after my emotional reaction passed, I realized that I was being traded for two very exceptional ballplayers and that my skill level was appreciated throughout the league. Other teammates told me how beautiful Seattle was and how much the Sonics's coach Lenny Wilkens really wanted me.

I gave in and headed to the beautiful Pacific Northwest.

SEATTLE

Seattle was a world away from Brooklyn. In New York, I had to go to Central Park or Prospect Park to see a tree. Trees were everywhere in the state of Washington. To the southeast, Mount Rainier boldly showed her majestic beauty, and the spectacular Olympic Mountains reigned to the west. A two- or three-hour trip would put you in breathtaking Vancouver, British Columbia, to the north, or to Portland, Oregon, to the south.

The people in Seattle during those days were kind and considerate. When they said hello to you, they meant it. Doors to homes were left open without fear. The city was so orderly that you could get a jaywalking ticket for crossing in the middle of the street and not at the crosswalks.

Seattle was the birthplace of Jimi Hendrix, which is still commemorated by a statue in the Capitol Hill neighborhood. The Seattle Center was built to house the 1962 World's Fair. In 1964, the Beatles stayed at the Seattle Edgewater Hotel during one of their rare U.S. appearances at the Seattle Center Coliseum.

That's also where we Seattle SuperSonics played basketball. In the cutthroat business of professional sports, Sam Schulman was the rare owner who showed some decency and compassion.

Zollie Volchok was the vice president and in charge of basketball operations. Bob Houbregs became the general manager who reported to Volchok. Bob was a standout player at the University of Washington before he came to the Sonics.

Brooklyn-born and All-Star Lenny Wilkens was the player coach. Lenny probably was the quickest and most intelligent guard in the league at the time, a fierce competitor who had acquired a short hook shot coming across the middle that was unstoppable. He was a left-hander, but he could still go around you if you forced him to the right. Rod Thorn, who got along great with Lenny, assisted him. Plagued by injuries during most of his eight-year career, Rod managed to average a respectable 10.8 points per game and knew the game inside and out. It was his love and enthusiasm for basketball that made him stand out.

When I met with general manager Houbregs, I felt very embarrassed to disclose my meager contract. Hayes and Unseld had signed huge three-year deals, plus bonuses, and my salary was pathetic, to say the least. Houbregs welcomed me to the Sonics and complimented my abilities. I was taken to my first practice, and there I met my new teammates, including center Bob Rule, who was about the same height as I was. He was from Colorado State and would turn out to be one of my favorite players. In looking around the gym, I realized that our team lacked height.

Rookie Pete Cross was six foot nine—not a good shooter but a fantastic rebounder. Tom Meschery, at six foot six, was limited by his advancing age and medical problems. Garfield Heard was from the University of Oklahoma, a fine forward with hands of steel. At six foot six and two hundred nineteen pounds, he could mix it up with the best of them. Dick Snyder was an incredible shooter who worked hard on defense. At six foot five and two hundred two pounds, Don Kojis was a "tweener" (neither specifically a guard nor a forward), who would score on fast breaks and drill midrange jumpers with accuracy. Barry Clemens was also a deadeye who most felt was the best shooter on the team when left unguarded.

Coach Wilkens averaged 19.8 points per game, but the stress of both playing and coaching began to take its toll. He still was a great player as he dished out 9.2 assists per game and shot 80 percent from the charity stripe. As a team, we were not tall, but we did have an advantage in speed and rebounding.

Leaping Lee Winfield was an excellent player who had amazing hang time and was a fan favorite with his athletic exploits. A Winfield dunk was one of beauty. He could also run the floor and stop on a dime.

I was even more amazed at Bob Rule. We called him the "Golden Rule," and that nickname was well deserved. A southpaw with huge hands, he bobbed and weaved himself into all types of artful moves. He had a lethal hook shot and if not played closely, that hook would end up right in your face. Reed, Russell, or Thurmond could testify to that.

Another amazing thing about Rule was that he never took care of himself, smoking cigarettes like they were going out of style. He would show up a mere forty-five minutes before game time and just destroy all the comers. At times, I thought he would collapse, since he worked very hard on the offensive end, breathing laboriously as he stooped over, holding his knees in exhaustion. I would think, "I wonder what this great player could do if he took better care of himself."

We had all the ingredients for a very good team. I was beginning to think that maybe the trade from Milwaukee was a blessing in disguise. We began the season at 7 to 4, beating solid teams. The combination of Rule and Smith was being talked about throughout the league. Lenny Wilkens and Dick Snyder made for a superb backcourt. Pete Cross, Don Kojis, Garfield Heard, and Tom Meschery produced quality minutes. With the Seattle crowd cheering us on, we were an exciting, high-energy act.

⇜⇝

Personally, I felt like I had been released from a two-year prison term. Milwaukee had boosted my morale, but Cincinnati had been a truly awful experience. I had been denied the expression of my gift: basketball. As I played each game, I furthered my mission to prove my worth and talent.

In the first ten games of the season, I had to face Bob Lanier, the newly named Kareem Abdul-Jabbar, and Willis Reed; I averaged 17 points and nineteen rebounds. On October 21, 1970, I recorded my high in rebounds with twenty-four against the Phoenix Suns. On October 28, 1970, with fire in my eyes and a point to prove, I scored twenty-five points and fifteen rebounds against the Cincinnati Royals. Our next game was played in Portland, and in that game I informed Coach Wilkens that I did not feel well and asked to sit out. When I returned to Seattle, I was seriously ill and was rushed to Overlake Hospital in nearby Bellevue.

After undergoing all sorts of blood and stress tests, I was diagnosed with pericarditis. I had to take medication to treat it. The doctor assured me that I could resume my career after the infection abated. Of course I was heartbroken. I thought, "My chance to become the star player that I know I can be is going to be denied me again!"

I then reflected on my career and past and saw where I had been fortunate. I remembered playing against Drake University in college and going in for a lay-up when my knee buckled. My career could have ended there. Or what if I had taken that whole mescaline tablet and had a coronary? What if I had succumbed to my peers' suggestions as a child in Brooklyn that I take a shot of China White heroin? What if Judge Mann had shown up in court and had thrown the book at me?

I knew I would come back and resume where I left off.

≈≈

Rule had torn his Achilles tendon, and in those days, that spelled the end of a career. After the loss of Rule and me, the Seattle SuperSonics were in trouble. The NBA rival American Basketball Association had great players who were available, such as Julius Irving, Rick Barry, George Gervin, and Artis Gilmore. However, the Sonics were sold on an amazing nineteen-year-old phenomenon named Spencer Haywood.

He was the 1970 Most Valuable Player of the ABA and Rookie of the Year. He had averaged an amazing thirty points and nineteen-plus rebounds a game for the Denver Nuggets, but he had run into trouble with the Nuggets management and was looking for a move.

Haywood hired agent Al Ross to represent him, and the deal went through, to the delight of Sam Schulman and the Sonics management. After a bitter fight (over switching from the ABA to the NBA) between Schulman, NBA head Walter Kennedy, Lakers owner Jack Kent Cooke, and the ABA, Haywood was cleared to play in the NBA.

A month had passed since I had been released from the hospital. Haywood was an upbeat individual with a very positive spirit. He would gather both Garfield Heard and me, and we would work out at the downtown YMCA. I was in shape, but not top basketball shape.

Even though Haywood was a great player, he had not been through the four years of collegiate competition that Heard and I had. The concept of cutting without the ball was hard for Spencer to visualize, since he had to have the ball to score. Assistant Coach Thorn would yell at me from the bench and say, "Don, move through!" When I did, I noticed that everything changed on the court. At times I would receive an easy pass for a dunk, or I could dish it off to Winfield or Snyder for a jumper. Like many great athletes, it was difficult for Haywood to adopt that philosophy of movement.

Then around late January, we caught on fire again. We began a drive that we hoped would get the franchise to the Western Division playoffs for the first time in history.

As a Seattle Sonic in 1971.

I used to meditate in my apartment before each game. During this period, we came up against the Cincinnati Royals in a game that stands out in my memory. While meditating, I imagined our team down by four points, with a minute to go. Then I saw a strategy that would give us the win. When

Wilt Chamberlain of the Los Angeles Lakers pulled a rebound away from the Seattle Sonics'
Don Smith in first-quarter action in a 1971 National Basketball Association game in the
Coliseum.

I got to the Coliseum, I was still visualizing the outcome of this game.

We played well against the Royals, but with four minutes to go, they were up by four. Tom Van Arsdale made two free throws. After shooting, Tom said, "I guess we have this game wrapped up!" to a teammate near the foul line.

I looked at them and said,

"Don't be so sure about that!"

We got the ball, scored quickly, and were now down by only four. On the next play, the Royals made a critical turnover, and we got possession and scored again with about ten seconds remaining. The Royals called a timeout. In our huddle, we discussed strategy and I realized this was the same sce-

Seattle SuperSonics versus Los Angeles Lakers Statistics

	Min.	FG	FT	Reb.	A	PF	TP
SEATTLE (115)							
Clemens	10	0–2	0–0	0	0	1	0
Haywood	47	8–19	8–9	15	1	5	24
Kojis	39	12–19	2–4	9	1	4	26
Rule	18	7–11	0–0	5	0	5	14
Smith	30	10–18	1–1	13	3	3	21
Wilkens	44	3–13	10–11	5	19	3	16
Winfield	21	2–4	0–0	1	4	0	4
Totals		46–94	23–28	50	32	21	115
LOS ANGELES (106)							
Baylor	30	8–19	1–1	12	3	5	17
Chamberlain	40	3–5	1–6	11	2	2	7
Cleamons	10	0–1	0–0	1	2	1	0
Ellis	8	0–5	2–2	5	1	2	2
Goodrich	43	8–21	2–2	4	7	1	18
Hairston	40	7–14	13–16	13	4	5	27
McMillian	26	2–8	3–5	4	1	4	7
Robinson	43	13–20	2–2	4	5	5	28
Totals		41–93	24–34	54	25	25	106
Los Angeles		24	28	29	25–106		
Seattle		15	35	38	27–115		

Min. = Minutes Played, FG = Goals; FT = Free Throws; Reb. = Rebounds;
A = Assists ; PF = Personal Fouls; TP = Total Points

nario I had seen in my meditation. I told guard Lee Winfield not to move so I could hide behind him.

Amazingly, this worked, even though Winfield was very thin (six foot two and around one hundred seventy-four pounds), and I weighed in at around two hundred forty-five pounds. The Royals threw the ball in and I moved out from behind Winfield, intercepted the ball, and dunked it at the buzzer to tie. We went on to win 132 to 131.

As we left the court, I walked over to Van Arsdale and said, "See, you can never count your chickens before they hatch." Tom just put his head down and walked off. In my personal vendetta with the Cincinnati Royals, I felt totally vindicated in that game.

≫ ≪

Our young team slowly began to understand teamwork, passing, and one another's tendencies and strengths. We were becoming a championship-caliber unit, with guys sacrificing for the sake of the team. We were a contending team, which the experts had not envisioned, and I was playing the best basketball of my life—superstar basketball.

On March 9, 1971, I scored twenty-eight points and hauled down eighteen rebounds against the Bucks. The next night we traveled to New York, and in an unbelievable game, we fought back from a twenty-six-point deficit to win. I had thirty-seven points and fourteen rebounds.

Two days later, as we blew out the Detroit Pistons—who had Dave Bing and Bob Lanier—I scored twenty-nine points and pulled down nineteen rebounds. During this spree, all the focus was on Spencer Haywood, who was playing at the top of his game. That was all right with me, since he deserved the attention, and I wasn't fond of the spotlight anyway. I was just happy that we were playing great ball as we began to dominate the Western Division.

Then in a game that was a must if our playoff hopes were to remain alive, we had to beat the Bucks (with Kareem and Oscar). On March 18, 1971, that game was held at the University of Washington before a packed house. We won in a thriller, and I had twenty-eight points and sixteen rebounds. Unfortunately, the San Francisco Warriors defeated the Chicago Bulls, and as a result, we were out of contention. We didn't quite make it, but we were hopeful that in the next season Bob Rule would come back in top shape, and we were adding a young guard to our roster by the name of Fred Brown. Things looked rosy for the Sonics and the city of Seattle.

At six foot nine, I had many advantages. I wasn't really a center but more a roaming forward. My strategy was to run the bigger centers like

Wilt, Kareem, and Thurmond. I had more problems with centers my size like Hayes, Cowens, and McAdoo. In this case my strategy was to overpower them with strength and speed. We were the same size but I was quicker to the ball, which made a big difference.

I was never intimidated by the greats on the court, and I had complete confidence in my game, but the press generally ignored me. There was continual buzz about Hayes, Unseld, Wilt, and, of course, Kareem, but I was rarely mentioned. I was playing star-level basketball, but I was never a media superstar. My shyness may have had a lot to do with it, as well as the fact that I was a loner and would never toot my own horn. Maybe being traded twice in two years lowered my standings throughout the league. I didn't really care about the press, but at that time, I wanted a great player like Oscar or Wilt to tell me, "Hey, you sure are good!" That never did happen, and ironically, I doubt I would have been able to enjoy it if it had, since I tended to discount compliments. So after the 1971 season, I could not wait for the next. I wanted to prove myself.

In the 1971–72 season, rookie Fred Brown was not known as Downtown Freddie Brown but the "Pillsbury Doughboy." His weight became a focus of concern for Coach Wilkens. I had played with Fred in pick-up games at Marquette University during the off-season and knew that even with his pudginess, he was a terrific player. Coach Wilkens, disciplinarian that he was, thought otherwise, and Fred had a tough rookie year. However, at the same time, Lenny began to slow down on the court. As a result, Fred was reluctantly played and we began to click as a team.

Unfortunately, that didn't last. Like a bad dream, everything began to fall apart for Bob Rule, me, Dick Snyder, Spencer Haywood, and the Sonics franchise—in that order.

Rule had injured his Achilles tendon that season, and he never fully recovered. He was later shipped to Philadelphia.

I remember that fateful kick, but paid little attention to it at the time. It happened in Milwaukee, as Kareem went up for one of his patented sky-hooks. I went to block it when Kareem extended his left foot and made contact with my right foot. I grimaced but continued to play. A week later we were at a game against the Celtics in Boston. With about two minutes to go in the first quarter, I suddenly felt a terrific pain about six inches above my right ankle. I tried to continue to play, but the pain was excruciating.

When I returned to Seattle, I saw an orthopedic physician who told the Sonics and me that I had a bruise and would be okay. I was put in a walking cast and told to rest for ten days. I traveled with the team to Portland about a week later. I tried to play but could not as the pain forced me to keel over. Back in Seattle, I met with the same doctor who had diagnosed the bruise and was X-rayed. The X-ray revealed a fracture, and I was out the rest of the season.

Next, Dick Snyder broke his right finger on a jump shot. Around the same time, Spencer Haywood met with a similar fate. On a rainy night in the Coliseum, he was going in for a shot when he slipped in a puddle of water that had dripped from the roof. Both Snyder and Haywood were out the remainder of the season.

Our team lost eight out of nine games and finished 47 to 35. Sam Schulman had no choice but to turn back to the ABA for help. Center Jim McDaniels was brought in from the Kentucky Colonels and became our next hope. My accomplishments in Seattle went unnoticed and unappreciated. All the twenty-point and twenty-rebound games that I had played were never reported.

I was like an invisible being. No one spoke about my skill level. No one talked about my having twenty-four points in the first half against one of the greatest players of all time, Wilt Chamberlain. No one discussed my multiple twenty-rebound performances against the NBA's greatest centers. No one mentioned the records I had set—twelve consecutive field goals (broken thirty years later only by Gary Payton) or the most rebounds in a quarter (twelve, which still stands today).

I did not want praise, but acknowledgment that I was a good player, that I was truly a number-one pick, and a two-time All-American from a university that was not known for having an elite basketball program at that time. I did not read the papers, and no one told me about the fact that I was being sold to the Houson Rockets.

No one told Lenny Wilkens either. While playing golf one day, he got the word he was being shipped to the Cleveland Cavaliers.

The Business of Professional Sports

_____

Haywood and I would talk, and I realized that I was taking everything too personally. He told me how he had been taken advantage of because of his youth and lack of business acumen. We began comparing notes, and it dawned on me that the superstar players of the day were great, but they also had equally great attorneys or agents representing them. Some agents or attorneys represented more than one player on a team, which put even more pressure on the management to treat professionally represented players with respect.

That was it! I was by myself and had no consistent representation, no one in my corner to deal with owners who would sell me to the highest bidder like aged prime rib. Haywood recommended Al Ross, who was representing some of the top names in the NBA.

I flew to Los Angeles and signed with Mr. Ross. About two weeks later I signed a three-year, no-cut contract with the Houston Rockets. The contract was triple what I was making with the Sonics. Although I was very happy with my new financial arrangement, I still felt unfulfilled professionally. Mr. Ross and I boarded a plane for Houston for the signing. Ray Patterson, who had moved from the Milwaukee Bucks to take over management of the Rockets, met us.

Ray, who was sorry that I was ever sent to Seattle in the first place, said that he was delighted to acquire me and that things would be different in Houston. I had a couple of reasons to believe Ray Patterson. The first was the fact that I had exploded for twenty-eight points and eighteen rebounds in a losing effort against the Bucks with Oscar and Kareem. During that game I had looked over at Ray during the last few minutes, and his eyes told me, "I'm sorry, you are a great player, but with the addition of Kareem you were very marketable!"

I responded in my stare, "That's okay Ray, I really respect you, no hard feelings!"

The other reason I appreciated Ray was that he knew and respected my mother. Ray had met her often and was impressed with her personality and wit. I appreciated Ray's kindness to me and my family. At the time I was unaware of the Alzheimer's disease that was creeping into her mind, and that would eventually sap her memory and take her life.

The Houston Rockets

I should have walked straight up to Coach Johnny Egan and said,

"Coach Egan, I was chosen in the first round, but now no one sees my abilities!"

I wanted to tell him about my background in Brooklyn and growing up without a healthy father figure, but you just don't do that in the NBA. It's a business, not a counseling service. So my stint with the Rockets began with me hardly listening to Coach Egan at all. At times I would stare off into space during practice. It was not directed at Coach Egan or Assistant Coach Larry Siegfried personally, but I saw Ed Jucker in them. It was my third team in three years—too many different cities and different faces. I felt like the boll weevil that everybody from Leadbelly to Brook Benton, Eddie Cochran to The White Stripes and The Presidents of the United States of America sang about. He was just looking for a home, but every time he found one, somebody set it on fire.

⋙ ⋘

Our Rockets team was a collection of very good players, but we were undisciplined and offensive-minded only. If we ever aspired to be contenders, we needed to learn the basic concept of team defense.

We had guys who could score at will. The great Calvin Murphy from Niagara University broke all the myths about the little man playing professional sports in the NBA. He stood only five foot nine, but he had the movements of a hummingbird. Left unguarded, Calvin could put up terrific numbers, like the fifty-seven points he scored in one game against the New

The 1973–74 Houston Rockets team. Front row: Cliff Meely, Rudy Tomjanovich, Don Smith, Otto Moore, George Johnson, E. C. Coleman, Jack Marin. Back row: Assistant Coach Larry Siegfried, Paul McCracken, Matt Guokas, Ed Ratleff, Stan McKenzie, Mike Newlin, Calvin Murphy, Dick Vandervoort, Head Coach John Egan.

Jersey Nets. He was a liability on defense, but he fought hard against the much taller guards like West and Oscar. He created serious match-up problems because no one was quick enough to keep up with him.

Calvin's best friend on the team was Rudy Tomjanovich, from the University of Michigan. Rudy was not the fastest of foot, but he could kill you with his patented jump shooting. He was also a tenacious rebounder who always found a way to the free-throw line, where he was a sure deadeye.

Jack Marin was a left-handed jump shooter who had played in Baltimore with Earl Monroe and the late Gus Johnson. Everyone in the league knew his offensive level and defensive liabilities.

Mike Newlin had a rebel-type personality who always seemed to be misunderstood, clashing with teammates and management weekly. He would dash out of practice after arguing with team members and return the next day like nothing had ever happened. But he was an extremely strong player, a deadly shot, and a fair defender, one I admired because of his work habits.

Houston Rockets versus Milwaukee Bucks Statistics

	M	G	GA	F	FA	R	A	P	TP
HOUSTON									
Tomjanovich	44	15	28	4	4	10	0	4	34
Newlin	36	7	18	2	2	4	1	4	16
Smith	38	7	18	7	9	18	4	2	21
Murphy	44	8	16	4	6	4	12	3	20
Guokas	30	2	6	0	0	2	3	1	4
Marin	17	3	8	3	5	2	7	1	9
Coleman	17	1	3	2	3	6	0	2	4
Meely	10	0	2	1	2	2	0	3	1
Ratleff	3	0	0	0	0	2	1	0	0
Johnson	1	0	0	0	0	0	0	0	0
Totals	240	43	99	23	31	50	28	20	109
MILWAUKEE									
Perry	35	6	14	1	2	17	7	5	13
Dandridge	41	11	20	6	9	12	4	4	28
A'-Jabbar	46	11	21	10	12	14	7	3	32
Robertson	36	5	9	3	3	5	5	1	13
McGlocklin	37	8	13	2	2	2	2	2	18
Williams	23	4	8	2	2	2	2	1	10
Driscoll	13	4	7	0	0	2	2	2	8
Davis	4	0	1	0	0	0	0	0	0
Lee	3	0	2	0	0	0	1	1	0
Warner	2	1	1	0	0	0	0	1	2
Totals	240	50	96	24	30	54	30	20	124

M = Minutes Played, G = Goals; GA = Goals Attempted; F = Free Throws; FA = Free Throws Attempted; R = Rebounds; A = Assists ; P = Personal Fouls; TP = Total Points

The best defensive player on our team was Cliff Meely, from the University of Colorado. I had played against Cliff in college and knew his potential. He was a good shooter and worked hard as he guarded the top players in the league.

Unfortunately, even with all this talent, the Rockets were a terrible defensive group. I did what I could to clog the middle to cover up our defensive deficiencies, but it became an overwhelming task. We were a helter-skelter, rollercoaster Houston Rockets team. At times it became almost comical as fights broke out in practice, but this chaos prevented any genuine team spirit from developing. Some halftimes when we were down, Ray, hoping he could inspire some good play, would holler "Reckless abandon! Play with reckless abandon! Have some fun!" We would get blasted one night, and the next night totally crush a top team.

≫≪

On the night of January 25, 1973, we were facing the Milwaukee Bucks in Madison, Wisconsin. I was pumped up, knowing that I would be facing Kareem. I had a point to prove in front of a Bucks crowd. I got my first three jump shots and then noticed that Kareem began to overplay me. I went backdoor and received a pass from Rudy Tomjanovich for a thunderous dunk. With eighteen minutes gone in the half, I was on defense when the "Comedian" Bob Dandridge came off a screen and slid on a wet spot on the court, slamming into my right knee. This time he wasn't funny! I felt a snap and grimaced.

Trainer Dick Vandervoort came running out onto the court and said, "Dynamite, I saw what happened and I don't want you to return! The way you were hit, I'm sure it was your ligament!" I really didn't want to come out, but I respected Dick and limped to the bench.

I was taken to the locker room and examined by a doctor who grabbed my right knee and twisted it. I felt an opening inside and then pure pain. To my horror, the doctor announced, "A torn or stretched medial collateral ligament. You'll be out about six weeks. Surgery will be necessary."

I just sat there as my team went on to win 129 to 125.

The next day I met with General Manager Ray Patterson. I could not look him in the eye. I was embarrassed and blamed myself for the injury. I should have seen Dandridge coming off the pick! I should have somehow seen the sweat puddle on the floor!

I reflected on the previous years. Getting benched in Cincinnati. Being traded when Kareem came to the Bucks. Rule going down. Haywood slipping on a puddle of rain. Snyder's broken finger. My chest infection. Once a durable and very strong athlete, I was beginning to experience physical and mental anguish. I thought, "Maybe my life is wrong. Maybe I'm missing something! What is my purpose besides running up and down a basketball court?"

I was fortunate to have two of the best surgeons in the world operate on me. I went to Los Angeles and met with doctors Robert Kerlin and Frank Jobe. They informed me that the surgery would take place in the morning. I was encouraged by their track record of operating on stars such as Wilt Chamberlain and Jerry West.

The only thing I remember about the surgery was trying to count with the anesthetist. I got to seven and I was out, going to a place that was tranquil and peaceful. Upon waking, I felt a terrific pain in my throat that was worse than the knee that had just been stitched. It had been about a three-hour operation during which I had to breathe through an oxygen mask, and my throat was raw.

Doctor Kerlin whispered, "The operation was successful, but you need to go on a weight-lifting regimen after we remove the cast in six weeks. If you don't do that, you might never play again." I don't know if he was just trying to scare me into following my therapy regimen, but I got the message.

I looked down, and then reached for the huge cast, which began at my hip and went straight down to my ankle. I caught a plane back to Houston with the purpose of life on my mind.

A GREATER PURPOSE

Abraham and the Prophets

I was crushed. Out for the season in a new town. I wanted to go home to New York, but I didn't have the strength.

My trainer Dick Vandervoort made up my mind for me as he told me, "Don, the doctor wants you to lift weights, but we don't have to wait for the cast to be removed." He pointed to a boot weight. "We can use this boot and put weights on the side so you can do leg lifts. If you do this, you can keep muscle tone, and your leg won't atrophy that much."

On Dick's suggestions, I began weightlifting with him, holding the weight straight so that it would not move. I worked out every other day, and the six weeks began to fly. At nights, I returned to reading spiritual texts again, which I had neglected because of my injury. I read and questioned all types of scriptures objectively. I wanted the truth.

I began my search by following what Jesus was reported to have said: "Seek the truth and the truth shall set you free." I somehow knew that truth had to have a continuum, like the numerical system or time itself. To me, truth had to progress systematically from century to century and individual to individual, passed down without breakage or corruption.

In studying the Bible, I went in with an open mind and the concept that Jesus was "God's son." I held this point of view not so much because I entirely believed in it, but because I had no reference that could give me a clearer choice. I went to the Old Testament and the Ten Commandments, seeking the truth that would link Moses and Jesus.

As I read, I found myself drawn to the teachings of Abraham, Moses, Jesus, and Muhammad. They all taught the importance of worshipping one god, continually reminding their followers of the dangers of creating idols. The First Commandment, "Thou shall have no other gods before me," was pretty straightforward. And yet, it seemed that many Christians worshiped Jesus rather than the one God he worshipped. Certain tenets of Christianity, especially the Trinity, just didn't resonate for me.

I continued the weight exercises on my leg during the day and the spiritual exercises of my mind at night. The weights helped my leg retain adequate muscle tone, while the spiritual search cleared my mind. About two weeks before my cast was to come off, I retreated again to deepen my spiritual quest.

≫ ≪

I learned about Abraham's spiritual conversion and some of the history of the time in which he lived. He is revered as a prophet in Judaism, Christianity, and Islam alike. Abraham was born in Ur, in what is now eastern Iraq. The society in which Abraham grew up was divided into three main castes: (1) Amelu, a higher class consisting of priests, state officials, and military personnel; (2) Mushkenu, the merchants, craftsman, and farmers, and (3) Ardu, or slaves. Since Abraham's father was a chief official of the state, Abraham was of the upper class. Like many people of conscience to this day, this class segregation troubled Abraham, which prompted him to consider the society of his time.

This society was also polytheistic, worshipping many gods and idols. This was thought to bring prosperity and success, but its logic troubled Abraham. For instance, the moon and sun were considered separate entities to be idolized, but Abraham felt that it made more sense that a single entity had created everything in the heavens and the earth. He finally decided to worship the single creator of the universe, the architect of existence, and was blessed by God for his choice (Genesis 17:20, 25:13–16, 17:3–5).

Abraham's blessing foretold that both of his sons Isaac and Ishmael would create great nations. Isaac's offspring included Jacob, Moses, and Jesus. Ishmael's descendents were the Arabs. There were many prophets from the House of Israel, but Muhammad was the first and only prophet from Ishmael's descendents.

≫ ≪

A few markers stand out as I consider moments in my life that nudged me to explore my relationship with God, including my frustration when a priest was unable to answer questions to my satisfaction when I was a child; my fervent prayer for help when I was in prison at sixteen and the miraculous circumstances that led to my release; and Kareem's casual but startling comment about the cross I wore as a young NBA player. Most of all, there were innumerable moments in my life filled with the yearning to integrate my faith in God and my outward life in the world.

Now I was consciously searching for the spiritual path that was right for me. I read voraciously during that period and *The Autobiography of Malcolm X,* in particular, made a huge impression on me. The book laid out his evolution from a young man filled with anger and antiwhite rhetoric to a mature man who believed deeply that God was colorblind and that humans should be, too. I could identify with many of the internal conflicts he described, and I was drawn to his conclusion that all humans deserve respect and compassion, regardless of creed or color. The fact that Islam was the path that brought him to that conclusion increased my interest in the Muslim faith.

I also began to notice Muslim people wherever I traveled and I was always impressed by the way they conducted themselves. Sometimes I wondered if one of my ancestors had been forced to outwardly abandon their Muslim faith, perhaps when enslaved to come to America. It wasn't anything I could put my finger on, but I had a feeling that perhaps that ancestor had made prayers that his or her descendents would find their way back to Islam. Perhaps in my spiritual search, I was responding to those prayers.

The spiritual, social, and health principles of the Islamic lifestyle also appealed to me. So many things pointed toward Islam. Finally, when I read Yusef Ali's translation of the Qur'an, it spoke to my heart.

I could not see how Jesus or Muhammad could be God, but I did see these great prophets as examples and guides for humanity. This led to my conversion to Islam.

So in April of 1973, I took my *shahada,* or testimony. I went to the mosque and repeated, "I bear witness that there is no god but God and that Muhammad is the prophet of God." I inwardly promised myself that I would follow these tenets:

1. Pray five times every day.
2. Fast in the month of Ramadan.
3. Give 2.5 percent of my earnings in charity.
4. Make Hajj at least once in my lifetime.

I made a commitment to abide by all the Islamic articles of faith: belief in angels, Paradise, and Hell, belief in life after death, and belief in divine decree.

Then all the people present uttered, "God is Great, God is Great, God is Great!"

People came up and embraced me. An older gentleman came up and said, "Congratulations, all your past sins have been forgiven and you are now as clean as a newborn baby!"

I then reflected on my childhood and how I had lacked a close family. How I drank wine and smoked marijuana and ate harmful pork products. I looked around and tears began to run down my face as I realized that I now had a family. Over one billion brothers and sisters were now my family and wished me peace. Yes, I thought, Don Smith has found success!

❧ ❦

The origins of Abraham are embedded in the very foundation of the world's three major religions, as is the Arabic culture and land. The U.S. wars against Iraqi dictator Saddam Hussein, the events of September 11, and other examples of Middle East dissent and conflict have deeply skewed the views of many Americans and other peoples around the world toward Arabs, Iraqi, and the Muslim culture in general.

Many Americans think that Iraq is a primitive, barbaric country, but it is literally the cradle of civilization. It existed as the ancient country of Mesopotamia over 4,500 years ago. Settled between the Tigris and the Euphrates, Mesopotamia was where Noah built his Ark and the Garden of Eden was found.

Arab contributions to civilization are many. The Arabs established the original postal system. Mounted soldiers delivered mail from city to city, and in areas where this regular postal service was impractical, carrier pigeons were used for communication, an ancient form of airmail.

The malls that we are familiar with today originated from the Arab *souk,* or bazaar. A souk could be seven-and-a-half miles long and stretch almost four miles wide. To make it easier for customers to find what they needed, merchants were strategically located within these massive souks.

The first paper mills probably opened in 751 B.C. in Samarkand, then Yemen, Spain, and Baghdad, to name a few. This proliferation of paper mills throughout the Arab world led to administrative recordkeeping. From this bound books, knowledge, and culture spread.

Educated Muslim women made a good living making copies of the Qur'an for newly established libraries. One library in Egypt contained over one-and-a-half million books! Calligraphers, masters of beautiful Arabic script, used both the angular Kufic script and a rounded cursive form, and knowledge spread rapidly.

Arabs also significantly contributed to science and education. The first *madrasah,* or university, was established in the eleventh century. In 1,000 A.D., Al-Biruni estimated the circumference of the earth and was only nine miles off. A book written in 869 A.D. gave information on over one hundred inventions such as service elevators, cold-water apparatuses, and mechanical toys.

Abu al-Qasim, a Muslim, wrote a comprehensive book entitled *The Art of Healing Wounds.* In this great work, he described where the surgeon's knife should be placed in surgical procedures. The study of medicine also triggered the creation of pharmacies. Ibn Sina's most famous works, the encyclopedic *The Book of Healing* and *Canon of Medicine,* were later translated into Latin and used by European physicians for five centuries. Abu Bakr al-Razi studied infections, including smallpox and measles, and explored the use of psychology on ill patients.

But the biggest Arab contribution to the world was the Prophet Muhammad. Moses was given the miracle of defeating the Pharaoh. Jesus was able to feed the masses and heal the sick. Muhammad was given the Qur'an. He could not read or write, but he lived in times when oral traditions and poetry abounded. When Muhammad was deep in prayer, the Angel Gabriel came to the prophet and urged him to recite the words revealed to him by God. In the span of twenty-three years, the Qur'an was revealed and lives as an ongoing miracle. Muslims all over the world learn Arabic to understand the Qur'an's verses as it was revealed to Muhammad. Today there are over 1.4 billion Muslims and the faith is growing daily.

In *Newsweek* on July 31, 1978, historian Michael H. Hart made a list of the most influential people in history. Hart made an effort to quantify the impact of individuals on civilization according to the number of people he or she influenced over history. The Prophet Muhammad was at the top of his list.

⇜⇝

As I continued to study, more questions arose. Things became clearer.

A ligament tear is a serious condition from which some athletes never recover from. I think my quest for truth really added to my overall healing process and state of mind. Instead of worrying about whether I was going to be the same high jumper I was before, I now began to give everything over to God, the creator of the heavens and the earth.

The National Basketball Association and its great players were also going to see the difference.

ZAID ABDUL-AZIZ

At first I was cautious and afraid to make physical contact with players. I remembered Dandridge crashing into my knee. But after a few hits and bumps, I realized that Don Smith was back. I hadn't lost any quickness or speed. Dunking was just as easy as it had been before.

Nothing had really changed athletically, but as a person I was completely transformed in that year of 1973. I began reading the translation of the Qur'an daily and to pray and fast on some days.

That year, with 11.7 rebounds per game, I placed in the NBA Top Ten in rebounding, and racked up almost eleven points a game. I was also a league leader in blocks, with 104. I possessed the rare combination of skills that allowed me to score, play defense, and block shots.

With Calvin Murphy and Rudy Tomjanovich's scoring potential, I decided to focus on rebounding and defense. I knew that it would take time and patience on my part for them to trust that I was back there to cover for them. We had others on the team who were great scorers, like Mike Newlin, Jack Marin, Cliff Meely, and Ed Ratliff, but gaining a collective understanding about team defense took time. Our team was young, and the thought of getting points was more appealing than stopping somebody. I knew that good defense was critical, but how could I convince the other eleven players? My strategy was to lead by example.

During the 1973 season, I played as well as anyone in the league. With time I felt our team could go far and possibly win a conference championship. As the season unfolded, I continued seeking spiritual truth with an open mind. Our team traveled to Chicago, and I decided to attend a Black

Muslim service.

During the 1970s, one of the most prominent voices for black people in America was the Black Muslim movement. Lynching, the Jim Crow laws, and general discrimination against blacks in American society had fostered the appeal of the Nation of Islam. Its message was for the black man to stop using alcohol and drugs and to refuse to rely on handouts such as welfare checks. It urged its followers to get educated, and it distributed handouts on how to eat right. Its message was more about self-improvement than spiritual in nature.

As I entered the temple, I could hear the minister speaking:

"I guarantee you that the white man is the devil. Look! Look where we are as a people: drug addiction, prostitution, and lynching. Oh yes, he is the devil!"

I glanced at the bow-tied speaker as he ended his speech. He was around thirty with a thin, athletic build. I looked at him more closely as he spoke. His skin was extremely smooth and shiny. The whites of his eyes were radiantly white, with dark pupils. His hair was carefully combed, each strand perfectly in place with the others.

I thought, "He really has the right code in life—I can see it."

He continued, "You see, we are the original people, the tribe of the original man who was brought to this country involuntarily!"

The crowd was now responding. "Speak on, brother minister!" a young man shouted from the right pew.

I had seen pictures of the inside of a mosque in my studies, so I was puzzled to see that the temple had pews like a church, rather than just a carpet. Today, all the pews were overcrowded with black faces intently listening to the minister's every word.

As he spoke, I thought about the plight of my people. Brought here and enslaved, segregated in the South, and forced into slavery, inferior schools, ghetto conditions, and separate restrooms. The minister was persuasive, and I would have bought his speech hook, line, and sinker except for one thing—my mind. I began to think about oppression in a broader sense. There were many tyrants in a myriad of colors and hues. The minister had a point, but not *the* point! Did not blacks kill Malcolm X?

The minister asked, "Who wants their X? Please, my brothers and sisters, we need workers! Those of you who want their Xs, please step forward!"

When people joined the Black Muslim movement, some chose to take an "X" as they relinquished their "white" names. I was tempted, but my gut told me that if I did, it would be only because of peer pressure. I needed more time to study and gather facts. On the other hand, I felt if I did not take my X right then, I would feel hypocritical to my people. I did not know what to do!

The minister increased his rhetoric: "Now's the time! Now, my brothers and sisters, raise your hands and be counted!"

I looked to my right and saw another gentleman (who looked very much like the minister), and I asked, "Brother, where is the men's room?" He pointed to the rear of the small temple. I headed in that direction, but as I approached it, I took a quick left and exited.

The Chicago air was freezing as I walked away from the temple, but I was burning up inside. Lifelong commitments had to be weighed and investigated. The leader of the Nation of Islam, Elijah Muhammad, seemed to have a message, but I needed to be 100 percent sure.

I hailed a taxi. I climbed in and said, "Sheraton Hotel, downtown, please." The south side of Chicago reminded me of Brooklyn. I thought about how all ghettos seemed to look alike everywhere in America.

As the taxi approached my hotel, I saw a huge mural of Mr. Muhammad across the street. When I reached my room I was exhausted and I had a game that night. I called the hotel operator and asked for a 4:30 P.M. wake-up call. I set my clock to 5:00 and fell asleep.

It seemed like only minutes had passed when I heard the phone ringing. I picked it up.

"Mr. Smith?" It was the same operator. "It's 4:30!"

I yawned and asked for room service. I ordered seafood parmeggiano, a large shrimp cocktail, orange juice, and cheesecake for dessert. My alarm clock went off as I heard a knock and the waiter entered. He rolled in the service cart, put it before me, and gave me the bill. I signed and reached for my wallet to give the waiter a tip.

After he left, I looked through my wallet and took out a folded schedule. As I ate, I read, "Houston Rockets versus Chicago Bulls, December 16, 1973, 7:30 P.M." I made ablutions, then fell on my face and prayed, asking God for strength and for the good of mankind. I asked Him for protection and for increased understanding. I asked Him to keep me on the straight path. Then I packed my equipment bag and headed downstairs.

"Starting at center, number 35, Don Smith," the announcer yelled. I ran out onto the floor but could not help but think about what had happened earlier in the day. The game began, and I was immediately fouled and went to the free-throw line.

"The white man is the devil," I thought as I missed the first shot. "No, there has to be a better way," I reasoned.

I looked around and saw thousands of faces and thought, "There *must* be a better way." Then all of a sudden I heard, "Boy, you must be cold!" in a southern twang, and I remembered the act of kindness that George Hamilton IV had shown to me as a boy so many years before.

"There must be a better way," I repeated to myself as I made the second shot.

We lost that game, but I won the spiritual battle of finding the correct path. It happened naturally at the free-throw line on that cold Chicago night.

☙❧

Nearly a year later, the Rockets and Bulls met again. By now, Kareem Abdul-Jabbar had plagued us for five years, but not this time.

Ask Bulls: Abdul-Aziz Better Than Don Smith

Bob Logan, *Chicago Tribune*, November 16, 1974

Decisively outplaying Nate Thurmond, Abdul-Aziz sparked the Rockets to a 105–96 victory over the Chicagoans. It was the first time they had beaten the Bulls since Dec. 17, 1971, snapping a string of 11 straight setbacks....

Four months later, on April 19, in the District Court of Harris County, Texas, I changed my name legally to Zaid Abdul-Aziz. On May 24, I married Tayyibah, whom I had met while in Toronto the previous year. I was now both husband and father as Tayyibah and three-year-old Atiya moved to Houston to join me.

In September, right before training camp, I went to the Rockets office and informed Ray Patterson of my name change. He was quite polite as he said, "If that's what you want to do, that's okay with me and the Rockets." I had a fondness for Ray and knew that's how he would respond.

Changing my name was likely to stir up a lot of controversy because Islam was not at all understood in the U.S. at that time. Even though I was not part of the Nation of Islam, any black who became a Muslim was assumed to be a nationalist Muslim. The Nation of Islam intimidated many people with its militant, antiwhite stand.

On September 22, 1974, I was featured in the *Houston Post* with the caption, "Rocket, Smith in the Pink." The article talked about how I had won the starting center position and the very good season I had had the previous year. But it was the last positive article written about me as a Rocket.

My name change became public knowledge, and I began to pray publicly, which caused some confusion with my teammates. They would watch as I pulled out my prayer rug at some airports to pray. Some teammates tried to act like they didn't see me.

One time I was praying, and a fan asked for my autograph, which I couldn't give him right then. Another time while I was praying, a person came up and said, "I'll help you. I'm always losing my contact lenses too!"

Some of my teammates may have thought I hated them because they assumed that I was now an antiwhite Black Muslim. Other teammates did not want to get too close to me, because their association with me could suggest that they had become Black Muslims, too. I guess they felt that their careers might be in jeopardy by even being near me.

My family thought that my change of religion and name might just be a fad, and I would grow out of it. I figured my father wanted to pull me over to the side and say, "What in the world have you done? You know you're going to catch more hell than you can ever imagine with this name change nonsense!" But he never said a word.

One day my mother handed me an article that said, "Joe Louis fought bravely but quietly." She was okay with my choice, but she felt I should just keep my religion to myself. I think she might have thought that I would get involved in some negative group or that I had been brainwashed. I could understand my parents' sentiments, but all I was trying to do was be a God-fearing man—a man who stayed away from bad things and tried do positive things in his short life.

I was grateful that God had given me the talent to play basketball and blessed me with money that I could have never imagined receiving. I just wanted to thank Him for everything more each day. Praying five times a day to show God my appreciation for His bounties was not enough in my mind, but that was the prescribed number in my new faith, which opposes excess in anything.

Others thought my decision was to model myself after Muhammad Ali or Kareem Abdul-Jabbar. No—my decision was to try and be a decent human being, just like the over one billion Muslims currently on the planet. It is true that some have caused a bad name for Islam, but a few people can corrupt even the purest endeavors. God has a way of dispensing with evil and replacing it with good.

Like any new convert, I was filled with enthusiasm and enormous energy. I wanted to do everything right and make every prayer on time. In my zeal, I fasted during our two-a-day practices in preseason training camp. I hadn't yet learned that I could make up for fasting days I missed after Ramadan was over.

Fasting placed unreasonable strain on my body because of the extreme physical requirements of my work. Dehydrated and weak from depleted vital mineral and vitamin stores, I became very agitated and moody and began to have a hard time falling asleep. I visited a doctor, who told me that I was on the verge of anemia. He suggested that I take some time off, but with the name change, I felt that no one would understand. I played for some time and felt miserable, but I improved after Ramadan was over, when I could eat and drink normally.

⇜⇝

I was also suffering from depression. I couldn't handle the stress of both the emotional conflicts of my new faith and the demands of my basketball career, and I really wasn't thinking clearly about anything.

I went to Ray Patterson again and said, "Ray, I don't want to play anymore. I'm tired. I retire."

Ray looked at me like I was crazy. "What do you mean?"

I said, "I'm going to get away and buy a farm."

Ray paused for a while, and then said, "If that's what you want, okay!"

I left the office and went home into "retirement." I hadn't even discussed this with my wife. The next day the news hit the media, and my father called me and asked, "What's going on with you? I saw on the *Today* show where you quit the team!"

But I could not explain my actions. I was in a depressed state and acting irrationally.

The next day I called Ray and told him I had made a mistake and did not want to retire. But the damage was done, and now my career was in jeopardy.

At the next practice, I was not allowed to play, and Kevin Kunnert, our seven-foot backup center, was given the job. In a way I could understand Coach Egan's position. Here he was trying to coach a team, he depended on me, and then I quit—amidst controversy. He decided to go with another player in my place and that was Kunnert. I probably would have done the same thing as coach.

Everything could have been resolved if things had been placed civilly on the table, but it did not happen that way. I was too much of an enigma and was not given that respect. My basketball skills were suddenly not as important as the issues around my change of faith and name. My playing time was reduced to not playing at all.

At one practice, Assistant Coach Larry Siegfried said, "We finally have our seven-foot center!" He had forgotten what I had done to some seven-footers in the league such as Wilt, Kareem, and Thurmond. On some nights I outplayed them, while on others I held my own. I was never intimidated by any of them. Some of my teammates knew that, in order to win, Zaid had to be played, but the whole situation was delicate for everyone involved.

The name change, the "retirement," my anemia—there were many factors to consider. I began to pray harder, asking God to forgive me. I asked for a friend, the success of our team, and a solution to the mess I had created. Eventually I got some playing time, although it was still limited. We made the playoffs that year and defeated the New York Knicks in a miniseries. I didn't play much, but I was a key factor in our victory. I hit a thirty-foot shot right before halftime, stole a pass, and went down for a dunk to win at the buzzer.

Our next opponents were the Boston Celtics. Kunnert was back in, and again I wasn't being played. At one game at the Boston Gardens, a fan held up a banner that said, "Why isn't Zaid playing?" My teammates and I were wondering the same thing. It didn't happen enough in that series, and we lost.

When I did have the opportunity to play, the response from the crowd was different. When Don Smith played well, they cheered; when Zaid Abdul-Aziz played, there was silence. It seemed like there were three entities on the court: the Rockets, the opponents, and then me. When Kevin Kunnert scored, the crowd went wild, but when I did, there was no more than a whisper. When I did manage to have a big game, nothing was mentioned in the *Houston Post* or the *Chronicle*.

After the playoffs, I left the Rockets under very unfavorable circumstances. Up until my one-day hiatus, I was playing the best of my career. I was putting up superstar points and rebounds and blocking opponent shots like a human flyswatter. But after my poor choices, I could hardly get five quality minutes on the court.

On top of this stress, I was concerned about a twenty-unit apartment complex I owned in Houston called Sunrise East. The building had a lot of possibilities, but primarily it served as a good tax write-off and provided some financial gain. I had friends move in and was not really concerned when they were late with their rent. I felt that I was taking responsibility for serving the less fortunate, but I was still learning what that meant. I was supporting my mother, who still lived in Milwaukee, as well as covering for some tenants in the complex who often paid no rent at all. As a result, I began to feel the economic strain. The building needed repairs, and the rent income wasn't even covering the general expenses.

I had reservations about evicting the tenants who didn't pay. What made matters even worse was that my contract ended that year with the Rockets. With the negative publicity of my quitting, I knew I was history as a Rocket, but I had no clue of what team I would play for or if I would ever play again. I contacted Spencer Haywood whom I had played with in Seattle. He suggested that I contact attorney Bob Mussehl, who had some connections in the league. Spencer was hopeful that Mr. Mussehl could get me placed again with another team.

Bob contacted the Seattle SuperSonics and about two weeks later informed me that I was a Sonic again, but at a very low salary. I agreed, and in

1975, after the birth of our child, Mariam, our family moved to Seattle as I headed for another disappointment.

≫ ≪

The coach of the Sonics was now Bill Russell. Russell was one of the greatest athletes to ever play the game, best known for winning eleven championships for the Boston Celtics. I was ready to run through a concrete wall for him.

However, I began to see that Russell was extremely self-centered. For our practice, he would often leave Bob Hopkins (Russell's cousin) to supervise the team, playing two games to ten. Bill would just sit there and not say a word, acting very indifferent as our coach. After the games were played, he would leave quickly for his noon tee-off at a local golf course.

Some coaches are X and O strategists. I came to find out that this was not Coach Russell's strength. Great players are often so naturally skilled that Xs and Os are not their strong point. Marginal players, on the other hand, have to learn everything to reach a level to make the team. The less gifted work harder on the fine points of the game and become better coaches. If you look at Don Nelson, Phil Jackson, Mike Dunleavy, and Don Chaney, you will see that they were average NBA players but astute X and O strategists. Larry Bird, Magic Johnson, and Kareem Abdul-Jabbar might have had a harder time being coaches for this very reason.

I definitely had problems trying to follow outlined strategies. Most of what teams did was in my head, and that's why X and O sessions usually bored me. I would know instantly on the court what was happening, but seeing a strategy outlined on a chalkboard during a timeout or in the locker room at halftime didn't make it sink in for me.

Once at Milwaukee, Coach Costello got the bright idea of having different-colored washcloths for our defensive strategy. When he held up a blue washcloth, we were in a full-court press. A red one and we were in a half-court trap. However, during the split second it took to look over at the bench to check the color of the washcloth, an offensive player would blow right by you!

I tried to have patience with Coach Russell. In practice I would dominate, but in games I still got little playing time.

Our center was seven-foot-two Tom Burleson who was a "project." Fred Brown and Slick Watts were our guards, with Leonard Gray the power forward. In 1976, we made the playoffs to face the Phoenix Suns. We opened at home and "split" (lost a game and won a game at home).

On our way to Phoenix, I remember being on the plane when Russell entered. He was very loud. He came over to me and said in a loud cackle, "Zaid, you don't drink, and you don't smoke, and you don't go out with women. What do you do for fun?"

I was shocked and didn't really have a response. That was the first time Bill had ever said anything to me or even looked in my direction. Fred Brown was sitting in the seat next to me and calmly said, "Yeah Bill, he used to do those things, but he doesn't anymore."

Coach Russell just walked away, cackling again, and didn't say anything more. That incident always baffled me.

We played Phoenix for Game 3 the next day. I didn't play in that game at all, and we lost. In Game 4, I played and scored twenty-two points and hauled down eight rebounds in only twenty-two minutes. After the game, the Phoenix center and All-Star Alvin Adams said, "I can't pronounce that guy's name, but he really can play!"

My Sonics teammates and I were hopeful. But in Seattle for Game 5 against Phoenix, Fred Brown scored forty-five points, but I did not play at all, and we lost. The series was over. I took that loss hard. I knew that the solution was to play me, but Russell chose not to, and to this day I still don't know why he made that decision. Many fans I have spoken with really felt badly about the whole affair, but what's done is done, and it was apparently meant to be that way.

I was not the only player to end up in Bill Russell's doghouse. John

Brisker was a great talent who also had problems with Russell. Brisker was known to fight on the slightest provocation. In one practice he got into a fight with Joby Wright, another tough player. Russell sided with Wright. In a game soon thereafter, Brisker had a career night in scoring in one game, but then he was benched. That was the end of his career. He never played again. He went to Uganda soon after that, ended up missing, and is presumed dead.

Some high school fans were perplexed that I wasn't getting time on the court. A group of Lakeside High School students started the "Fans for Zaid Club." At first I thought that they were mocking my name (since that was not unusual at that time), but in February of 1977, when I returned to the Sonics after playing for the Braves, they sent me this letter:

Dear Zaid,

When Buffalo came to play the Sonics last December, you may remember that a group of young gentlemen approached you in order to inform you of a group created in your name—the Zaidist Youth Organization.

We would like to tell you about the Z.Y.O. which was formed around what we believe are the teachings that you have shown us as a pro ball player here in Seattle. We consider ourselves the first to be enlightened by the lessons you have displayed on the basketball court and we are committed thoroughly to the body of ideas that originated with the Sonics game of April 4, 1976 and their diffusion.

In this letter we would like to inform you fully of our organization, our ideology, our goals, and some of our projects. Enclosed you will find a copy of a pamphlet we are publishing that we would like you to O.K. before distribution and give your criticism; plus a copy of a recent article which appeared in our school newspaper.

We want to make sure that you know that this is not a religious cult and doesn't interfere with previous religious beliefs.

From our recycling projects we have developed a bank account which is used to defer the costs of some of our other projects.

This group has gained high esteem among school officials and many throughout our community. Thus, during a week of special projects at school this month we were allowed to conduct a Zaidist Workshop during which we visited rest homes, picked up litter from our school's campus and various locations in Seattle, painted the inside of the gym, and worked on this letter and the pamphlet.

Hopefully this will be the beginning of continued correspondence between us. We would like to share with you more of our philosophy and answer your questions.

Thanks so much for your time and efforts.
Respectfully & Reverently yours, the Z.Y.O.

I really appreciated that a group of teens could see me in such a positive light, and I cracked up at the article they wrote in their school paper to explain "Zaidist Principles." A lot of it was tongue-in-cheek, as if this were one of the many radical movements of the day. But the bulk of the article was a list of how they intended to be good members of the human race.

They first explained the origin of their philosophy:

… Zaidism was founded as a few people watched Zaid Abdul Aziz play the game of basketball. We realized that he embodied what we believed were ideals and basic concepts of the game. He strove to be the best ball player he could possibly be—to fulfill his potential. He always kept a positive attitude, even on the bench. He did things that didn't always get him personal glory but helped the team succeed at its goals. He always worked to better the team. …

Then they listed the reasons they were sharing the philosophy with others:

- *So the community can help us help others help themselves*
- *To gain a greater insight into Zaidism*
- *To implement Zaidist principles and put them into productive action*
- *To cooperate to achieve community involvement*
- *To effect change with a non-violent organization operating within society*
- *To encourage unity, happiness and solidarity among ourselves and the human race*
- *To help to gently, non-imperialistically inZaidiate the world*
- *To help people realize their potential and to help them be positive*
- *To change what is wrong, not to leave or condemn it.*

Those funny, creative kids were thinking seriously about their personal impact on the world, and giving me some credit for their direction. I did meet with them once, but unfortunately I didn't really keep in touch with them. It was partly because of my self-perception. I couldn't quite accept that I would have such a positive impact on others. Like so many other times, I was embarrassed. But at the same time, their cheerful, idealistic perspective of my approach to the game of basketball was a great gift to me during a time when I was feeling anything but confident about my future as a ballplayer.

As I look back, they were great role models for me.

⁂

The next couple of years, I played for the Buffalo Braves and very briefly with the Boston Celtics. I can't recall too much of what happened in Buffalo, but I do remember the snowstorm of 1977. It seemed that the snow would never stop falling, and when it did, blistering cold followed.

Also I remember being challenged and surprising the whole Braves team. At one practice, Adrian Dantley was shooting baskets alone at the opposite half of the court. Someone asked (I think it was John Shumate), "Zaid, block Adrian's shot!"

I looked down and saw Adrian at the left sidelines. I yelled, "Hey Adrian, try and dribble to the basket, and I'll block your shot!" Adrian laughed and dribbled to the basket for a lay-up. I sprinted down and as Adrian faked and tried to shoot, I went up and threw his shot into the stands.

Everyone was shocked. Players came up and asked, "Zaid, how did you do that?" I smiled and replied, "I don't know." That sort of thing was just natural to me, and I honestly couldn't tell someone else how I'd done it.

One great thing about being picked up by the Boston Celtics was seeing John Havlicek honored in different arenas. There is a mystique about the Celtics that few NBA teams have ever enjoyed. People remember Russell, Cousy, and Havlicek as Celtics. There was Dave Cowens, the Jones boys, Heinson, and Bird; Len Bias, Jo Jo White, and Kevin McHale also joined these elite ranks. Yes (and however briefly), Zaid Abdul-Aziz got to wear a Celtics jersey!

In 1977 my son Adam was born, and the reality that my career was coming to an end began to sink in. After my short stint with the Celtics, the Rockets picked me up for the rest of the season and I played some, but not much. Coach Tom Nissalke wrote me a letter saying that he was happy with what he saw and was looking forward to the next season when I could come to camp, get in shape, and earn a spot. Sure, I thought, I knew that my NBA career was finished.

Looking back, my career was actually very successful. If you factor in the Cincinnati disaster and the period when I was only played sparingly due to politics, I would have easily averaged double-rebound and double-point stats. I played 505 games and had 4,065 rebounds for an 8-rebound-a-game average. I also tallied 4,557 points for a 9-point-a-game average. I blocked a shot a game, which is not bad.

In 1978, I officially retired from the National Basketball Association. I had come farther than I had ever anticipated—from the streets of Brooklyn to collegiate and NBA fame. I am respected and remembered by my peers as one of the highest jumpers who ever played.

The time had come in my life to move out of the world of the NBA and on to the next thing, but I wasn't quite sure what that next thing was. I had a made a few efforts to establish some long-term income while I was still playing, but the business part of it had never been my strong point.

I still had that apartment complex in Houston and a couple of other investments. One spring afternoon in 1976, when I was still playing for the Sonics, Fred Brown and I traveled to Vashon Island near Seattle to relax, and I saw a beautiful house there. It sat on two acres of land with an incredible view of Mount Rainier. I could not resist. The islands near the city had not yet caught on as a hot real estate market, and I thought it would be a future gold mine. I took the paperwork home and eventually bought it.

A few years later, a professional volleyball league was developing in Seattle and Wilt Chamberlain was promoting it. I invested in the local franchise, the Seattle Smashers. We all thought that professional volleyball would catch on.

꧁꧂

After I retired from the NBA, a friend came to me who worked in Saudi Arabia. He said he could get me a position as a coach, and I jumped at the proposal.

"Wow!" I thought, "What an opportunity: to be able to live in Saudi Arabia, go to Mecca, and learn Arabic." The possibility that I could pass down my knowledge of the game to the youth there and be respected as a Muslim NBA player was mind-boggling.

The wheels were set in motion for the Saudi Arabia position, but it took over a year for it to come together. This would be a huge change for my whole family, and I was looking forward to being employed again. The good news came that I had been hired, travel plans were made, and we launched into a completely new world.

The first thing I noticed when we got off the plane in Jeddah was the heat. That fall day it must have been 115 degrees. I looked around and saw men in turbans and women in veils. I heard the voices of people speaking Arabic and was dazzled by the beautiful ancient dwellings and buildings everywhere.

My family and I went to a hotel, and later I met with an official from the university, who explained the terms of the contract. I would earn thirty-five thousand dollars annually and be given a two-bedroom apartment in a building owned by the university. In the summer I would be off for two months of paid vacation, and I could route my ticket back to the States any way I wanted, which would allow us to visit other countries. It seemed like a great opportunity in all regards.

My job consisted of counseling during the day and coaching the university basketball team at night. It is so hot there that everything is done in split shifts, with midday as a time of rest. Since basketball was not very popular in the Middle East, I had players who had to be taught the game from scratch. Most Saudis were focused on soccer, but a number of private clubs existed with good basketball teams.

At six foot nine, I probably was the tallest guy in the city. I was a celebrity, not only at the university but also throughout Jeddah, and I became quite popular. There were some basketball players who knew about the NBA, and word got out about my professional past. At the university, the youth enjoyed playing basketball, and they listened intently to what I had to say. I was a patient coach, and in about a year's time, our young team became fairly competitive. We began to hold our own with the premier basketball clubs in the city.

The main reason our team excelled was Ahmad Falatha. Ahmad was only about six foot two, but he was a great shooter with very quick reflexes. He was a coach's dream, since he did exactly what I suggested. He became our team leader, and under him our team became very good. We were unselfish and played tough defense, which most Jeddah teams neglected. We began to be feared by the local clubs when we beat a few of them, much to the chagrin of their coaches. This was all done in my broken Arabic, with Ahmad translating.

While in Jeddah, Tayyibah and I traveled to historical and religious sites when our schedule allowed. I also made the Hajj, the pilgrimage to Mecca, again. It is most important pilgrimage Muslims make.

Tayyibah and I had made the Hajj once before, in 1977, long before I worked in Saudi Arabia. But that first time we were not prepared for some of the logistical problems that the pilgrimage involves, and we took our very young children. Atiya was six and Mariam was only two. The long trip from the U.S. was exhausting, and as we stepped off the plane, the temperature was scorching. This heat was like nothing I had experienced before, but it was especially hard on the children.

Between two and three million people visit the holy sites at the same time. The actual visitation of the sites begins on the first day of *Zul Hajj*, which means "the month of Hajj" in the Islamic lunar calendar. People visit Mecca at other times of the year as well and the holy sites are less crowded then. These journeys are important, but they are considered lesser pilgrimages than the Hajj. They are called the *Umrah*.

So, as we arrived in Mecca, the heat and travel were challenging, but we were in good spirits. However, a few days into the ten-day pilgrimage, we had a terrifying experience. One afternoon, we were in our tents when a fire broke out. Smoke and flames spewed everywhere and I was separated from Tayyibah and the girls. We anxiously searched for each other for hours amidst the panicked crowd.

My friend Khadir and me after Hajj.

The fire was eventually brought under control, and as the smoke and confusion cleared, we found each other. We were exhausted, but everyone in the family was safe. Others, however, were injured that afternoon, and many died. We felt blessed because we were all safe. We finished the pilgrimage and returned to the United States.

≫ ≪

Six years later, I made the Hajj again, this time with a better understanding of the commitment I was making. In the interim, I had continued my studies. The more I studied, the more God showed me that the difficulties I had experienced in my career were for a purpose. They brought me closer to God, and helped me develop my commitment to worship Him devoutly for the rest of my days.

As He had blessed me with a talent for playing basketball, so He blessed me by allowing me to make the Hajj. It is a great blessing when the Creator allows you to make that pilgrimage and to see the miracles of the faith first-hand. So when I made the Hajj in 1983, I was not concerned with my past career. I looked toward my eternal future.

The Kaa'ba, the holiest place in Islam. When Muslims pray, they face the Kaa'ba.

The Qur'an states, "In Mecca are manifest signs. Pilgrimage, therefore, is a duty men owe to God—those who can afford the journey; but if any deny faith, God stands not in need of any of his servants."

Pilgrims from all over the world—now nearly five million annually—gather to perform this sacred duty. The men wear the all-white *ihram* (a two-piece covering). Women dress simply, also in white. This mass of white-clad pilgrims circles the holy Kaa'ba, the house that was built by Adam and rebuilt by the Prophet Abraham and his son Ishmael. The blackest men and women from Africa meet with the whitest men and women from Europe. Asians, North and South Americans, Australians—people from every continent in the world are

In Jeddah right before leaving for Mecca.

there. The rich mingle with the poor, the strong with the meek, and the young with the old. All this exemplifies true brotherhood and love for one another.

With Muslims from all over the world, I witnessed the holy Kaa'ba. I moved between the two mountains, Safa and Marwa, just as Ishmael's mother, Hagar, had as she searched for water for her infant son. I drank from the well of Zam Zam, which sprang from the spot Ishmael kicked the ground.

> *And God heard the voice of the lad; and the angel of God called to Hagar from heaven; and said to her, "What troubles you, Hagar? Fear not; for God has heard the voice of the lad where he is. Arise, lift up the lad, and hold him fast with your hand; for I will make him a great nation." Then God opened her eyes, and she saw a well of water; and she went, and filled the skin with water, and gave the lad a drink. And God was with the lad, and he grew up; he lived in the wilderness, and became an expert with the bow. He lived in the wilderness of Paran; and his mother took a wife for him from the land of Egypt.*

—Genesis 21:17–21

I was blessed to be on Mount Arafat with all the pilgrims at once as we asked God for forgiveness just before sunset, in the same place where Adam and Hawa (Eve) had wept and prayed for forgiveness. Mount Arafat is also called *Jabal-i-Rahmah*—the Hill of Mercy—because that is where Allah forgave Adam and Hawa.

After the ten days of Hajj is complete, pilgrims exchange their white garments for new clothes they have brought from home. When I made the Hajj, after wearing and seeing only white clothing for ten days, I was struck by the beautiful array of colors and designs from so many cultures. When one's Hajj is accepted by God, he or she is spiritually changed forever. The pilgrims return home to share the wonderful news of their experiences with those who have not yet had the opportunity to experience the Hajj first-hand.

⇜⇝

I was certainly transformed by my experience. My life seemed to have made a complete change from the turmoil of the last years of my NBA career. By 1984, we had four wonderful children. Adam was born in 1977 and Yusef in 1981. I knew everyone on campus and I enjoyed my job. Tayibbah was studying Arabic and the Qur'an and taking care of our children. Everything seemed to have fallen into place.

Then my investments in the United States began to unravel. I got word that the tenants at the Houston apartment complex had not been paying their rent and that the property was in the red. I sent funds to cover major damages from a rainstorm that had gutted five apartments on the ground floor. I was also informed that the fledgling professional volleyball league was having problems, and the Smashers needed more money for operating expenses. I gave more funds, hoping the league would make a comeback.

Then I heard from different people that my mother was acting strange. During summer break I went to see her in Milwaukee. I learned that she was behind in her rent and faced eviction. I was happy to pay for her housing, but sadly, I saw the beginnings of dementia in my mother's eyes and her actions.

To make matters worse, when I returned to Saudi Arabia, I was told that the university would no longer continue covering the school fees for my children, and I would have to pay nearly thirty thousand riyals yearly (ten thousand dollars) to keep them in the school they were attending.

My wife and I were worried. A lot of money was going out and little was coming in.

A WRONG MOVE

In May of 1984, the vice president of a prestigious Jeddah sports club approached me. I was offered a contract of nearly seven thousand dollars a month, a villa, and a car. I signed a two-year contract, which specified that if I was released after my probation period of three months, then I would be given the full balance of my contract, plus severance pay. The package deal amounted to $170,000, and with this, I expected financial stability at last.

I resigned from the university but was told that the villa that had been offered to us was not quite ready. So we were moved into a small temporary apartment in an industrial area. We stayed there for nearly four months, and during that period, I never received my salary on time.

The club's Egyptian treasurer told me that funds were running short because Tele Santana, who was currently coaching the club's soccer team, had to be paid and as a result, no cash was available. Tele Santana was the Brazilian who coached soccer superstar Pelé. His contract was rumored to be nearly $30,000 a month, plus a new Mercedes and a free airline ticket to go anywhere in the world he wanted. Santana's salary was not my business, but it looked like my funds had been taken to pay him, and I was angry.

I went home and spoke to my wife about the whole affair. We came to the conclusion that, in hindsight, leaving the university had not been a good idea. Even though my salary had nearly tripled, we had no guarantees. I was also learning that these clubs had bad reputations for not paying and that firings were common—but this lesson came too late. I had thought that my NBA status was respected and that I was making a contribution to a local sports program, but that didn't really amount to much within the club's social structure in Saudi Arabia.

One morning before breakfast I heard a scream from our small kitchen. I rushed to the kitchen to find my wife, terrified.

"It was a rat! I opened the cabinet door to get the cornflakes and a rat jumped over there!" She pointed to the sofa in the living room.

I looked in that direction and noticed four huge rats jumping around like they were playing a volleyball game. We packed up the family immediately and checked into a nearby hotel. I went to the club and told them what had happened.

The treasurer said, "I also have mice in my house!"

I yelled, "They were not mice, but huge gray rats!"

I asked for my salary, and he said, "We'll have something next week," and walked away.

That night my son Yusef became very ill. He went into breathing distress and at one point turned blue. We rushed him to a local hospital, where I was told that the fur from the rats had caused an asthmatic reaction. The doctors put him on large doses of cortisone and albuterol. It was touch-and-go, and we were concerned that our three-year-old son would die.

Yusef survived, thank God, but I was determined to confront the treasurer to make sure our housing situation improved. We got into a verbal argument, and I was branded "a problem." I was given my dismissal letter and replaced by an Egyptian coach who had been waiting in the wings all along.

I asked for the terms stipulated in the contract, but instead I was given only two months' salary and released. The club refused to pay for our airline tickets back to the United States or our moving costs. This process financially and emotionally devastated our family. I contacted my representative in Washington, D.C., who wrote to the Saudi embassy. The embassy wrote back, "We are processing your case."

I was hopeful. I wrote a letter to my NBA colleague, Senator Bill Bradley, who was gracious enough to send a letter to the Saudi ambassador. The response came back that I should have gone through the employment griev-ance procedures while I was over there.

"Yeah," I thought, "Win my case and lose a child!"

❧ ❧

The next two years, I tried everything to get my contract fulfilled. I contacted all the mosques in America, and most of them supported my claims. Then one day I received a letter from Saudi Arabia. Foolishly thinking that it was a positive response to my claim or even a check, I opened it quickly. The letter was from an American coach there who apologized for what he had heard had happened to my family and me. He went on to say that his employer, a prince who sponsored a different club, would be in Los Angeles soon. He asked if I could arrange for the prince to meet Kareem Abdul-Jabbar.

My initial reaction was, "Not in a million years!" But when I looked at it more closely, I realized that I could ask both to help me with my case. I wrote back and agreed to be the Kareem Abdul-Jabbar conduit. A short time later, I received seven hundred dollars for a plane ticket and expenses. Even though I didn't have Kareem's address or telephone number, I was confident I could reach him.

The Lakers had just won the NBA championship, and I heard that a parade would be held, so I knew Kareem would be in town. Before I left Seattle, I tried to get in touch with him through mutual friends, but to no avail. I felt like he was avoiding me. I arrived in Los Angeles and rented a room at the airport. I called the Lakers and left a message, but two days later I still had received no response. I tried and tried and still could not contact Kareem. Finally, while I was having dinner in the hotel, Kareem called but left no return telephone number.

The Prince's attaché, a man by the name of Eli, called and asked if I had contacted Kareem. I told them that I had and would contact them for the meeting arrangements. Eli asked me to move to a hotel in Bel-Air, closer to theirs.

I knew that Kareem had just purchased a home around the area where tours of the stars' homes were conducted. I went to Beverly Hills and got on a tour bus. I asked the driver where Kareem's house was, and he showed me on a map. I memorized the address and when we were nearby, I disembarked.

I walked to the beautiful mansion at that address, went up to the door, and rang the bell. A maid opened the door and asked, "May I help you?"

I said, "Yes, could you tell Kareem that Zaid is here!"

She said, "Okay," and walked up a hedged path. Five minutes later she returned and said, "Come with me!" She took me up the path, where I found Kareem sunbathing and reading a book.

"Assalaam alaikum," I said.

"Wa alaikum salaam," Kareem replied.

I handed him an unopened letter from the prince. I also gave him the letter I had received to give him an idea of why I was there.

"It's nothing negative, man," I said, unable to disguise my disappointment. "I've been here two days, and I couldn't figure out why you didn't call me back."

"I'm sorry, Zaid. I did call the hotel but didn't leave my home phone number. I should have called you back."

Kareem began reading the letters. He said he would be glad to meet the prince.

I asked to borrow a phone and called the number Eli had given. We agreed to meet at my hotel at 7 P.M. the next day. After I hung up, I told Kareem about my horrible experience in Saudi Arabia and asked if he could help.

The next day at 7 P.M., I met the prince and Eli. They were very cordial as we headed to Kareem's in a beautiful Mercedes. The prince discussed the sports program in the Kingdom and particularly basketball. We pulled up to Kareem's house, where a huge gate lifted at the entrance to his driveway. After we pulled up in front of the house, Eli asked me to take a long cardboard box from the trunk while he removed a smaller square one. We entered Kareem's house, and I reflected on the first time I saw him, years ago in the 52nd Street station.

A short time later, Kareem appeared.

The prince began, "We in Saudi Arabia are very proud of you and want to offer congratulations for winning the NBA title. I pray that you win next year also!"

Kareem said, "Thank you for your kindness, and it's good to know that we are making positive strides in basketball in Saudi Arabia."

Eli began taking photos of Kareem and the prince. Then the prince said, "On behalf of the Kingdom of Saudi Arabia, I want to offer you a personal invitation to visit us."

Eli handed Kareem the square box and motioned to me to give Kareem the long box. Kareem opened the square box and gasped. It was a beautiful, pure gold teapot. Then he opened the long box and pulled out a pure gold sword with what appeared to be precious stones embedded in an ivory handle. Kareem was awestruck and expressed his gratitude to the prince.

Eli looked at his watch and said, "Well, the prince has to be going now!"

I was stunned by the lavish gifts, and also because the meeting ended before my case was even discussed. We left Kareem's house and headed back to the hotel.

We went to the hotel restaurant and sat down to order. I then said to the prince, "I have something to talk to you about…" and before I could finish my sentence, the prince said,

"Zaid, I know about everything that happened to you with the club. If you want to, you can come back and coach my team. I promise that we will honor our agreement." Then he handed me three hundred dollars.

I was so disappointed. I felt like I had helped him and Kareem, and now I was being brushed off with a few hundred bucks.

I thought about his offer, and for a moment, it appealed to me. I had enjoyed my time in Saudi Arabia up until the problems with the athletic club. But I couldn't risk putting my family through anything like we had experienced again.

I said, "Wa alaikum salaam," and left.

That was the last time I saw the prince, or Kareem for that matter.

Liens, Judgments, and Faith

My financial situation was now in serious peril, and I was fearful.

Wilt Chamberlain dropped out of the professional volleyball league venture, and the stock I had purchased in the Smashers was now worthless. My entire investment disappeared in one day, and I ended up in a lawsuit regarding liabilities for the financial obligations of the failed Smasher's franchise.

Other major expenses seemed to crop up every day. The house on Vashon Island needed repairs and the property taxes were due. My mother, who was still living in Milwaukee, was ill and her bills were getting larger. When I returned from Saudi Arabia, I began to work as a drug and alcohol counselor. The work was rewarding, but compared to my past income and my financial obligations, my salary was just a drop in the bucket.

⋙ ⋘

We had been in Saudi Arabia over a period of four years and had often stayed in the Vashon house during the summers, when we returned to North America for breaks. Now we moved to Vashon full time, primarily for financial reasons. It was here where our wonderful daughter Saara was born in 1988.

I rode the ferry into Seattle to my counseling job each day. As a counselor, I noticed a shocking change in the black community in the four years I had been gone. The youths in Seattle's Central District had begun using crack cocaine. This insidious drug was everywhere. It was not uncommon to see mobs of black youths running in and out of alleys, smoking crack. They began fighting and wearing the colors of the gangs they showed allegiance to, such as the Cripps and Bloods. This drug culture was devastating Seattle's black neighborhoods.

As I witnessed this tragedy, I felt that God had moved us to Vashon (not something I would have done without the financial problems) to protect my children. If they had lived in the city, there was a strong possibility they would have been influenced by the drug epidemic. Certainly, we felt isolated on the island, which was mostly rural and mostly white. But Vashon was a safe, healthy place for our children to attend school, and eventually, when they were more mature, they found their way back to their black roots without ever having been caught in the crack craze.

⊰⊱

No one ever plans to divorce. But after the troubles my wife and I went through abroad, our relationship began to change. My wife's confidence in me was shattered by what had happened. The financial pressures we faced after we returned to the U.S. and the isolation she felt on Vashon added to our troubles. We were broken from within.

I knew that I had made some unwise decisions, but I also felt that times of trouble are opportunities when you pull together as a family. In retrospect, I underestimated the stress my wife was experiencing.

As a child I had lived on the streets, so while these troubles seemed unfortunate, I had survived much worse conditions. However, my wife came from a better family structure, and these hardships overwhelmed her. She began working as a nurse's aide, and I started driving a taxi to supplement our income. I would come home after breathing carbon monoxide all day and just pass out from fatigue. Exhausted, I wouldn't even speak to my children. At times I was very irritable, causing even more family communication problems.

On top of this, I was also going through my own identity problems. Here I was, a former NBA player and collegiate Big Eight great, driving a taxi. Even though the taxi was my own, I had trouble accepting my fate. I could have called the NBA office and gotten a small loan, but I was too shy and embarrassed to make that call. I didn't want anyone to know my financial plight.

One day I was in the taxi line at the Four Seasons Hotel, and Abe Pollin, the president of the then Washington Bullets, climbed into my car. He looked at me, paused for a moment, and said, "Hey, I know who you are. You're Zaid! Why in the world are you driving a cab?"

I felt horrible. I thought, "Yeah, why am I driving a taxi?" I began to reflect on my whole career, and tears began streaming down my face. How had I gotten into this mess, and how would I ever get out?

I can't even remember what my response was, but that moment was a turning point. I began to have more faith that I would learn why my life was unfolding this way. Even though I was fragile financially, I was growing stronger spiritually.

My wife, however, had come to the conclusion that things weren't going to get better, and she filed for divorce in 1996. She moved out and took the kids with her. Although I felt devastated, I prayed more, asking God to assist and guide me. I got a better counseling job and sold the taxi.

I was still strapped for money, so I chose to take early retirement for my time in the NBA. I foolishly refused to face the divorce, thinking we would reconcile. When I received any mail from the lawyers or the court, I would just toss it into the garbage. I guess my attitude was, "How in the world can a judge tell me what to do with my children and property?"

I saw my children as frequently as I could. I brought groceries over and hoped my wife would drop the divorce proceedings. I honestly could not imagine my future without my family, so I continued to assume that, if I was patient and had faith, it would all work out. But month after month passed, and my wife was still determined to go through with the divorce. I finally accepted the fact that reconciliation of our marriage was not part of the plan.

Casablanca and Mina

I was disappointed over the divorce, but I realized that I needed to go on with my life. For a change of scene, I visited Khalid, a friend I had known since I lived in New York. He lived in Ann Arbor, where I had often visited him during the summer. We had known each other over twenty years and had seen each other through the vicissitudes close friends often share.

Khalid's children were studying in Casablanca, Morocco, and he had friends who lived there. He asked me if I was interested in eventually remarrying. That may seem like an unusual question considering that I wasn't divorced yet. But in the Muslim community, family is very important. A responsible adult should be married, and potential spouses are often introduced through families and friends. He wanted to introduce me to friends in Morocco who were interested in meeting me. I told him that I had to resolve the divorce and my financial problems first. I was getting ready to sell the house in Vashon, and I felt that when I did, I would be financially stable enough to remarry.

To be honest, I look back at this timeline, and it all happened so fast that it is hard to make sense of it. But once I realized my wife had no interest in getting back together I was ready to move on. Soon after my visit to Ann Arbor, on Khalid's introduction, I traveled to Casablanca. I stayed there for a month. There I met Mina. She was a beautiful, intelligent biologist. Her family was also wonderful. And before I returned to Seattle, we became engaged.

Hardships and Healing

I went back to Seattle to put my affairs in order. Unfortunately, since I had never responded to the letters from the court, I had little say in the final divorce settlement. When I finally went to a lawyer to prepare for the divorce, he asked,

"Why didn't you reply to the letters from the court?"

I said, "I was so depressed. I just didn't care!"

My lawyer said, "If you knew what it says in these letters, you would have cared!"

He began to explain that because I had neglected to respond to the letters, I was facing serious consequences. He wasn't sure if he could help me because most of my rights had been waived when I failed to respond. I was terrified! I was going to lose almost everything I had.

When the Vashon house sold, the bill collectors came out of the woodwork. I had enough to resolve my financial obligations, but once that was done, there was less left than I had envisioned. Even so, I felt very positive about the future because I had a lead on a job that seemed very promising.

I contacted the NBA and applied for a position as a counselor. I had become a certified Chemical Dependency Professional in the state of Washington since my return from Saudi Arabia. The work I did provided treatment plans for persons with drug and alcohol addictions, as part of a three-point program in association with a physician and a psychologist.

The recruiting doctor came to Seattle and interviewed me. He later wrote back and said that I would represent the Western region as a chemical dependency counselor on an ad-hoc basis. I was to meet with NBA players, and if I suspected drug abuse, I could request a random urine test and report the findings to the league. I went through the counseling procedure with my first player-client and created a treatment plan. When I contacted the doctor, he had apparently changed his mind. He would not send me the list of the other players I was supposed to monitor, so I could not continue my work as planned.

To make matters worse, he did not even send me payment for the work I had done. I was really disappointed, because this seemed like an ideal opportunity to meld my NBA experience with my counseling background. Now this too was falling apart.

✥

I went back to Morocco to marry Mina in a wonderful ceremony. Her family, highly respected in the Casablanca community, is wonderful. They are gracious hosts and welcomed me into the family. My father-in-law is very religious and God-fearing, and we hit it off right away. After the wedding, we bid Mina's family goodbye and came to Seattle to begin our new life together.

I had a small amount of savings in the bank, but not much for a man of my age starting a new family. In Morocco, a person marries when they are financially ready—a good tradition. I certainly intended to honor that tradition, but at this point, I still had to keep faith that I could turn things around!

By 1997, the stress of Saudi Arabia, the divorce, and my bleak financial condition began to take its toll. I had no energy, and after some tests I found that I was again suffering from anemia. I called my friend Khalid in Ann Arbor, who suggested that I move there to be close to friends who could support us through this time of crisis. Too hastily I decided to go. Mina and I packed our things and left for Ann Arbor. Upon our arrival, the snow was piled high, and the temperature a mere five degrees Fahrenheit.

I thought, "Why did I move us here?" We were newlyweds, and we had left Seattle for Michigan! I was also so far from my children.

I was confused and sick, and Mina was very patient. We stayed with Khalid and his family for a while, and then we moved in with another dear friend, Jami. I had hardly any strength at all, and mentally I was pretty much bankrupt. Naturally, people began talking and wondering what in the world was wrong with me.

I got a counseling job in Detroit and Mina worked at a department store in Ann Arbor. She never complained about working, and neither did she say anything negative about the frigid weather. We would awaken at 5 A.M. to pray, and then I'd get a ride with another friend to Detroit. It was difficult, but I was making an effort.

Then on Thanksgiving Day, I got sick and went to the University of Michigan Hospital. After testing, I was told that something was wrong with my heart and that I could die at any moment. They wanted me to stay in the hospital, but I was so confused that I didn't. I was also so depressed that I felt that perhaps death was better than feeling the way I did.

I resumed my work schedule in Detroit but didn't tell anyone, even Mina, about my medical problem. Then one day I met a woman in a health food restaurant who was crying. She told me that her uncle was dying of cancer, and she had come to get him some carrot juice. She asked me where

I was from and why I was in Michigan. When I told her my story, she said, "Son, I have been a nurse for over forty years and I know what's wrong with you. It's happening to many people. Go back home and get a test for *H. pylori!*"

Later, when I told Mina what the woman had told me,

Me, Mina, and Nurah, 2005.

we decided to return to Seattle.

One cold morning, we just "upped and left" Michigan without telling a soul.

In Seattle, we stayed at a hotel near the airport. I did what the lady recommended, and both Mina and I were tested. The tests came back positive, we were both put on medication, and miraculously, we both revived. Soon I was able to run a couple of miles.

I learned during that experience that illness can be a result of the depletion of vital nutrients. The culprit is often stress and poor eating habits, resulting in complete exhaustion and mental confusion. People who knew me during this illness were disturbed by my symptoms (as was I!) and they really didn't know how to respond to me. That caused even more stress, perpetuating the cycle. Mina, however was very understanding, patient, and supportive. The initial medication helped, but, in my case, I had lost a lot of calcium, magnesium, and potassium. I augmented my intake of these minerals and took a hormone supplement. Weeks passed, and gradually everything began to clear up for me, both physically and cognitively. The cobwebs were gone!

⤳⤛

On April 9, 1998, my beloved mother Juanita Louise Smith died. I was crushed, but I actually felt relieved for her. She had put up a courageous fight against an overwhelming opponent, Alzheimer's.

As life came back together, I resurrected my career as a drug counselor. On July 26, 2001, our beautiful daughter Nurah was born. Just as I had been with the birth of all of my children, I was on top of the world. It seemed like finally Mina and I were healthy, finances were improving, and we were beginning to settle into our life together, raising our new daughter.

Then just a month and a half after Nurah's birth, on September 11, 2001, the world awoke to the tragedy that would change world politics and the experience of every Muslim in the United States.

September 11

When I awoke to the news of September 11, not only did it have that surreal quality that many people experienced—as if it were some sort of horrible dream—but I also had personal anxiety for my family and friends who lived in New York City.

The last time I saw my sister Beverley was in lower Manhattan, right across from the World Trade Center's twin towers. She was there for a friend's wedding. At first, she didn't see me, but then I honked the car horn and, like finding something lost, our eyes met.

My sister is a real survivor. She never complains about anything. When her son Kevin was arrested for murder and named "The Token Booth Killer," she persevered. When her youngest son Binky exited an alley and found a dead man with his wallet in his back pocket, Binky thought, "What the heck, he's dead and doesn't need the money!" He took it and before you could say "Willie Sutton," he was arrested by two detectives who were watching him. Binky was only fifteen years old and had a pretty clean record, but the system showed him no mercy. Even though the charges were circumstantial and weak, he was sentenced to twenty years. He did fifteen before he was released.

Back in 1970, I had persuaded Beverley to move to the Seattle area. She and her children moved to Redmond. It is now famous as the home of Microsoft, but at that time, it was a small city on the east side of Lake Washington. Beverley didn't stay. She missed New York, and she soon moved her family back to the Big Apple.

My father was still living in New York, too. At 81, he was getting up there in age. He had a number of serious health problems, but like my sister he never complained.

After his disastrous discharge from the NYPD, he decided to pursue freelance photography. My father took photos of Jackie Robinson as a rookie, Frank Sinatra in concert, and Sammy Davis Jr. in Las Vegas. He worked very closely with Governor Nelson Rockefeller and became his personal photographer. Before his death on April 6, 2003, he was working with Al Sharpton's presidential campaign.

So, when I first heard about the World Trade Center tragedy, my initial thoughts were of my sister and father. It was a strong possibility that they could have been killed that day.

≫≪

Throughout my life, I had always wanted to help the folks back home overcome drug and alcohol addiction. I felt that was my true calling from childhood. I had never expected to become a professional ball player. Life's circumstances had, however, turned out differently, and now I was living in Seattle.

I had worked very hard to earn my certification credentials, which required three thousand hours of hands-on experience and a rigorous state examination. After I became certified as a chemical dependency professional (CDP), it didn't take me long to see that some CDPs were recovering abusers themselves. Some knew that I had never used drugs habitually, so they thought I could never truly understand the addiction process. That seemed odd to me, because as a child, when my friends were shooting up heroin, I had to resort to basic survival skills to deal with them and handle myself.

"Funny," I thought, "live clean and you're the enemy and don't know it! They should be breaking down the door to see how I did it!" I decided to ignore such criticism, and continued to reach out to young people who would listen.

On September 11, 2001, it was very early when I arrived at Mountlake

Terrace High School where I worked as a counselor. Located about ten miles north of Seattle, Mountlake Terrace is a very quiet, conservative community with just a sprinkling of minorities. Students are affluent and often travel to school in their own cars, a sharp contrast to the neighborhood where I grew up.

Outside, the school was totally quiet. As I entered, I heard sobbing and students yelling, "Oh no!"

I went to the lounge, looked at the television, where time and again videos showed the awful events as the towers of the World Trade Center crashed to the ground. Then more crashes were reported—the Pentagon had been hit, and another plane had gone down, which had apparently been headed for the White House. Bad news came in all day. As that awful day progressed, school officials informed the counselors to implement crisis counseling for the traumatized students.

"Who is going to give crisis counseling to us counselors?" I thought.

I became numb as the news announcers began identifying the hijackers. The names were Arabic. At that moment, I understood how Japanese-Americans must have felt after Pearl Harbor, or how vulnerable German-Americans must have been as Adolph Hitler perpetrated his crimes across Europe. The United States was my home, but by the night of September 11, I felt that most Americans would view me as a foreigner in my own country. Most of all, I was concerned for my family and friends.

As the week progressed, I began to notice that I was becoming the center of attention. I started to be watched in the staff lounge as if I were going to plant anthrax there. Students and staff who had previously been friendly were now only barely cordial.

Freedom of religion is a constitutional right, but now I understood how that right had loopholes. I became concerned about the female Muslim students in particular, because they were so highly visible. I looked them up in the school directory and called them all to my office, one by one. I told each of them to be brave and keep in close contact with one another. I also urged them to let me know if they were harassed or abused in any way. They all agreed.

The question that played over and over in my mind was, "Who would do such a horrible thing and why?" Of the 1.4 billion Muslims in the world, why would a few individuals choose to completely violate Islamic tenets and kill innocent people? Nowhere in the holy Qur'an did it say to do such a thing, and it was hard for me to imagine any Muslims I had ever met committing this awful crime. I began considering alternative explanations, including conspiracy theories that I heard from others. Perhaps someone was trying to start a world war, devising a plan in which a homing device was left on board the airplanes that was timed to go off. But who would do this, and why?

Hundreds of other scenarios crossed my mind, but then I thought, "Humpty Dumpty was pushed!" In a defensive and comparative way, I tried to compare the act with others. In Guyana on November 18, 1978, the Peoples Temple leader and ordained minister Jim Jones convinced 914 of his Christian followers to commit a mass suicide. Under his orders, they drank grape drinks laced with cyanide, along with sedatives such as liquid Valium, phenegren, and chloral hydrate. It took about forty-five minutes for this cyanide mixture to kill them. Some followers were murdered by injection! A total of 638 adults and 276 children died. Jim Jones then took a gun and blew his brains out.

Going into overdrive, my mind began to compare Christians killing Christians. No! I reminded myself that Christianity is a major religion, which Jim Jones left and turned into an evil cult. Jones should be blamed and indicted, not the religion of Christianity. No, I went on, I would not blame an entire religion for the acts of a few. That would be utter madness!

Then the irrational part of my mind began again. On April 19, 1995, at 9:03 A.M., the largest terrorist act ever committed in the U.S. prior to 9/11 took place in Oklahoma City. The accused was a churchgoing soldier named Timothy McVeigh. The crime was blowing up the Alfred P. Murrah Federal

Building by putting a massive bomb inside a rental truck. The dead numbered 168, and nineteen of them were children. Over eight hundred more were injured. McVeigh proudly took full responsibility for the bombing, and before his execution on June 11, 2001, he declared, "I am the master of my fate. I am the captain of my soul!" He called the deaths of the children "collateral damage."

I recalled that the statement, "The white man is the devil," could apply in this isolated tragedy. With this thought I realized I had to get a grip on my rationale, or I would surely go insane. I thought of history and what I had read. Was it not the missionaries who took Bibles to the American Indians while speaking of "peace"? Were not woolen blankets that were infected with the smallpox virus given out to eliminate entire villages of native tribes? Were not Crazy Horse and Geronimo called "terrorists," who had to flee from their ancestral homes? Did not "white" and "colored" water fountains exist in most southern states? And what about the infamous Jim Crow laws? When playing a Big Eight Conference game in Colorado during my junior year at Iowa State, did I not hear the word "nigger" yelled from the stands as we were running out on to the court for warm-ups?

Then I paused. I thought, "I have not lived half a century for the events and horrors of September 11 to turn me into a reactionary bigot. I will find a solution and a positive strategy to offset the evil that was done."

Then, like a miracle, I flashed back to when I was young and repeated that line from the pledge of allegiance: "One nation, under God, indivisible, with liberty and justice for all!"

The answer and solution were right there and had always been there, but America was too blind to implement it. "No," I thought again, that's wrong. The politicians were too blind to implement it. It was those who would pimp Miss Liberty or drape the American flag around themselves solely for the sake of financial gain who were blind and misguided.

I began reviewing my NBA career for an answer, and I found it. On commercial flights, when turbulence and bumpiness causes concern, the pilot announces over the loudspeaker, "Ladies and gentlemen, we are experiencing choppy winds. We will drop down to thirty thousand feet for a smoother ride. Please keep your seatbelts fastened. We apologize for any inconvenience. Thank you!"

There it was! So simple and so plain! Fasten your seatbelts and hold on! The bumpiness will abate! Love one another. Help one another and pray to God, your true pilot, daily. Learn to respect people of all creeds, religions, and cultures. Now is the time to practice what America has always preached, but not always acted on. Despite the September 11 tragedies, don't fall victim to more hate and broken promises.

⇜⇝

In looking back on my life, there is very little that I regret. I was given enormous talent and did the best that I could. I played with and against some of the greatest players in basketball.

I never got a championship ring or even came close to it. Some say that because I played with the greatest, I was overlooked and underappreciated. Maybe so, but that's what God wanted for me. Very few people remember me as a ball player, but I take some pride when they do.

Not long ago, a police officer approached me in downtown Seattle. He was coming out of the courthouse when he spotted me and said, "How tall are you?"

I responded, "Six foot nine, officer."

He then asked, "Did you ever play basketball?"

I replied, "Yes."

He then asked, "What's your name?"

When I told him, he became very animated and said, "You're the great Zaid Abdul-Aziz, Don Smith?"

I had a hard time with that because the word "great" bothers me. To me, "great" should refer only to God's greatness, not mine. He then pulled out a piece of paper and reached for a pen in his shirt pocket. "Could you please autograph this for my son?"

All I could say was, "Sure, officer. I'll be honored to do that."

That officer's act of kindness helped offset the negative experiences and racial profiling I have endured since my retirement. Like the time I was accused of being a seven-foot-tall black bank robber who was a suspect at the time. On that occasion, detectives surrounded me with guns drawn. It happened at my own bank while I was making a deposit to my account, and the teller still said that I was the guy!

Another time I was accused of using a fraudulent ATM card at a local grocery store. The security guard said that he had watched me, and when he saw how much cash I was receiving from the machine (all of one-hundred-fifty dollars), he became suspicious and called the police!

Being six foot nine and black can be stressful at times in this society. When I was playing basketball, it was hardly ever stressful because people saw me as a celebrity. Now on some occasions, whites run from me in total fear! When I approach, they act as if they are making calls on their cell phones as a defense mechanism, like "If you come any closer buddy, I want you to know that I am on the phone with the police." Welcome to the real world, Don Smith, All-American! I just smile and let it go.

I have travelled all over the world and met people of many cultures. That experience has taught me that people are people. Black friends, white friends, and yellow friends, I love them all!

UNPROFESSIONAL
PROFESSIONALISM

At times, the things I see in this society frustrate me and make me sad.

Take the NBA, for instance.

A few years ago I settled down to watch an NBA playoff game in April 2001 between the Los Angeles Lakers and Portland Trail Blazers, and I witnessed something that I had never seen before. Rasheed Wallace was arguing, like he always does, and to prevent him from getting a technical, his teammate, Arvydas Sabonis, tried to pull him away. Rasheed grabbed a wet, sweaty towel and hit Sabonis right in the face with it.

"Wow," I thought, "Rasheed is lucky that wasn't me. I probably would have broken his hand!" Rasheed is a very gifted seven-foot-tall player, and he possesses a touch that is rare for a big man. His three-point range is equal to that of a point guard who is a foot shorter. He has a good overall concept of the game. However, if he had been around in my era, Rasheed could never have played for me if I were coach because of his attitude.

Some NBA players act like spoiled brats and crybabies, despite the fact that they are highly paid professionals. The game is in trouble if these seven-foot whiners continue to shame it.

Don't get me wrong—Kevin Garnett, Jason Kidd, and even Gary Payton (who has done his share of whining) are throwbacks to the old days because they have solid fundamentals. I marvel at the picks and rolls of John Stockton and Karl Malone. I respect their unending service and respect for the game.

Even the opinionated Charles Barkley has the heart of a lion and the fearlessness of a warrior. The much-talked-about and tattooed Allen Iverson shows great professionalism as he gets beat up nightly by today's Goliaths.

I reflect back on ten years of arenas, schedules, and games, and I think of Jerry West as he wore facemasks to protect the nose that had been repeatedly broken. I remember Willis Reed limping onto the floor to encourage his team after seriously injuring his knee, spurring the Knicks on to the NBA championship that year of 1970.

I recall my rookie season with the Cincinnati Royals, when we played eight games in eight nights in eight different cities, and Oscar Robertson saying with only slight annoyance, "I can't believe this crazy schedule!"

Today the professional game is chock-full of entertainment and merriment. Mascots, such as the Sonics's Squatch, spring off trampolines to flip and do reverse dunks. Whistles and indoor blimps with flickering lights circle the arenas, dropping prizes and T-shirts down to the enthusiastic crowd. Tickets are gobbled up by corporations, making it almost impossible for the "common folk" (whom these athletes were at one time) to attend.

Certain things annoy me! Like why Spencer Haywood was never inducted into the NBA Hall of Fame. His enormous talent and career both in the ABA and NBA qualify him to at least be considered. And the fact that players ran up into the stands to fight with the fans is an embarrassment. To this day I have not viewed the huge brawl that took place on November 19, 2004, between players of the Indiana Pacers and the Detroit Pistons.

NBA players are out in front of the world. They have the opportunity to inspire or disgust fans with their behavior. When I think about the players whose egos seem to be as inflated as their salaries, I can't help but compare them to a young man I met about a year after I started writing this book.

I was on my way to Shoreline Community College, which is just north of Seattle. While stopped at a light, my attention was drawn to a young man who seemed to have trouble walking. I could see that his legs were twisted and that he walked with extreme effort. My first thought was of sympathy for this poor guy. I watched him closely and saw that he had a radiant smile on his face. I was so moved that I honked the horn and waved at him. He looked in my direction, saw me smiling, and grinned even more brilliantly. It was a typical rainy Seattle day, but at that moment, it felt like a summer's day. For weeks, that wonderful image stayed with me, and one day I saw him again, in the same location. I honked again, he smiled again, and the sun came out.

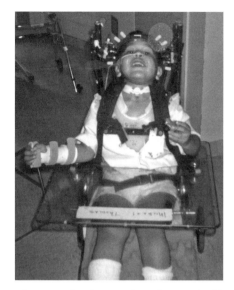

Lamont when he was about three years old.

One day not long after that, I was at the library and he sat down at the seat across from me. I whispered,

"You are the guy I have seen walking to the college!"

"Hey! You're the guy who honked!" That smile filled up the entire library. We wanted to talk a bit, so we stepped outside. He introduced himself as "L. J." (his nickname for his real name, Lamont) and told me his story:

"At the age of eighteen months, I had just learned to walk. For some reason, I decided to leave my house and cross the street. A car came speeding down the street. The elderly woman who was driving didn't see me and smashed into my body, dragging me about one hundred feet. The only thing I can remember was the pain I felt as I went into a coma. It was excruciating. I slipped in and out of consciousness for many days. The doctors said that I would never walk again and that I would be severely mentally retarded. They told my parents that I would have to undergo many medical procedures, and that even so, I would always be paralyzed on one side. They also said that I would have to take all sorts of painkillers and medications.

At that young age, I didn't really understand what they said, and as I got older, I never really believed it, either. I thought, 'I was hit by a car and

I am in pain, but I am not defeated!'

I managed to put a smile on my face through all that pain, and deep from within, I knew that despite the accident, I was the equal of other kids. I refused to see my challenges as a liability, but rather as an asset."

Then Lamont looked at me with a clear, direct gaze and continued.

"Never give up. You can do whatever your mind can envision. Don't take life for granted. Keep your spirit up. Dreams are attainable if you believe!"

At this point, I felt like crying, but I thought that Lamont would say, "Don't cry for me!"—even though it was the beauty of this kid, not pity, that moved me. Instead of crying, I asked him about how he had been treated by his peers as he grew up.

"In the third grade, some eighth graders pushed me down a flight of steps. They called me a "retard" and "cripple" as my body hit the final step. I got up and went home and prayed for all of them to be guided. I knew that I was not a retard, but a person who had had something happen to him."

Then Lamont reached into his duffle bag and gave me a photo. It was a picture of him a year after his accident. There he was, his twisted young body in a wheelchair. Smiling. My whole body began to smile, and Lamont said with a grin,

"You know, I can run a mile in 7 minutes and 35 seconds."

I smiled and said, "That's great, son!"

Then, as naturally as if I had known him forever, Lamont picked up his duffle bag and said, "Well, I must be going, Dad," and he walked away.

I realized that a new person had just been added to my family. Lamont and I have been friends ever since that day and he is a constant source of inspiration.

The NBA needs a few young guys like Lamont! Where have you gone, Magic Johnson and Larry Bird? The league cries out for more of your kind. (Sung to the tune of "Mrs. Robinson.")

THE RETURN FULL CIRCLE

In 1998 I was inducted into the Iowa State Hall of Fame. I went back to Iowa for that ceremony, and it was the first time I had returned to Iowa in over thirty years.

After the murder of my friend Willie, I had some huge chips on my shoulders about ever coming back. In addition, while I was playing professionally, an Iowa sportswriter wrote an article about me for a local ISU publication, which basically said that Don Smith, the poor boy from Brooklyn, New York, should have stayed there instead of ever coming to Iowa. I was really hurt by that article. I thought I was helping the ISU sports program by cooperating with the sportswriter, but he had nothing good to say about me. I went to the induction, but the feelings I had regarding Iowa really hadn't changed much.

Then in 2004, I was contacted by ISU and invited to a ceremony in which my jersey and the jerseys of five other Iowa State basketball All-Americans were to be raised to the rafters of the gymnasium. Happily, this trip was different. I met once again with the people of Ames and my old teammates, and I felt more relaxed and at ease.

⇜⇝

When I saw my old college teammate John McGonigle, I remembered our recent conversation. I had called him to see if he could attend the jersey ceremony.

Elated, he said, "I wouldn't miss it for the world! I'll get in touch with some other teammates to see if they can make it, too."

Then John said, "Zaid, after all these years, I want to thank you for saving my life."

John was known to have a comical side, so I waited for a punch line, but it never came. Still thinking it was some kind of a joke, I asked him what he was talking about.

Amazed that he'd have to remind me, John tried to jog my memory.

"Willie—Willie Muldrew!"

I asked, "What about Willie?"

The story John shared stunned me.

"We were at a party, playing pool. Everybody was relaxed and having fun; then Willie came in. He was angry about something, and he may

have been drinking. Then, out of the blue, Willie pulled a gun on me and said, 'I'll kill you.' Everyone else backed away, leaving me standing there with Willie pointing that gun at me. But you walked right up to Willie, relaxed as could be, and said to him, 'Hey, Willie, what are you doing? This is just John. Relax.' Then you took the gun right out of his hands."

John McGonigle and I at the jersey-raising ceremony at Iowa State on February 14, 2004.

I didn't remember that incident at all, but as I gripped the phone, I realized that my hands were sweating. I had carried around resentment about Willie's death and the subsequent publicity and trial for thirty-five years. Until that moment, I had always felt that Beth had been acquitted based on racist representations of Willie's character.

For the first time, I saw that Willie might not have been quite as innocent as I had always assumed. I knew that racism was a part of that tragedy, but now I understood that Willie's anger and drinking may have contributed. I began to feel spiritually lighter. I thought about Willie and began to love him more. I thought about Beth, who had shot my friend, and began to forgive her. I thought about John McGonigle and the fear he must have suffered as the gun was pointed at him. I thought about that *Sports Illustrated* article in which I had said, "I would not recommend Iowa State University to any black athlete who wanted to be happy."

In my mind I then heard "Boy, you must be cold!" and thought about my childhood meeting with George Hamilton IV. I considered the times we lived in then, and it all began to make sense. The chip on my shoulder was supposed to fall away at this time in this small Midwestern city so I could grow in my understanding. A large piece of the puzzle of my life was becoming clearer to me, and I felt free.

At the jersey-retiring ceremony with four of my children in Ames in 2001. From left to right, Yusef, Mariam, me, Saara, and Adam.

Standing at midcourt, I watched the jerseys lifted to the rafters. I looked at my beautiful wife and five children, and I thought about my journey. I had experienced such contrasts, from Brooklyn to Iowa, from America to Mecca, and from Don to Zaid. I looked at my children and thought, "When I am no longer here, you can bring your children to Ames, point to that jersey, and say, 'That jersey belonged to your grandfather.'"

That thought brought me great satisfaction. And yet I also understood that that kind of recognition is eventually dust in the wind. I was ready to move on to more important issues … eternal issues.

Epilogue

One day not long ago, I got on the bus with my young daughter, Nurah. She is five now, and curious about everything she sees. We sat down in the front seat and she noticed a black oval sign near the seat directly across from us.

Nurah asked me to read it to her, so I did.

"It says, 'Seat dedicated in honor of Rosa Parks. 1913–2005.'"

She asked me why it was there.

"Rosa Parks was a great lady who passed away not long ago." I told her. "This plaque is a way of saying thank you for what she did for all of us."

Nurah wanted to know just what Rosa Parks had done. So I told her that Rosa Parks had ridden the bus in Birmingham, Alabama, long before Nurah was born. Rosa's bus was segregated, which meant African-Americans had to sit in the back. I told her that Rosa Parks was a brave, upright woman, who had always followed the law. But one day she was so tired, she just didn't want to move all the way to the back of the bus, even if the law said she should. When the bus driver and even the police insisted she move, she stayed put. She had decided that she would no longer abide by a law that was unjust.

Nurah was sitting up as straight as an arrow, listening attentively. When I told her that Rosa Parks was taken to jail because she sat in the front of the bus, she said,

"Daddy, that's not right!"

By this time, everyone on the bus was listening to our discussion. Heads began nodding in agreement with Nurah.

"Yeah, honey, I know it wasn't right, but that's what happened. Rosa

Parks stood up for what she believed in. Fortunately, some other good folks stood up with her. Eventually, lots of bad laws about what African-Americans could and couldn't do were changed. Rosa Parks was one of the people who got the ball rolling."

Nurah sat very still for a moment. Then she moved across the aisle and sat in the Rosa Parks seat. Her arms were crossed and she wore a look of determination on her small face.

That day, sitting on the bus, I witnessed a very young lady who is both learning about her past and moving toward her unique future. In one breath, I wonder what miracles life has in store for her, and pray that she will never have to experience the cruelty of prejudice.

❦

Well, that's the end of my story so far. It was challenging to get it down on paper, but I did it.

The story of my life is like no other journey I could ever imagine. I wish you success, because in this life, anything is possible.

If you are ever in Ames, Iowa, look up in the Hilton Arena rafters and you'll see old 35 up there. Or if you are ever in Brooklyn, think of me, because I will always be thinking of you.

Career Statistics

Chronology

1965–1968	Iowa State University
1968–1969	Cinncinnati (Royals)–Milwaukee (Bucks)
1969–1970	Milwaukee (Bucks)
1970–1972	Seattle (SuperSonics)
1972–1975	Houston (Rockets)
1975–1976	Seattle (SuperSonics)
1976–1977	Buffalo (Braves)
1977–1978	Boston (Celtics)–Houston (Rockets)

College (1965–1968)

- Led the Big Eight in scoring in final two seasons, averaging 24.8 points per game as a junior and 24.2 as a senior

- Led Big Eight in rebounding 1965–68 (13.7)

- One of only two Big Eight players to score 600 points in a season twice—619 in 1967 and 604 in 1968 (Wilt Chamberlain was the other)

- One of only two Big Eight players to accumulate more than 1,000 points and 1,000 rebounds, for a total of 1,672 points and 1,025 rebounds

- Two-time All-American selection, three-time Big Eight selection, 1968 Big Eight Conference MVP

- Selected for U.S. Olympic team in 1968

- Changed NCAA history by triggering ban on dunking in 1967 until its repeal in 1976

PROFESSIONAL (1968–1978)

- Selected fifth overall in the 1968 NBA draft by the Cincinnati Royals

- High points—37 against World Champion New York Knicks in 1971 at Madison Square Garden

- Nineteen defensive rebounds in a game during the 1972–73 season

- Averaged 13.8 points and 11.3 rebounds for the Seattle SuperSonics in the 1971-1972 season

- Held Seattle SuperSonics record for most consecutive field goals (12), which was broken only by Gary Payton (13)

- Along with Jim Fox and Bob Rule, one of only three players to have 12 rebounds in a single quarter; ranked sixth among Seattle SuperSonics in rebounding per minute

- Scored a total of 155 double doubles in his NBA career

PERMISSIONS
ACKNOWLEDGEMENTS & CREDITS

The author wishes to gratefully acknowledge numerous organizations and sources for the articles and photos in this book.

FRONT COVER

Boy Dribbling the Ball in a Barn, © Richard Smith/CORBIS.

BACK COVER

Clockwise from top left: Bert Smith, courtesy of author; Sonics uniform, courtesy of NBA Properties, Inc.; Juanita Smith, courtesy of author; Williamsburgh Bank Building, courtesy of Tom Fletcher, nyc-architecture.com; Hattie Coombs, courtesy of author; Hajj photo, courtesy of author; ISU photo, courtesy of Iowa State University; Dorothy Erskine, courtesy of Gary Erskine.

CHILDHOOD

7	Excerpt reprinted courtesy of *Sports Illustrated,* from "The Black Athlete, A Shameful Story"; by Jack Olsen, July 1, 1968. Copyright © 1968. Time, Inc. All rights reserved.
12	Billie Holiday, © Bettmann/CORBIS.
15, 17	Juanita Smith and Hattie Coombs, courtesy of author.
19	Cyclone Rollercoaster, courtesy of The Brooklyn Historical Society.
22, 31	Bert Smith and Brooklyn, courtesy of author.
32	Williamsburgh Bank Building, Tom Fletcher of nyc-architecture.com.
40	Excerpt of song lyrics from "Lonely Teardrops": Words and music by Berry Gordy, Gwen Gordy Fuqua, and Tyran Carlo. © 1957 (Renewed 1985) Jobete Music Co., Inc., Old Brompton Road, and Third Above Music. All rights reserved in the U.S. for Jobete Music Co., Inc. and Old Brompton Road. Controlled and administered by EMI April Music, Inc. All rights reserved. International copyright secured. Used by permission.
40	Excerpt of song lyrics from "Why Do Fools Fall In Love?": Words and music by Morris Levy and Frankie Lymon. © 1956 (Renewed 1984) EMI Longitude Music and EMI Full Keel Music. All rights reserved. International copyright secured. Used by permission.

43	Courtesy of George Hamilton IV.
44	Zaid and George Hamilton IV, courtesy of author.
50	The Drifters, Hulton Archive/Frank Driggs Collection/Getty Images.
53	Don Smith and Gene Smith, 1968, © Roy DeCarava.
53	Courtesy of Michael Davis.
59	Courtesy of Roy Killens.

Adolescence

66	Beverley and Zaid, courtesy of author.
79, 80	Courtesy of Howie Jones.
89	Brooklyn House of Detention, courtesy of author.
96	Song lyrics from "Strange Fruit," by Lewis Allan. Copyright © 1939 (Renewed) by Music Sales Corporation (ASCAP). International copyright secured. All rights reserved. Reprinted by permission.
97	Two Men Are Lynched in Marion, Indiana, © Bettmann/CORBIS.
100	Hank Whitney, courtesy of Iowa State University.

Iowa State University

111	Information used from Ames Chamber of Commerce website (www.ames.ia.us), 2006, and 1960 Census Bureau.
112	The Fountain of the Four Seasons, Courtesy of Iowa State University.
119	Blue Book, courtesy of author.
127	Dorothy Erskine, courtesy of Gary Erskine.
133	ISU 1964 Cyclone team, courtesy of Iowa State University.
140	All photos courtesy of Iowa State University.
141	Don Smith and John McGonigle, by Bert Smith.
141	Courtesy of Iowa State University.
142, 145	Dave Fleming, by Iowa State University, courtesy of Beth Fleming.
150	Willie Muldrew, courtesy of John Chism.
154	Don Smith Night, by Bert Smith.
155	Don Smith Night program, courtesy of Iowa State University.

155   Excerpt from "Smith Honored By His Own," by Dick Wade, March 6, 1968. Reprinted by permission of the *Kansas City Star*.

157   King Kong Attacking Manhattan, © Bettmann/CORBIS.

159   "Praise for Smith," by Fred Wright, March 4, 1968. Reprinted by permission of the *Ames Daily Tribune*.

GOING PROFESSIONAL

173, 175   Excerpts from *Milwaukee Bucks Media Guide* and "Bucks Logo and Nickname" history from National Basketball Association website, 2006, courtesy of the Milwaukee Bucks and the NBA.

178   1969–70 Milwaukee Bucks team, courtesy of the Milwaukee Bucks.

191   "Smith May Sue Bucks, NBA," Sec. 2/p. 11, by Bob Wolf, September 22, 1970. Copyright © 1970 *Milwaukee Journal Sentinel*. Reprinted by permission of *Milwaukee Journal Sentinel* via the Copyright Clearance Center.

197   Don Smith, courtesy of NBA Properties, Inc.

198   Bruce McKim/ *The Seattle Times*.

207   1973–74 Houston Rockets team, courtesy of NBA Properties, Inc.

A GREATER PURPOSE

217–218   Information used from "Spark of Noah's Ark," Robert N. Mullins, *The Seattle Times*, April 24, 2004, and *Arabs in the Golden Age (Peoples of the Past)*, Mokhtar Moktefi, 1996, Millbrook Press, Minneapolis, Minnesota.

224   Excerpt from "Ask Bulls: Abdul-Aziz Better Than Don Smith," by Bob Logan, November 16, 1974, reprinted by permission of the *Chicago Tribune*.

237   Zaid and Khadir, courtesy of author.

238   Kaa'ba, courtesy of the Saudi Information Office, Washington, D.C.

239   Hajj, courtesy of author.

254   Courtesy of author.

265   Courtesy of Lamont ("L. J.") Thomas.

268   John McGonigle and Zaid, courtesy of author.

269   Zaid and family, courtesy of author.

271   Courtesy of Iowa State University.

ABOUT THE AUTHOR

Zaid Abdul-Aziz (formerly Don Smith) was born in Brooklyn, New York, in 1946. He started playing basketball at the age of six. He attended Iowa State University, where he was a two-time All-American. After graduation, he went on to play ten successful seasons in the National Basketball Association. He accepted the Islamic faith in 1973. He now works as a chemical dependency professional in Seattle, where he lives with his wife and daughter.

 SUNLIGHT
PUBLISHING,
INC.

Sunlight Publishing, Inc.
Order Form

Telephone Orders: Call 1-877-244-4009 toll-free.
Please have your credit card ready.

Email Orders: Email us at info@darknesstosunlight.com

Postal Orders: Clip and mail this completed form to
Sunlight Publishing, Inc., PO Box 75184,
Seattle, WA 98175-0184.

Name _____

Address _____

City _____   State _____   ZIP _____

Phone _____   Email _____

DARKNESS TO SUNLIGHT

Pricing: $22.95 each x _____ **No. of Books** = _____
Shipping & Handling For First Book: *Add $4.05*   _____
Each Additional Book: *Add $1.00*   _____
Sales Tax: (8.8% for WA State Residents only)   _____

Total   _____

For quantity discounts, contact Sunlight Publishing, Inc.

PAYMENT METHOD

❏ *Check* ❏ *Money Order* ❏ *Visa* ❏ *MC* ❏ *Amex* ❏ *Discover*

Card Number _____   Exp. Date _____

Name on Card _____

Signature _____

If you wish to contact Zaid Abdul-Aziz for speaking engagements or consulting,
please call him at 1-877-244-4009, or email him at zaid@darknesstosunlight.com.
Visit our website at www.darknesstosunlight.com.